Estate planning and taxation

WILLIAM J. BOWE

Professor of Law, University of Colorado
Tax Counsel, State Farm Insurance Co.

 THIRD C.L.U. EDITION • 1972

RICHARD D. IRWIN, INC. *Homewood, Illinois 60430*
IRWIN-DORSEY LIMITED *Georgetown, Ontario*

ISBN 0-256-00455-2
Library of Congress Catalog Card No. 72-79317

Printed in the United States of America

To George R. Davies, A.B., L.L.B., C.L.U.
Who over the years has continued to inspire
and stimulate my interest in the uses of life
insurance in estate planning.

Foreword

This edition of the author's text, *Estate Planning and Taxation*, has been prepared primarily for insurance agents studying for the Chartered Life Underwriter designation.

The chapters on Forms in the basic text have been eliminated. Lengthy quotation from Regulations and court decisions have been deleted as well as some of the more technical discussions of complex legal points. The text cites by name and gives the facts of many court opinions. However, footnote citations to the original sources do not appear in this edition in the interest of conserving space and because the life underwriter will not be concerned with looking up the original cases. Some new materials have been added and occasionally principles have been restated in what is hoped to be simpler language.

In spite of the above, the book is still basically a text on the law of taxation and, to a lesser extent, on the law of other areas relating to estate planning. The life underwriter must, to properly serve his clientele, acquire a considerable amount of general knowledge of law as it relates to estate planning. Much insurance is purchased to provide liquidity to meet death costs. If the underwriter is to suggest the amount of insurance that may be needed for this purpose he must be generally familiar with the types of property included in the gross taxable estate and with the allowable deductions. This requires a study of the estate tax law. Frequently insurance will be given away by the insured to remove it from his estate. Here the basic principles of the gift tax law become important.

On the original issuance of a policy questions of beneficiary designations arise. Whether to use one of the optional settlements or to create a revocable life insurance trust to receive the proceeds is a question frequently raised by the prospect. These call for at least general tentative suggestions by the underwriter as to the advantages and disadvantages of these devices. The list of illustrations could be continued indefinitely. The underwriter must know something of the law as it pertains to partnerships and corporations as he urges upon his business prospect the wisdom of a business purchase agreement.

But while the underwriter should have a general background in several areas of the law he must refrain from making any but the most general suggestions with respect to the application of legal principles to any particular fact situation. This is the function of the lawyer whose training and experience give him the necessary background to plan the overall estate. The underwriter should be alert to introduce the prospect's lawyer into the picture at the earliest moment when any over-all planning is contemplated or where any other than routine questions arise. The student should at this point turn to Chapter II, Sec. 2.4 and carefully study the opinion of the Standing Committee on Unauthorized Practice of Law of the American Bar Association which is reproduced there.

August 1972   WILLIAM J. BOWE

Table of contents

10. The federal gift tax   168

I

A quick survey of basic estate tax planning

1.1 Historical background

Pliny the Younger argued that an inheritance tax was an unnatural tax in that it augmented the grief and sorrow of the bereaved. Unfortunately this laudable sentiment never gained any headway in English or American law. As early as the 15th century there were death taxes, clients who desired to avoid them and estate planners sufficiently ingenious to devise techniques to accomplish their clients' objectives.

The early common law attached many burdens to the holding of legal title to land. Under the English feudal system the lord of the manor was entitled to a "relief" or money payment when the land descended to the heir of full age, to the rights of wardship and marriage when the heir was a minor, and to "aids" upon the marriage of the daughter and the knighting of the eldest son. These burdens fell upon the holder of the legal title.

To escape these exactions the estate planner of that day ad-

1

vised his client to convey his land to a carefully selected person, in whom he had explicit trust, with the understanding that the grantee would permit the client to use the land during his life and, upon his death, would give the *use* of the land to such person or persons as the client might designate in writing. The client and his designees were said to hold the *use,* the person selected as the grantee held the naked legal title. By transferring the legal title to two or more persons jointly (whose number was renewed from time to time) with right of survivorship, the burdens incident to the descent of land were avoided. This device also eliminated any forfeiture for crime or treason since peace-loving and law-abiding law clerks were generally selected to hold the title. Further, the creditors of the client could not reach his interest in the land. In addition, since dower attached only to the legal estate, this plan could be successfully used to deprive the widow of her rights in the estate, if this were desired. Lastly, it furnished a method of designating beneficiaries who were to be given the land at death during the period when wills devising real estate were not permitted by English law.

The transfer to uses, as this type of conveyance with retained benefits was called, was the beginning of our modern law of trusts. The reserved privilege of designating the person or persons to succeed to the use was the forerunner of the power-of-appointment technique so widely used in estate planning today. Thus the history of estate planning can be traced to the very beginnings of English common law.

1.2 Five basic principles

The object of estate tax planning today, as to a·very considerable extent it was in those early times, is to so arrange the transmission of property from one generation to the next as to provide for minimum tax burdens, both at death and during life, consistent with the estate owner's nontax objectives. Below are listed five very elementary principles of current application. They may be characterized as the basic estate planning tools. While almost too obvious to mention, applying one and overlooking another of these principles can cause tax catastrophes, as the example under 2 below indicates.

1. *Lifetime gifts*   If property is given away during life, it will not be a part of the donor's estate at death. Further, the earnings from such property will normally be taxable to a lower bracket donee. Thus, the lifetime gift will avoid death taxes and shift income taxes to lower brackets.

2. *Creation of successive life estates*   If a life interest in property rather than complete ownership is given to the primary donee, there will be nothing to be taxed in his estate at his death, since his ownership ceases at his death. He owns nothing he can transmit. While this is obvious, it is frequently forgotten. Here is what has happened when this principle was overlooked.

A wealthy industrialist gave his wife $300,000 in the stock of his company in 1940. He paid a gift tax of $60,000. His wife died in 1946. An old will was discovered in which the wife dutifully left "my entire estate to my beloved husband." Thus the stock came back to him but only after $56,000 was paid in estate taxes. He was back where he started except for the $116,000 that went to the United States Treasury. Had he given her the stock for life only and upon her death to the children, the $56,000 tax on her death would have been eliminated and the property would not have been burdened with the later tax on his death.

3. *Use of trusts*   Trusts may be be used to create additional tax entities or second tax pocketbooks. Under our progressive system, the tax on $30,000 is obviously much more than it would be if the $30,000 were spread among three taxpayers.

While the unlimited throwback rule discussed in section 6.12 has placed some limitations on the income tax savings formerly available, the use of trusts will in many cases still save income as well as estate taxes.

Trusts not only create additional tax entities but the proper use of powers over the trust assets, some vested in the trustee, some in the beneficiary, make possible extremely flexible dispositions that enable the donor or testator to give his primary donee or legatee most of the benefits of ownership without the attendant tax burdens.

4. *Use of the gift tax privileges*   The $30,000 lifetime exemption, the $3,000 annual per donee exclusion, the gift tax marital deduction, and the gift splitting option are privileges that exist only during life. If not used they are irrevocably lost since there is no carry-over to the decedent's estate.

5. *Use of the estate tax marital deduction*   It should be used only when and to the extent indicated in each particular case. In many cases it may be costly to use it at all, in others it ought to be used to the fullest permissible extent. Care should be taken not to qualify property in excess of the maximum allowable deduction.

1.3   *Testamentary plans—The unmarried estate owner*

a) *Estate taxes*   A specific illustration will show the tax consequences of a bequest of a life estate as contrasted with a bequest of complete ownership. Assume a relatively simple situation and the effect of federal taxes only.

Mrs. Brown inherited $115,000 from her husband several years ago. She has a son, John, 30. He works in the local bank, manages her funds, and will ultimately inherit them. Mrs. Brown wants a simple one-page will leaving everything to John. Investigation disclosed that John has a home worth $25,000, $15,000 of stocks and bonds, and $50,000 of life insurance. He is married to a young lady whose assets are nominal but with fairly good prospects of inheriting a respectable amount of property from her family. They have three children. If Mrs. Brown leaves her estate to John, he may expect to receive, after taxes and administration expenses, about $100,000. On his later death his taxable estate will amount to:

Inheritance from Mother	$100,000
Life insurance	50,000
Residence	25,000
Stocks and bonds	15,000
Miscellaneous	5,000
	$195,000

Assuming no further increases in his estate, his death costs (federal only) may be estimated as follows, if he does not use the marital deduction as seems likely due to his wife's prospects of inheriting from her family:

Gross estate..		$195,000
Less administration expenses....................	$15,000	
Specific exemption........................	60,000	75,000
Net Taxable Estate...		$120,000
Federal tax on $120,000 (before credit for state taxes, if any)....		$26,700

If instead of an estate of $195,000, John's gross taxable estate is reduced to $95,000 by having his mother create a trust for his benefit, his federal taxes will be reduced to about $2,700.[1] Thus, by giving him a life interest in the property rather than the full ownership, $24,000 in death taxes will be saved. There will also be a saving in administration expenses.

Are there any objections to gifts in trust that may cause Mrs. Brown to hesitate? Trusts may be associated in her mind with spendthrifts and incompetents. John does not need another to do his investing for him. Trusts tie up property. She wants John to have a free hand and, as to the latter, John would agree. Since tax considerations ought not outweigh other factors, perhaps John ought to be given one fourth or one third outright but the bulk of the estate may better serve family purposes if it is put in trust. The advantages are at least worth investigating.

Of course a trust is not the same as outright ownership. If it were it would not be possible to save the $24,000. But under a carefully drawn trust John can be given most of the benefits of ownership without the attendant tax burdens.

In addition to the income, a study of the power of appointment section of the Code will show that without adverse tax consequences:

1. John may be given a right to withdraw $5,000 a year from the capital at his mere whim and pleasure.

---

[1] This assumes about $7,000 of debts and administration expenses.

2. John may be given the right to demand additional sums from capital if needed to maintain his accustomed standard of living.

3. The trustee may be given the power to pay capital to John at any time, in any amount, and for any reason that the trustee, in his discretion, may deem proper. Here reliance is placed upon John's persuasive abilities.

4. John may be given the power to direct the trustee to distribute capital to John's wife or children at any time and in any amount that John shall decide.

5. John may be given the power to dispose of whatever capital remains at his death to and among his family and such other persons as he may wish, provided only that he may not designate his estate, his creditors or the creditors of his estate as recipients of the fund.

With all of the above flexible provisions he will have most of the advantages of ownership without the estate tax disadvantages. If he had unlimited control, he would use it only for his family's benefit and his own. Under the trust it will be available for such purposes and to a very considerable extent John's decisions will determine the particular uses to which it will be put. He may have $5,000 a year for any purpose, he may demand more if needed to maintain his usual living standard. Only if he wants sums in excess of $5,000 and beyond his needs, must he persuade the trustee he ought to be given them. He may make gifts of the property to his wife or children during his life. At his death he can will the property as though it were his, provided he foregoes the doubtful privilege of being able to include his creditors among the beneficiaries.

b) *Income tax savings*   In addition to the estate tax savings, the trust plan offers income tax saving opportunities. Since Mrs. Brown's property will ultimately go to John's children, the fund at her death may be divided into as many shares as there are children of his, in this case at least three, each share to be held as a separate and distinct trust but all to be administered as a unit. John may receive the income from all three trusts until his death, following which event each child will receive the income and, on distribution, the capital from the fund created for his particular benefit. The separate trust technique[2] provides three entities among which to spread the income. Since capital gains are normally taxed to the trust, it is obviously preferable to spread any capital gains among three taxpayers rather than lump the entire gain in a single return. Under the unlimited throwback rule accumulated trust income and capital gains of complex trusts are initially taxed to the trust in the year realized and will be later again taxed to the beneficiaries on distribution with a credit for the taxes paid by the trust. There may be occasions where this may result in a refund to the beneficiaries. See the discussion of the unlimited throwback rule—section 6.12.

While Mrs. Brown wants the income to be paid to John, it is too bad to force it upon him and thereby make it taxable to him at his top bracket. It he gets it all, whatever is left after taxes is going to be used for his children. Would it not, therefore, be better to direct the trustee to pay the income from each of the trusts either to John or to the child of John for whom the particular trust was set up? Then the trustee may pay all the income to John, if this seems desirable. But, if not needed by John, he may, with an eye to the tax burden, pay it directly to the children for deposit in savings accounts or for other investments, thus spreading the income among three taxpayers. Were it to be paid to John, the entire amount would be taxed at his top bracket. This device is known as a spray or sprinkle trust and offers tremendous income tax saving opportunities.[3]

Perhaps the trustee should be given authority to accumulate income or to use it for the purchase of life insurance on the lives of the trust beneficiaries. This will relieve the beneficiaries of the burden of carrying insurance and free the proceeds from estate tax on their deaths. Any income accumulated or used for the payment of premiums will be initially taxable to the trust subject to later tax and tax credit to the distributees under the unlimited throwback rule discussed in section 6.12.

---

[2] See 6.18.

[3] See 6.22.

The effect of partly accumulating to buy insurance and partly paying out to the children is to spread the tax burden initially over six entities.

Thus use of the trust plan will save income taxes:

1. Through the creation of separate trusts;
2. By adoption of the sprinkle technique;
3. By provisions for accumulation and purchase of insurance.

c) *Planning for the family*   Planning is never complete unless it considers the family as a unit and integrates the plans of the several members. In the Brown case it might be well to have John remove his life insurance from his taxable estate by transferring it to an irrevocable trust for his children. Mrs. Brown's will could then leave enough capital to this trust, in states permitting "pour overs," to produce the income needed to pay the annual premiums. Under such a plan the income used to pay the premiums would then be first taxed to the trusts and later to the beneficiaries under the unlimited throwback rule discussed in section 6.12. If pour overs are not permitted an inter vivos gift could be made by her. Such a plan would increase the estate tax savings at John's death indicated above, even if he were given outright $25,000 or $35,000 of his inheritance.

1.4   —The married estate owner

a) *Where one spouse has the bulk of the wealth*   Prior to the introduction of the marital deduction in the Code there were two traditional methods of leaving the estate to a spouse: (1) outright and (2) for life with remainder to the children. Since 1948 it has become common practice to leave one-half outright and one-half for life in order to get the benefit of the marital deduction.

It is interesting to compare the federal tax costs of ultimately passing the family wealth to the children under each of these plans. Assume an estate of $200,000 and ignoring debts, administration expenses and the credit for the state death taxes, the results are as follows:

1. Husband leaves his entire estate to his wife outright.

Husband's gross estate.........................		$200,000
Less marital deduction........... $100,000		
Specific exemption........... 60,000		160,000
Taxable estate...............................		40,000
Federal estate tax..		$4,800

On the later death of wife.

Wife's gross estate............................		$200,000
Less specific exemption............ $60,000		60,000
Taxable estate...............................		140,000
Federal estate tax..		$32,700
Combined federal estate tax on both deaths....................		$37,500

2. Husband leaves his estate to his wife for life.

Husband's gross estate.........................		$200,000
Less specific exemption............ $60,000		60,000
Taxable estate...............................		140,000
Federal estate tax..		$32,700

On the later death of wife, there will be no tax since she has only a life estate.

3. Husband leaves his estate to his wife, one-half outright and one-half in trust.

Husband's gross estate.........................		$200,000
Less marital deduction........... $100,000		
Specific exemption........... 60,000		160,000
Taxable estate...............................		40,000
Federal estate tax..		$4,800

On the later death of wife.

Wife's gross estate............................		$100,000
Less specific exemption............ $60,000		60,000
Taxable estate...............................		40,000
Federal estate tax..		$4,800
Combined federal estate tax on both estates....................		$9,600

Summary

Tax costs under outright bequest plan............................	$37,500
Tax costs under life estate plan....................................	$32,700
Tax costs using marital deduction but not qualifying excessive amount of property..	$9,600

Care should be taken to include a simultaneous death clause. The law is clear that the wife must survive in order for the husband's estate to qualify for the marital deduction. However, the regulations provide that if there is no evidence as to survivorship then state law or the provisions of the will govern. Since the Simultaneous Death Act (law in practically all states) provides that each spouse, as to the distribution of his estate, is deemed to have survived where there is no proof to the contrary, the marital deduction will be lost, if reliance is placed on local state law. If, however, the will of the spouse desiring to provide for the marital deduction (the husband in the cases discussed) contains a clause stating that "if the order of our deaths cannot be established by proof my wife shall be deemed to have survived me," then the marital deduction will be preserved, if the spouses die in a common accident and, as so frequently happens, there is no proof as to the order of their deaths.

b) *Where both spouses have substantial wealth*   There will be many cases where use of the marital deduction is less clear. The wife may have nominal assets but prospects of inheriting a substantial estate from her father—how much and in what form he may not tell and, of course, daughter and son-in-law are hesitant to ask. If all is to go to her in trust, her husband ought to use the deduction; if it is to come to her outright, using the deduction could prove extremely costly. In other cases both spouses may have substantial estates.

Suppose each has $300,000, use of the deduction will cut the tax on the death of the first to die from $62,700 to $17,900 but will swell the tax on the second death to $110,500. The combined taxes with the marital deduction on the first death will amount to $128,400. Where no marital deduction is provided and the entire estate of the first dying spouse is left in such a way as to be sheltered from tax on the second death, combined taxes will be $125,400. Here it may be considerably more expensive to use the deduction when state taxes are considered. But it is believed that one should not lightly decide against providing for the deduction. It may be better to delay the payment of the bulk of the tax as long as possible.

as a transfer in contemplation of death. But a study of chapter 12 should convince the reader that this possibility should not act as a deterrent since such gifts generally avoid some tax, and frequently result in very substantial savings.

Form of gift

To remove the property from the estate of a donor the gift must be complete. This means that he may not reserve a life estate, either in the form of the income or the use of the property. He may not retain any power to amend or revoke the gift or change the beneficiaries. While remote possibilities of reverter do not have the same disastrous effect they once had, the only sensible transfer is one that completely divorces the donor from any interest in or control over the property.

It is possible under the new Code to delay the possession and enjoyment of the donee. Frequently donors are willing to give, provided their donees do not get the use of the property until the donor's death—they want to retain the satisfactions that belong to the holder of the family purse strings. Under the 1954 Code a trust with directions to the trustee to accumulate the income until the death of the donor, may be created without adverse estate tax consequences.

Gifts of present and future interests

1. *Adults*   To obtain the $3,000 annual exclusion the gift must be of a present interest. That means the donee must be given something he can presently enjoy. If the income is to be accumulated or if it may be accumulated in the discretion of the trustee or if it may be sprayed among two or three beneficiaries the exclusion may be denied. Further, a gift in trust of $3,000 will not get the full exclusion since it is in part a gift of a future interest. Only the right to the income is a present interest. How much this right to the income is worth will depend on the age of the donee since the value of his right is measured by his life expectancy.[5]

---

[5] See 10.11, 10.12.

2. *Infants*   Prior to the new Code there was substantial doubt whether any gift in trust to an infant would qualify. Congress has now provided that if the income and principal may be paid to or applied for the benefit of the minor and any unexpended income and principal will pass to him at 21 or, if he be dead, to his estate or his designees under a general power of appointment, the exclusion shall not be denied because of his infancy. But this may be paying too high a price for the exclusion. Generally it is not possible to foresee what kind of person the infant will be at 21 and whether it will be in his best interests to have the property forced upon him.

As a generalization too much attention is sometimes given to obtaining the $3,000 exclusions. They may require the sacrifice of too many sound family objectives and income tax saving techniques to justify the slight saving in gift taxes they achieve.

Gifts in trust

It may be well to conclude with the suggestion that substantial gifts should generally be to trusts rather than outright.

Trusts avoid estate taxes on the deaths of the donees. See page 3 for the example of the wealthy industrialist who gave the stock to his wife and got it back a few years later by inheritance but only after the government collected $116,000 in taxes.

Trusts, in spite of the unlimited throwback rule, offer tremendous income tax saving possibilities. They serve as second tax pocketbooks. By creating separate trusts for each primary beneficiary a number of additional tax entities are provided. By authorizing the trustee to purchase insurance on the lives of the beneficiaries,[6] a part of the income may be made initially taxable to the trustee. By giving the trustee discretionary power to spray income among the family much of it may be kept in the lowest tax brackets.

---

[6] Other than on the life of the grantor or his spouse.

1.6 Assembling the necessary information

Before any planning is possible the family and financial picture of the estate owner must be obtained. For this purpose a checklist will be helpful in suggesting the kind of information that should be obtained.

A. Personal
  1. Name of client
  2. Date of birth
  3. Permanent residence address
  4. Other residences
  5. Period of time resident within the state of permanent residence
  6. Name of wife
  7. Wife's date of birth
  8. Names of children and dates of birth
  9. Whether any children married, and if so, names of spouses
  10. Names of grandchildren and dates of birth
  11. Names of any adopted children or grandchildren
  12. Names of parents and ages, if living
  13. Names and ages of any dependents, not noted above
  14. History of any divorces in the family
  15. Health of client, spouse, and immediate family
  16. Names and addresses of:
      a. Attorney
      b. Accountant
      c. Life underwriter
      d. Bank
  17. Estimate of client's annual cash requirements
  18. A brief statement of how the estate owner disposes of his property by will
B. Property
  1. Residence
      a. Individually owned or jointly with wife
      b. Date acquired (this may have gift tax significance)
      c. Cost
      d. Portion of purchase price paid by client
      e. Mortgage, if any
      f. Cost of any substantial improvements, date and by whom paid for
  2. Real estate owned in client's individual name. List each piece separately

15

          a.   Date acquired
          b.   Cost
          c.   Current value
          d.   Mortgage, if any
          e.   Net rental

3. Real estate jointly with wife or others
   a. Date acquired
   b. Cost and current value
   c. Portion of purchase price paid by client
   d. Extent of client's interest
   e. Joint tenancy or tenancy in common
   f. Name of co-owner or owners
   g. Mortgage, if any
   h. Net rental

4. Stocks owned in cilent's individual name. List each holding separately. (Omit stock of any business interest; see C below)
   a. Date acquired
   b. Cost
   c. Current value
   d. Approximate dividend

5. Securities owned jointly with wife or others
   a. Date acquired
   b. Cost
   c. Current value
   d. Approximate dividend
   e. Portion of price paid by client
   f. Extent of client's interest
   g. Joint tenancy or tenancy in common
   h. Name of co-owner or owners

6. Average bank balances
   a. Check accounts $
   b. Savings accounts $
   c. Joint accounts $
   d. Names of persons with whom joint accounts maintained

7. U.S. Savings bonds, Series—
   a. Maturity value
   b. How registered

8. Other bonds, notes and mortgages. List separately with approximate yield

9. Life insurance on life of client. List each policy separately. Obtain policies for actual inspection
   a. Name of company
   b. Amount
   c. Type of policy (term, endowment, ordinary)

        d. Owner

        e. Beneficiary

        f. Method of payment of proceeds

        g. Cash surrender value

        h. Amount of annual premium

   10. Life insurance on other family members (same information as above)

   11. Social security coverage

   12. Tangible personal property

        a. Household furnishings

        b. Automobiles

        c. Boats

        d. Jewelry

        e. Art objects

C. Business Interests. List Each Separately

   1. Sole proprietorship or partnership or corporation

   2. Percentage of interest of client if stockholder or partner

   3. Names of co-owners and their percentage interests

   4. Estimated fair market value of client's interest

   5. Book value of business

   6. Average earnings for last five years, after taxes and allowances for salaries to client and co-owners

   7. Current arrangements, if any, for disposal of interest at death

   8. Is buy and sell agreement funded with life insurance?

   9. Who owns the policies?

  10. Who pays the premium?

  11. Does the business own any key man insurance?

  12. On what lives?

  13. In what amounts?

  14. Does the business have a pension or profit sharing plan?

  15. Does the business provide group insurance?

D. Property of Other Family Members (What is asked in B above will be suggestive. Care should be exercised to avoid duplication. Here the information may be considerably less detailed)

E. Gifts and Trusts

   1. Amount of prior gifts

   2. Names of and amounts given to each donee

   3. Amount of client's lifetime exemption still available

   4. Amount of wife's lifetime exemption still available

   5. Has client created any revocable trusts?

   6. Has client created any irrevocable trusts?

   7. Is client beneficiary of any trusts?

F. Expectancies

   1. Sources of likely inheritances by client

   2. Approximate amounts

3. Whether outright or in trust
4. Sources of likely inheritances by wife or children
5. Approximate amounts
6. Whether outright or in trust

1.7   How to use the information when assembled[7]

The significance of the various items of information called for in the checklist (section 1.6) will become apparent if a hypothetical set of facts and figures or an actual case is used. The following procedure is suggested to determine opportunities for improvement of the estate plan, with particular emphasis upon life insurance needs.

1. *The gross estate*   List all the estate owner's assets, showing current values. Total these values.

a) Include all jointly owned property to the extent it has been paid for by the estate owner. If he paid the full purchase price, include the full value; if half, include half; if none, include nothing; if received by gift or inheritance (so that neither owner paid anything), include half.

b) Include the face amount of all life insurance on the life of the estate owner owned by him, and the cash surrender values of all insurance owned by him on the lives of others.

c) Watch particularly for the valuation of business interests.

d) If the estate owner has interests in trusts, ascertain the nature and extent of those interests.

e) If there are substantial expectancies, it may be advisable to make two separate calculations to illustrate the present estate and the likely estate.

2. *Deductions (estimated)*   List all liabilities, including mortgages on assets listed above. It will be necessary to estimate debts and administration expenses. These vary widely from state to state and among individuals. Ten percent of the gross estate is probably a fair average figure, diminishing as the estate exceeds $150,000. Also, if the assets include jointly

---

[7] This material is taken from the author's State Farm Life Insurance Company Handbook, Advanced Underwriting and Taxation.

owned property and life insurance, the administration expenses will be proportionately less, since these assets are not subject to executor's commissions and are not generally included in the basis for attorney's fees.

The estimated figure, since it is at best a very rough approximation, may be fixed in an amount which will round off the taxable estate. Thus, if the gross estate is $186,415, debts and administration expenses may be estimated at $16,415, giving an adjusted gross estate of $170,000.

3. *Federal estate taxes and state inheritance taxes*   These computations should show the taxes with and without the use of the marital deduction. It is always well to consider the extent of the burden of state taxes though frequently the federal tax computations alone (before the credit for state taxes paid) will be sufficient to illustrate insurance needs. State taxes are generally lower, because the rates are lower, and not all items included in the federal tax estate are included for state inheritance tax purposes. Thus, life insurance is frequently wholly exempt or exempt up to a stated amount. Further, many states include only half the value of jointly owned property even though paid for in full by the decedent. Some exclude such property entirely.

4. *Marital deduction*   The brief statement of the dispositive provisions of the estate owner's will should indicate whether he has taken advantage of the marital deduction. If he has not, its use may be indicated in appropriate cases after study of the possible tax savings. Frequently the entire estate will be left to the wife outright. This qualifies for the marital deduction, but may be inadvisable in that it unnecessarily increases taxes on her death. Assume Husband leaves Wife his estate of $200,000. The tax on his death, because of the deduction, will be $4,800. But, on Wife's later death, it will be $32,700, whereas it would have been only $4,800 had he given her half outright and half in trust.

In studying this problem, the wife's assets, if any, should be listed. Also note whether she already owns the life insurance on her husband's life. If so, or if her estate is substantial, doubt may arise as to the wisdom of using the deduction.

5. *Will of wife*   It may be a mistake for her to leave her entire estate to her husband, thus needlessly increasing his estate.

6. *Jointly owned property*   Watch for too much jointly owned property. It qualifies for the marital deduction, but may create too large a tax on the later death of the wife. Assume $200,000, all jointly owned but paid for by the husband. On his death the tax will be $4,800 because of the deduction, but, on her later death, it will be $32,700. It need only be $4,800 on each death if they divide the property or hold it as tenants in common, and each leaves his estate in trust for the other.

7. *Wife insurance*   The marital deduction computations may immediately suggest the need of insurance on the life of the wife. Thus, the federal estate tax on $300,000 is $62,500 without the marital deduction. It is $17,900 with the deduction. In this case the premature death of the wife is the costly risk to be insured against. Her death, before the husband's, will increase his death costs by $45,000.

Insurance to meet this additional expense may be on either the life of the husband or the life of the wife because, while the risk is her death, the cash will be needed at the later death of the husband. The policy on either life probably should be owned by the wife to keep the proceeds out of the husband's estate. Care should be taken that her will does not leave the policy to him, should she predecease him; and, of course, if it is on her life, he should not be the beneficiary. The policy or the proceeds should probably go to a trust under the wife's will so that the funds will be available at the husband's death.

8. *Transfer of ownership of insurance on life of the estate owner*   Consider whether the husband should assign ownership in the insurance on his life to his wife in order to remove the policies from his taxable estate. Also, if there are policies on the lives of the children, consider if these should not be owned exclusively by the wife, and if she should not be the sole beneficiary, for the same reason.

9. *Qualification of insurance for the marital deduction*   If the husband continues to own the policies on his own life, the means for qualifying the proceeds for the marital deduction

should be integrated with the provisions of his will. Note, however, the advantage of the installment options in order to obtain the $1,000 special interest element exclusion for the surviving spouse. This is available whether or not the proceeds qualify for the marital deduction.

10. *Beneficiary designations of insurance owned on the lives of others*   All policies owned by persons other than the insured should be checked to avoid inadvertent gift tax consequences on the death of the insured. Thus, if Mother owns $50,000 on the life of Father, with Child as revocable beneficiary, Mother will incur a tax on Father's death when the proceeds are paid to Child. As a good general rule, where a policy is owned by someone other than the insured, the owner should also be the beneficiary.

11. *Purchase of insurance on the lives of children*   Parents or grandparents sometimes want to reduce their estates by making small annual gifts to the children. Life insurance on the lives of the children presents an ideal means by which this objective can be accomplished. The annual premiums constitute gifts which qualify for the $3,000 yearly exclusion ($6,000 if the payor is married and his spouse consents), provided the policies are owned outright by the children.

12. *Long-term insurance trusts*   Sometimes the parent or grandparent will be interested in creating a funded trust to purchase life insurance on the lives of the children. The transfer of $50,000, for example, to such a trust, would:

a) Eliminate this amount from the estate of the donor. If he has $200,000 it will save $15,000 in Federal taxes.

b) Cause the income used to pay the premiums to be taxed initially to the trust at its beginning bracket of 14 to 17 percent rather than at the top bracket of the donor.

c) Permit the gift to be charged to the lifetime exemptions of the donor and his wife. Thus, no gift tax need be incurred. The gift will not qualify for the $3,000 annual exclusion, however, because it is a gift of a future interest.

d) Prevent the insurance proceeds from being taxed at the death of the insured since the policy will be owned by the trust.

e) Permit the proceeds to be made available to the insured's executor to serve normal insurance purposes through the purchase of nonliquid assets from his estate.

13. *Short-term insurance trusts*   The parent may not want to part with his property permanently. Instead of the long-term trust, therefore, he may create a ten-year trust, the income to be used to purchase a ten-pay policy on the life of the child. At the end of ten years, the capital will be returned to him and the paid-up policy will be given to the child. Meanwhile, the income will be taxed to the trust (at 14 to 17 percent) instead of to the parent (at fifty percent, sixty percent, or whatever his top bracket happens to be) and later to the children under the throwback rule; see section 14.14.

The gift tax consequences are negligible. The measure of the gift is about 44 percent of the capital placed in the trust. Thus, if $50,000 is transferred in trust, the value for gift tax purposes is about $22,000 and, while not chargeable against the annual exclusion, it may be charged against the $30,000 lifetime exemption.

14. *Business insurance*   See chapters 16 and 17.

2

Professional conduct

2.1 Introduction

This chapter sets forth the National Statement of Principles of Cooperation between Life Underwriters and Lawyers, the Statement of Guiding Principles for Relationships between Life Underwriters and Trustmen, and the Recent Opinion on Estate Planning by the Standing Committee on the Unauthorized Practice of Law of the American Bar Association. These statements should be studied with great care by the life underwriter so that he may constantly keep foremost in his mind his place on the estate planning team. He must be ever watchful not to attempt to give advice in areas beyond his competence or to engage in any activities that could be construed to constitute the practice of law.

2.2 National statement of principles of cooperation between life underwriters and lawyers

In February, 1948, the National Conference of Lawyers and Life Underwriters issued its *National Statement of Principles of Cooperation between Life Underwriters and Lawyers.* That Statement reads:

Foreword

The National Conference of Lawyers and Life Underwriters was constituted on July 17, 1946, by representatives of The American Bar Association and The National Association of Life Underwriters upon due authorization by the governing bodies of the two Associations. Its purpose shall be to promote cooperation and understanding between life underwriters and lawyers and to eliminate, as far as possible, misunderstandings and causes for complaint by either against the other in relation to any practices which do not appear to be in the public interest.

The National Association of Life Underwriters has a membership of 52,500; its members are estimated to sell and service more than 70 percent of all life insurance in the United States. There are affiliated with it 41 state and 505 local associations throughout the country. It and its members have for many years sought to maintain and uphold a formal code of ethics adopted by them. The Association has created the American College of Life Underwriters through which have been established university and college courses leading to the designation of 'Chartered Life Underwriter' after a recommended course of study of three years; all of this has been done toward the end of developing competency and a professional point of view by the life underwriters.[1]

The American Bar Association has, for many years, adopted its Canons of Professional Ethics and maintained its Standing Committee on Professional Ethics and Grievances to aid the Bar in their interpretation and observances by lawyers.

The American Bar Association is recognized as the national representative of the organized Bar of this country.

In 1940, a National Statement of Principles of Cooperation between Life Underwriters and Lawyers was published. The present Statement is intended to supersede the 1940 Statement. It, like its predecessor, is intended as a guide to the professional conduct of attorneys and life underwriters in respect to one another and in relation to the public.

Statement

In recent years, much of the actual negotiation of the sale of life insurance contracts involves estate planning. The acquisition of life insurance has become a complex problem by its ever increasing relation to plans of testamentary disposition, wills and living trusts, to partnerships

---

[1] The author recognizes that since this statement was issued in 1948, the program of the American College of Life Underwriters has been broadened considerably and contains five courses which normally require four to five years for their completion. Similarly, the membership of the National Association of Life Underwriters has greatly increased.

and close corporation contracts, and to problems of taxation. The solution of such problems requires a man to make far-reaching decisions. These decisions often are, or upon the happening of death become, irrevocable. The American public should therefore receive not only expert insurance service and disinterested advice but also skilled and disinterested legal guidance and advice when necessary; both are often required in problems arising out of negotiation for and use of life insurance, and when this is the case, the simultaneous and harmonious attention of a representative of each profession in solving the problems of the same client will provide the safest and most efficient service.

Fair dealing with the public and an observance of laws which have been enacted throughout the United States require that all legal service and advice should at all times be given by an individual trained in the law and duly licensed to practice; anyone who gives legal advice should be solely devoted to the interest of his client and permit no personal consideration whatsoever to weaken his exclusive loyalty to his client.

In this connection, it might well be remembered that the courts consider communications between an attorney and his client as privileged, that is, they do not compel their disclosure, while communications between a life underwriter and his client are not so considered. This distinction should, for the protection of the public, be borne in mind by the members of both professions.

For the guidance of life underwriters and of lawyers, and to insure that the public shall be protected by receiving authorized and disinterested legal advice on life insurance problems, such as those hereinabove referred to, the National Conference states:

I.

The National Conference considers it to be in the interest of cooperation between life underwriters and lawyers and of better service to the public, that all lawyers be guided by the opinion of the American Bar Association's Standing Committee on Professional Ethics and Grievances, dated February 10, 1940, issued in reply to an inquiry from that Association's Standing Committee on Unauthorized Practice of Law. That opinion in full is as follows:

"In the opinion of the Committee, the Lawyer's conduct in each of the following situations is ethically improper and should be condemned:

"1. A life underwriter recommends a certain transaction, for example, the purchase of business life insurance. The client presents the proposed transaction to his attorney for approval or disapproval. The attorney then demands of the life underwriter, as a condition for his approval, a share in the life underwriter's commission.

"2. An attorney promises a life underwriter to recommend him to

25

the attorney's clients, provided the life underwriter will pay to the attorney a share of his commissions resulting from any business obtained from the lawyer's clients.

"It should be noted, in this connection, that in most of the states participation in commissions on life insurance contracts by any person other than a duly licensed life insurance agent, has been condemned by statute or by court decision and has been declared unethical for life underwriters by their professional organizations.

"3. A life underwriter proposes a certain life insurance plan to a prospective client; the client submits the proposed plan to his attorney for his legal opinion. The attorney approves the plan, but for reasons of personal advantage to himself advises the client to divert the business and to purchase the necessary life insurance not through the underwriter who submitted the plan but through another underwriter whom the attorney recommends although the interests of the client do not require such substitution.

"4. An attorney promises an underwriter that if he, the underwriter, will induce his clients to refer legal business to the attorney, the attorney will pay to the underwriter a share of the fees resulting from such business.

"5. To advertise himself and to promote his sale of life insurance, a life underwriter desires to use a lawyer's legal opinion in relation to a specific plan by using the lawyer's name and opinion in a general circular or as a selling document. At the underwriter's request, a lawyer furnishes such an opinion knowing (*a*) that the attorney's name will be thus advertised and utilized by the underwriter and (*b*) that the opinion may mislead the person to whom it is exhibited to his detriment unless it is adapted to the facts of his particular case. This form of business solicitation by life underwriters has been condemned by their profession and by this Association's Committee on Unauthorized Practice of the Law."

II.

The National Conference considers it to be in the interest of cooperation between life underwriters and lawyers and of better service to the public, that all life underwriters be guided by the following principles:

(1) A life underwriter has no right to practice law or to give legal advice or to hold himself out as having such rights. He should not attempt to do so directly or indirectly. Therefore, he must never prepare for execution by his client legal documents of any kind, such as wills or codicils thereto, trust agreements, corporation charters, minutes, by-laws, or business insurance agreements. When submitting an involved mode of settlement, or one which may affect a client's prior disposition of property by his Last Will and Testament, the life underwriter should suggest that the same be submitted to the client's attorney for approval.

In estate planning, all transfers of property, except simple modes of settlement under life insurance policies or changes of beneficiary thereof, should be recommended subject to the approval of the client's attorney. Since these decisions should in the final analysis be subject to the approval of the client's attorney, it is important for the life underwriter to collaborate with his client's attorney as early as possible in the negotiations so as to afford his client the safest and most effective service.

It is improper for a life underwriter, in submitting to his client an estate planning report, to attach thereto or insert therein any forms of legal instruments or of specific legal clauses.

(2) A life underwriter should never dissuade a client from seeking the advice of legal counsel. It is improper for a life underwriter to attempt to divert legal business from one attorney to another.

(3) It is improper for a life underwriter to furnish attorneys who will give legal advice to the life underwriter's clients or prospective clients.

(4) A life underwriter must never share or participate in an attorney's fee; a life underwriter must not pay directly or indirectly any part of his commission to an attorney or any other person not a life underwriter, whether or not such sharing in commissions is known to the insured.

It should be noted, in this connection, that in most of the states participation in commissions on life insurance contracts by any person other than a duly licensed life insurance agent, has been condemned by statute or by court decision and has been declared unethical for life underwriters by their professional organizations.

(5) A life underwriter may properly obtain legal advice or a written legal opinion from an attorney for his own guidance; it is improper conduct, however, to circularize any such legal opinion, or to use it as a selling document.

Nothing herein contained is intended to restrict or limit the life underwriter's legitimate activities in measuring the client's need for life insurance, determining the amount and type needed, developing a comprehensive life insurance program in relation with the client's other plans and affairs, and selling such insurance; the ethics of his profession require him not to recommend the purchase of additional insurance unless needed. Such activities are for the benefit of those insured and their dependents only insofar as they are consistent with the foregoing statement of principles.

III.

The National Conference of Lawyers and Life Underwriters recommends to state, district and local bar associations and to state and local associations of life underwriters that cooperative action be taken by them to secure adherence to the principles contained in this Statement and to dispose of misunderstandings between the two groups. The National Conference is authorized to act in an advisory capacity as a clearing house for suggestions and complaints, to aid in establishing, as far as may be practical, a country-wide recognition of these principles, and to aid in the setting up of similar conference groups in the various states and localities. It gladly offers its services in this respect to state, district and local associations of the bar and life underwriters.

2.3 Statement of guiding principles for relationships between life underwriters and trustmen

In September, 1968, the Executive Committee of the National Association of Life Underwriters and the Executive Committee of the Trust Division of the American Bankers Association issued a *Statement of Guiding Principles for Relationships between Life Underwriters and Trustmen*. That statement reads:

Life Insurance—Trust Relationships Logical. The existence and continuance of active and cooperative relations between life underwriters and trustmen are not only logical but also mutually beneficial because life underwriters and trustmen deal frequently with closely related aspects of the same estates. Consequently, life underwriters and trustmen should have a clear understanding of the basic principles and practices underlying these relationships.

Relationships Focus in Estate Analysis and Insurance Settlement. Life Insurance—Trust relationships focus principally on human and financial aspects of estate analysis. Life underwriters analyze estate assets to determine insurance needs and trustmen analyze estate assets to determine trust needs. In the analysis of the same estate it is desirable for the life underwriter and the trustman to coordinate their efforts so that each may bring to bear upon the analysis his special points of emphasis. Such an analysis usually leads to the realization of the need for a will or trust and a determination of how best to deal with life insurance. Since the mode of settlement of the life insurance is an integral part of the general estate plan, it is desirable in such cases for the life underwriter and the trustman to cooperate toward reaching a recommendation concerning the disposition of the life insurance proceeds which can be presented to the individual's lawyer for consideration.

Life Insurance—Trust Mode of Settlement. The life insurance trust might be likened to a mode of settlement, but, unlike the others, it is a method that requires the introduction of a trustee involving continuous flexible management of the insurance proceeds vested in the trustee. Every mode of settlement has is special function and no single mode is equally appropriate for all cases. Consequently, life underwriters should acquaint their clients with the special and distinctive functions of trusts and modes of settlement and help them select the method best suited to their needs. Trustmen should present the life insurance trust as one, but not as the only method of settlement.

The Use of the Terms "Option" and "Trusts." When not payable in lump sum there are two principal methods of distributing life insurance proceeds—(1) through the optional settlements of the life insurance policies, and (2) through trusts administered by trustee. The term "trust" implies a fiduciary obligation that is enforceable in a court of equity as distinguished from a contractual obligation that is enforceable in a court of law. For the sake of clarity and common understanding of terms a mode of settlement of insurance should be referred to as a "trust" or "trust settlement," only in those cases in which the relation between the life insurance company or the trust institution and the beneficiary is, in fact, an equitable relationship of trustee and beneficiary and not a legal relationship of debtor and creditor such as exists under policy "options."

Life Insurance Options. Both life underwriters and trustmen realize the value and advantages of the optional settlements provided in life insurance policies.

Insurance Trusts. The life insurance trust is a method of settlement especially to be considered in the following situations:

1. When flexibility of administration and the exercise of discretionary powers are needed to meet situations which cannot be foreseen or requirements of beneficiaries that cannot be provided for beforehand;
2. When, in connection with business insurance, there is need for an impartial and responsible third party to carry out the plan under which the insurance was effected;
3. When the immaturity, inexperience, or incompetence of the beneficiaries creates a need for the services of an experienced and objective financial adviser;
4. When the primary purpose of the insurance is to safeguard the estate against complications and shrinkage due to debts, taxes, and administration expenses.

Advice of Life Underwriters and Trustmen Restricted to Their Respective Fields. While life underwriters should be familiar with the basic principles of trust, and trustmen with the basic principles of life insurance, neither life underwriters nor trustmen should give specific information or advice on matters that lie within the province of the other. Instead of offering specific advice or information on trust matters, the underwriter should consult with or call into conference a trustman of the individual's choice; and instead of offering specific advice or information on life insurance matters, the trustman should consult with or call in a life underwriter of the individual's choice.

Life Underwriters and Trustmen Mutually Cooperative. Life underwriters and trustmen are both engaged in the processes of estate creation, conservation, administration and distribution for the same persons. The best interests of the individual and his beneficiaries should be paramount. In promoting the best interests of the individual, the life underwriter and the trustman will work together in mutual respect and cooperation.

2.4 Opinion on estate planning

The Standing Committee on the Unauthorized Practice of Law of the American Bar Association issued the following opinion in 1959.

This Committee has received inquiries concerning the propriety of the conduct of corporations and individuals who are not lawyers but who, through advertisements, brochures, orally or otherwise, solicit legal work or hold themselves out to the public as being available to give legal assistance in the field of estate planning or to do the whole job of planning an estate.

The phrase "estate planning" has come into existence in recent years to refer to the orderly arrangement of an individual's assets so as to provide most effectively for the economic needs of himself while living and of those dependent upon him after his death. At the outset it should be recognized that there are certain lay activities which are legitimate aspects of estate planning and which do not involve legal work, but which are in the nature of an analysis of the facts and assets of an estate in relation to economic needs, and may extend to giving general information as to laws affecting the disposition of estates, though without any specific application thereof to a particular estate or individual situation. These activities may be properly performed by persons who are not lawyers, and are discussed later in this opinion. In general, however, pursued to its proper conclusion, estate planning necessarily involves the application of legal principles of the law of wills and decedents' estates, the law of trusts and future interests, the law of real and personal property, the law of taxation, practice in the Probate and Chancery Courts, or other fields of law. When such is the case, the work involved in estate planning includes legal research, the giving of legal advice or the drafting of legal instruments.

There can thus be no question that estate planning, except where it is in the nature of an analysis of the facts and assets of an estate as above described, involves legal work and constitutes the practice of law. When engaged in by an individual who is not a lawyer, or by a corporation, it is the unauthorized practice of law. Nor does it become any the less the practice of law because the suggestion is made that the legal advice given or legal work done should be reviewed by an attorney. It is well settled that both corporations and laymen are prohibited from practicing law directly, and that they may not practice law indirectly by hiring lawyers to practice law for them. Accordingly, neither corporations nor laymen may engage in estate planning by soliciting the legal work involved and then hiring lawyers to perform it. This is also the unauthorized practice of law. In addition, under Canon 47 of the Canons of Professional Ethics of the American Bar Association no lawyer shall permit his professional services, or his name, to be used in aid of, or to make possible, the unauthorized practice of law by any lay agency, personal or corporate.

It is elementary that under Canon 27 lawyers are forbidden to solicit legal employment by circulars, advertisements, or otherwise. Thus, no lawyer may solicit legal work in the field of estate planning or be employed to do such work for a corporation or a layman which does. But the public could not be protected by prohibiting the lawyer from soliciting legal work in the field of estate planning, if at the same time laymen and lay agencies were permitted, in any guise, to advertise a claimed legal competence in this field. It should be clear, therefore, that the holding out by any lay agency to the public, directly or indirectly, overtly or subtly, of its willingness to perform legal services in the field of estate planning is itself the unauthorized practice of law. Also, no lay agency may hold itself out to the public as willing to do the whole job of "estate planning" without becoming engaged in the unauthorized practice of law.

In addition, the lawyer-client relationship requires a duty of absolute loyalty to the client, and undivided allegiance. Under Canons 6 and 35 of the Canons of Professional Ethics the lawyer cannot permit his professional services to be controlled or exploited by a lay agency intervening between him and his client.

Also, under Canon 34 lawyers may not divide fees with laymen, and this principle applies to fees for legal work in the field of estate planning. Moreover, the sharing by a layman of a lawyer's fees constitutes the unauthorized practice of law.

Illustrative of the treatment of the subject in the Courts is the decision of the Superior Court of Cook County, Illinois, in *Chicago Bar Association* v. *Financial Planning, Inc.,* decided March 21, 1958, in which the court held that certain estate planning services involved the giving of "legal advice on some of the most important problems which can arise during a man's lifetime and after his death," adding that "Even if this advice were confined to tax savings alone, it still would amount to the practice law . . ." and "the contention that the advice is comprised merely of suggestions, and is always subject to be reviewed by a lawyer, is no excuse for the conduct of the defendants. The practice of law should be confined to lawyers without the interposition of unauthorized practitioners who solicit this business directly or indirectly."

The decree in this case permanently enjoined the defendants, their agents and employees from:

"(a) Giving legal counsel and advice,
"(b) Rendering legal opinions,
"(c) Preparing, drafting and construing legal documents,
"(d) Preparing estate plans which embody legal analysis, counsel and advice,
"(e) Holding themselves out as persons who prepare estate plans embodying legal analysis, counsel and advice,
"(f) Charging and collecting fees for legal counsel, advice, or services rendered by them, or their agents, or employees,
"(g) From practicing law in any form, or holding themselves out as having a right to practice law, or soliciting employment to prepare estate plans embodying legal analysis, counsel and advice, or from charging, or collecting fees, or payments for legal services rendered by said defendants and each of them or their agents, or employees."

It is not intended by the opinion of this Committee to proscribe activities of those groups which serve various fields related to estate planning unless they involve the performance of legal services as outlined herein. Activities geared to motivating the individual concerned to do something about his affairs and to seek the advice of his own lawyer as early as possible, preferably from the outset, with regard to the development of an overall estate plan, are in the public interest. Advice on matters of law with respect to the prospect's particular factual situation, however, must not be given.

The activities of lay groups described above should conform to the standards of propriety set forth in the several Statements of Principles developed through the Conference method between the American Bar Association and various business and professional groups. Moreover, because of the shadowy borderline between an analysis of facts and assets of an estate and the application of legal principles to them, it is clearly within the spirit of the several Statements of Principles that the activities of these groups should be performed in close cooperation with the client's own attorney. It is contemplated that any disputes which may arise with respect to the activities of such business and professional groups shall be governed by such Statement of Principles. The understandings reached in these Principles have served to encourage the public to seek proper legal guidance, the lay groups not to transgress upon the sphere of activity properly reserved for the legal profession, and to bring about better understanding and cooperation between those groups and the Bar.

3

The federal estate tax in brief

DEDUCTIONS

EXEMPTION, RATES, CREDITS

In general

3.1   Introduction

As death taxes, in the more substantial estates, often cause the largest single item of shrinkage, it is always desirable to prepare a federal estate tax table of assets and liabilities, in order to make an estimate of the likely taxes that will be incurred. This is the initial step in determining what, if any, tax savings are possible without departing significantly from the client's basic objectives. For this reason the present chapter is devoted to a discussion of the federal estate tax.

3.2   The theory of an estate tax

The federal government imposes an estate tax as distinguished from an inheritance tax. An estate tax is a tax on giving. An inheritance tax is a tax on receiving. Most states have inheritance taxes, with varying exemptions and rates for each beneficiary. For example, there may be a $10,000 exemption for a spouse, with rates from 1 percent to 10 percent, $5,000 for children under 21 and $2,500 for adult children, with rates from 3 percent to 12 percent, $1,000 for brothers and sisters, with rates from 5 percent to 15 percent, etc. Frequently there is no exemption for strangers and the rates are considerably higher. An estate tax, on the other hand, is not concerned with the recipients. There is a single exemption (in the case of the federal tax $60,000) and a single set of rates. Each type has its merits. From time to time it has been suggested that the federal government should adopt an inheritance tax, but the change now seems unlikely. Indeed some states have shifted to an estate tax. The classification of property in both taxes is much the same, though in state inheritance taxes there will be found many variations in the treatment accorded the different types of included items. Thus state laws will vary as to the extent to which the proceeds of life insurance, jointly owned property, and assets subject to powers of appointment are to be included in the tax estate.

3.3 Constitutionality

The constitutionality of the federal estate tax was sustained in *New York Trust Co.* v. *Eisner* against the argument that it was a direct tax and therefore invalid since it was not apportioned as required by the federal Constitution for all direct taxes. The Supreme Court held it was not a tax on the property itself, but rather was an excise on the privilege of transmitting property. The tax is imposed on the transfer or shifting of relationships to property at death. It is not levied upon the property as such. For this reason it was held in *United States Trust Co. of New York* v. *Helvering* that the proceeds of war risk insurance were subject to estate tax even though section 22 of the World War Veterans Act of 1924 provided that such insurance "shall be exempt from all taxation." Similarly, municipal and state bonds owned by a decedent are includible in his taxable estate.

The Supreme Court has sustained the constitutionality of the inclusion of various property interests in the estate of a decedent, even though such interests were not technically "owned" by the decedent at the time of his death. For example, the proceeds of life insurance purchased and controlled by the decedent, property held by the decedent and his spouse as tenants by the entirety, property irrevocably transferred in contemplation of death, revocable transfers requiring the consent of another person, transfers with reserved life estates, may all be included in the taxable estate.

3.4 Retroactivity

In the beginning days of the federal estate tax serious questions were raised as to the retroactive application of the tax. The usual argument was that a tax on transfers that antedated the statute was arbitrary and therefore unconstitutional since the taxpayer could not have foreseen the consequences at the time of the transfer. But these doubts have been virtually eliminated by such cases as *United States* v. *Jacobs* and *Fernandez* v. *Weiner.*

In the *Jacobs* case the decedent had created a joint tenancy long prior to the enactment of the estate tax. The full value of the property was, nevertheless, included in his estate because he had paid the full purchase price. The Court, in rejecting the argument of retroactivity said, "There was at death a distinct shifting of economic interests . . . . Neither the amount of the tax nor its application to the survivor's change of status or ownership was in any manner dependent upon the date of the joint tenancy's creation."

However, as will become evident in subsequent chapters, there has been a general congressional policy against retroactivity. Statutory modifications ordinarily are made applicable only with respect to decedents who die after the date of the amendment, and often only as to transfers made after the passage of the statutory change.

Property owned by decedents

3.5 *The probate estate*

Section 2033 of the 1954 Code requires the inclusion in the gross taxable estate of all property, including real property situated outside the United States, "to the extent of the interest of the decedent therein at the time of his death." Speaking generally, this section corresponds to the probate estate, i.e. property subject to disposition by will. Stocks, bonds, mortgages, bank accounts, household furnishings, art objects, claims, the family residence, and other real estate fall within this section. Prior to 1962 the Code excluded real property situated outside the United States due to doubts with respect to the constitutional power to tax such property. The 1962 amendments provided that foreign real estate would be taxable as part of the estate of a citizen or resident if he died on or after July 1, 1964, regardless of the date the real estate was acquired. For those who died prior to July 1, 1964, such property is included only if acquired after January 1, 1962. Thus persons who had relied upon the prior law were given an opportunity to dispose of their foreign real estate since in many cases it may have been acquired or held primarily because of the tax advantage under the prior law.

3.6 *State law determines the existence and extent of the interest*

On the question of the nature and extent of the property interest owned by the decedent at the time of his death, the federal courts and the Commissioner are bound to follow state law. Until 1967 the courts had held that if a state court had decided a dispute over ownership of property or construction of a will or other document the federal court hearing a tax dispute was not free to make an independent judgment as to applicable local law but was required to follow the decision of the local court. Thus in *Commissioner* v. *Rhodes* it appeared that on the death of Mr. Rhodes, his estate, consisting in large part of International Shoe Co. stock, passed in equal shares to his wife and four children. Later the children executed an instrument assigning all their interest in the stock to their mother. She subsequently attempted to dispose of the stock in her will. However, a state court proceeding was instituted after her death to reform the assignment to show that only a life estate was intended to be conveyed by the children. After a full hearing the state court decreed that the "assignment be and the same hereby is reformed, as of the date of its execution, to read that the children hereby jointly and severally grant, transfer and assign to our said mother . . . an estate for her life only."

The Commissioner attempted to include the full value of the stock in the estate of the mother. But the Board of Tax Appeals, now the Tax Court, held nothing was to be included in her estate since she had only a life interest under local law. "The determination of whether the decedent owned only a life estate in the property assigned in 1925 by her children or whether she owned an absolute interest is clearly a determination of property rights and, as such, is controlled by local law." Similarly a state court's decision that a decedent had made an effective gift of bonds, even though the bonds were found in his safety deposit box, was held conclusive in *Sharp* v. *Commissioner*.

However, in 1967 the problem was reexamined by the Supreme Court. Probably because state courts had tended to unduly favor taxpayers in their decisions, the Court in *Bosch* held that while deference was to be shown to the adjudications of lower state courts a federal court was free to make its determination as to state law as it applied to the particular case unless the law had been settled by the highest court of the state.

In practice the federal courts have tended to follow the decisions of local probate courts where there appears to have been an adversary proceeding, i.e., one in which the litigants had conflicting interests and where each was attempting in good faith to prevail, in other words, where the question was actually litigated. On the other hand, where there was a default or consent decree the courts have disregarded the determination. In these latter cases it is generally apparent that a genuine dispute as to construction or ownership did not exist and that the litigation was simply an attempt to dress up the title in appropriate garments for the anticipated tax inspection. In these cases and in cases where the issue of local law has not been litigated the federal courts in the tax litigation will make their own independent determinations of the applicable local law.

3.7 Beneficial ownership

If, under local law, the decedent is found to have only a bare legal title to the property, as where he is trustee or nominee for the real owners, nothing is to be included in his estate. Thus, in *Reed* v. *Commissioner,* on the death of their mother the children conveyed to their father all of their rights in the mother's share in the community estate, the father orally promising to leave the property to them by will. Since under Texas law an oral trust is enforceable the father was found to have a beneficial interest which ceased with his death. Hence the Court held no part of the property includible in the tax estate. Again in *Doerken,* the president of a corporation individually signed an application for a life insurance policy. It was issued in his name but all premiums were paid by the corporation. The corporation carried the policy as an asset on its books, dealt with the policy as owner, and was designated beneficiary. The Court held Doerken was merely the nominal owner and nothing was to be included in his estate because of the policy. On the other hand in *Harter,* realty and securities were transferred to a wife with the private understanding that the donor husband would have the income from the property for his life. The value of the property was included in his estate, the Court saying, "The language of 811(c)(I)(B) (the former version of section 2036 1954 Code) does not contemplate, as the taxpayer has contended, that the retained interest must be set out in the instrument of transfer, nor does the language of that Section require that the retained interest must be one that could be enforced against an objecting transferee. Section 811(c)(I)(B) poses a factual test. Under the clearly apparent facts of this case the decedent retained what amounts to a life estate in the property."

3.8 Claims

In order for an asset to be included in the decedent's estate he must have had an interest therein at the time of his death. For this reason wrongful death recoveries form no part of the taxable estate since the decedent never had any interest in the cause of action. On the other hand, a cause of action arising prior to his death which survives, under statutory provisions, for the benefit of his estate may be included unless the value is so speculative as to be worthless. Care should be taken not to undervalue doubtful claims and other causes of action since, as a practical matter, the estate tax value governs the cost basis of the asset for income tax purposes, in the event of a later recovery. In one case a $500,000 note was valued at $200,000. The note was later collected in full with unhappy income tax consequences, since the income tax on the $300,000 taxable gain was very considerably higher than the estate tax avoided through the lower valuation of the note.

3.9 Voluntary employee benefits

In *Estate of Salt* v. *Commissioner* the decedent's widow received $40,000 as a "Regular Death Benefit" from his former employer. At the date of decedent's death the company plan provided for pensions and other benefits if, in the discretion of the committee administering the plan, the committee authorized the payment of a specified amount to persons related to a deceased pensioner. The $40,000 was paid pursuant to order of the committee. The payments were excluded from the tax estate on the ground that all the decedent had during his life was an expectancy. "At the time of his death the decedent had no vested interest in the $40,000 nor did his widow have an enforceable right" to it. But if the death benefit must be paid in accordance with a plan in effect at the date of death, even though the company reserves the right to discontinue the plan at any time, the payment is taxable as it becomes indefeasibly vested at death. This area is now covered by the new Code section dealing specifically with annuities. See section 3.19.

Under the Code the first $5,000 of any death benefit paid by an employer by reason of the death of an employee, whether the payment is made pursuant to a contract or voluntary, is exempt from income tax. In some cases voluntary payments in excess of $5,000 were held to be gifts and therefore exempt. However, as under the 1962 amendments to the Code deductions by employers for gifts are limited to $25 (plus, of course, the $5,000 referred to above), gifts in excess of $5,000 will rarely be made by employers.

3.10 Rights to future income

Any rights to future income which have accrued prior to the decedent's death such as rents, interest, dividends, his share of postdeath partnership profits, etc. are includible in his tax estate. In *McClennon* v. *Commissioner,* the decedent was a partner in a Boston law firm. Under the partnership agreement his share of the profits during life was 8 percent. The contract provided that the same percentage of profits was to be paid to his estate for 18 months following his death. It was held that the value of this right, as of the date of his death, was to be included as part of his estate since it represented payment for his interest in the partnership assets, books, fixtures, receivables, goodwill, etc. On the other hand the mere right to participate in future earnings of a partnership, without more, may not constitute an estate asset in the rare case where the partnership has no tangible property or other assets. Thus in *Bull* v. *United States* the decedent was a partner in a ship brokerage business. The partnership had no capital and no tangible assets. Goodwill inhered in the partners rather than in the partnership. All the estate succeeded to was the privilege of becoming a partner and sharing profits and losses on the same percentage basis that the decedent had participated. But cases falling within the *Bull* rule will be extremely rare.

Rev. Rule 55–123 held the right of a deceased lawyer to receive compensation for legal services on a contingent fee basis constituted an interest in property under Code Section 2033.

This inclusion of future income items resulted in very considerable hardship prior to the adoption of the Code Section 691. If lawyer A had died a week after collecting a $25,000 fee, the cash was obviously part of his estate but his estate received a deduction for the income tax liability which receipt of the fee entailed. Assuming he was in a 50 percent income tax bracket, the net increase in his taxable estate therefore amounted to $12,500. But if his client had paid the fee a week after his death, the full $25,000 would be includible in his estate but no deduction would be available, since the estate or legatee rather than the decedent would then be burdened with the income tax. To alleviate this hardship Code Section 691 now provides an income tax deduction to an estate or beneficiary for the estate tax attributable to the "net value" of such an item. The valuation of the income item included can be no greater, however, than the amount included in gross income and is to be reduced by the expense items deducted in computing the net estate. This can best be illustrated by an example.

Suppose our lawyer had an estate of $200,000, including the uncollected fee of $25,000. He had unpaid expenses of $5,000 which would have been deductible by him if he had paid them and which are deducted as claims on the estate tax return. The net value of the item is therefore $20,000. If the estate had not included this item the estate tax would have been about 30 percent less. Thus the estate tax attributable to the net receivable of $20,000 is about $6,000. Assume his sole legatee Y collects the fee. Y would deduct from his taxable income in the year the fee is reported, $6,000. The problem becomes more complicated where the receivable is valued at less than face, as will usually be true, and where it is collected in part by the executor and in part by the legatee. But the statute roughly eliminates the inequity that existed.

3.11   Executory interests

Assume a lifetime gift "to A and his heirs but if A dies without issue, to B and his heirs." If A dies, leaving issue, the full value of the property will be part of A's estate, since the fee will pass under his will. Suppose B dies while A is still alive. B has a transmissible estate, which may or may not ever come into possession and enjoyment. If A has three children at the time of B's death it is worth very little; if A is 60 and has no issue, it is worth a great deal. Whatever it is worth must be included unless the right is so speculative as to be worthless. While the cases treat the problem as one of vested or contingent remainders, the true test is believed to be whether the interest survives and can be transferred.

3.12   Contingent remainders

In *Commissioner* v. *Rosser,* the testator left three daughters. His will directed his executors to continue his business so long as they deemed it advantageous to the estate and so long as it was satisfactory to the legatees or a majority of them. Meanwhile the daughters were to receive the income. Upon the discontinuance of the business the residue was to be paid to the daughters and, if any were dead at that time, to their issue. The business was continued until 1926. One daughter died in 1924, survived by a child. The Commissioner attempted unsuccessfully to include one third of the value of the business in the estate of the deceased daughter. The opinion discusses at length the difference between vested and contingent interests and found the interest to be nonincludible because contingent. The real reason, however, would seem to be that it was not transmissible. Her estate terminated with her death and this would be true whether it was contingent or vested, subject to divestment. Thus from an estate tax planning standpoint indefeasibly vested remainders are to be avoided; "to A for life, remainder to B and his heirs" will incur estate tax on the death of B during A's life whereas "to A for life, remainder to B but if he fail to survive A, then to his issue" will avoid any tax if he predeceases A.

3.13 Speculative interests

In some cases a transmissible interest may be excluded because its value is speculative and remote. Thus land may be given to a church "so long as it is used for church purposes." Here it is possible that the gift may terminate and the property return to the donor or his heirs since conceivably the church may close due to population shifts etc. But such possibility is so remote that it will be disregarded. On the other hand in a case of a gift of property to a widow so long as she remains unmarried, the donor's possibility of getting the property back, while far from certain, is very real. Here the value of the interest must be included, even though it presents a very difficult valuation problem.

3.14 Community property

Eight states—Arizona, California, Idaho, Louisiana, Nevada, New Mexico, Texas, and Washington—operate under the community property system.

In the jurisdictions noted above all property acquired by husband and wife during the marriage, other than by gift, devise, bequest, or inheritance, is community property. In some of these states but not in others, income from noncommunity assets becomes community. Where it is not possible to trace particular assets there is a presumption in favor of their being part of the community. The husband is the manager of the community property and generally, short of fraud, may deal with it as he will, although in some states his power to make gifts is limited. Upon his or her death the deceased spouse may dispose by will of his or her share of the community. In New Mexico this right is denied the wife who predeceases her husband. The same was true in California prior to 1927.

Before 1942 there was no specific federal legislation governing the estate taxability of community interests. The courts had generally held that only the one-half owned by the deceased spouse was includible in his estate but the result depended on local law. Thus in California the wife's share under pre-1927 law was a mere expectancy and the entire value of the property was included in the taxable estate of the husband.

The federal estate tax law was changed in 1942 to require inclusion of all community property in the estate of the first dying spouse except that portion shown to have been received as compensation for personal services actually rendered by the surviving spouse, but in no event was the amount includible to be less than the value of the community property subject to his or her testamentary power of disposition. While this was intended to equalize the tax burden in all the states and to destroy the advantage that had theretofore adhered in community ownership, it actually worked a hardship on residents of community property states.

Prior to 1942 the community advantage was tremendous where the husband was the sole breadwinner. Thus, if he amassed a fortune of $200,000, the tax on his death was only $4,800, whereas in the noncommunity state a citizen similarly circumstanced paid a federal tax of $31,500. Of course, the latter could avoid any later tax on the death of his wife by giving her an interest in his estate for life only. In community property states this tax on the wife's death could not be avoided as to her half of the community. However, since it would amount only to $4,800 on our assumption of $100,000 as her share of the community, the residents of community property states were better off, on the estate assumed, by almost $22,000.

After the 1942 Act the shoe that pinched was on the community foot. The tax was the same everywhere if the husband died first. But if the wife predeceased him, her half was subject to tax. Further, the local law presumption that all property was community and the tax presumption that threw the burden of proof on the survivor to show the share attributable to his personal services, made the 1942 solution unacceptable to the community states.

The Revenue Act of 1948 attacked the problem from a diametrically opposite approach by conferring the benefits of community ownership upon common law owners rather than forcing the hardships of common law ownership on community owners. This was accomplished through the introduction into the Code of a marital deduction for bequests to spouses. The extent and limitations on this deduction form the subject matter of chapter 4.

Lifetime transfers

3.15 *Marital rights*

Many state courts had held, in interpreting their inheritance tax acts, that a dower or curtesy interest of a surviving spouse was not includible in the tax estate of a decedent because no new rights were created at death in his surviving spouse. The federal Revenue Act of 1918, however, specifically required the inclusion of the value of dower and curtesy interests and statutory shares in lieu thereof, and the present Code Section 2040 is substantially the same. Thus, if the deceased had owned Blackacre, worth $40,000, but subject to his wife's dower interest, worth $8,000 the full value of $40,000 is taxable as part of his estate rather than the $32,000 interest, which is all he really owned at his death and all he could transmit by will.

3.16 *Joint ownership*

Code Section 2040 requires the inclusion of the full value of jointly owned property with right of survivorship in the estate of the first dying owner except to the extent that the survivor can show that he contributed to the purchase price. Thus, if husband and wife own Blackacre as joint tenants with right of survivorship, or as tenants by the entirety, its full value will be included in the estate of the first dying spouse, unless the survivor can show that she made contributions to the purchase price from property that originally belonged to her and had not been received or acquired from the decedent for less than a full and adequate consideration. In the typical case this means that the full value is taxed as part of the husband's estate. However, if the wife dies first, there would be nothing included in her estate assuming the husband used his funds to pay the purchase price and that he was able to establish this by proof. Where the husband contributes 75 percent and the wife 25 percent, 75 percent of the value will be taxed in the husband's estate, if he dies first. Where neither contributes anything, as where the property is acquired by gift or inheritance, then half the value is included. If the property is owned as tenants in common or without right of survivorship, then only the half owned is included without regard to the source of payment.

Joint ownership and the problems it presents form the subject matter of chapter 8, to which the reader is referred for a more detailed discussion of this topic.

3.17 Gifts in contemplation of death

The value at the date of death of all property transferred during life by a decedent, for less than a full and adequate consideration, in contemplation of death is included in the tax estate. The Commissioner may not, however, include any transfer made more than three years prior to the date of death, no matter how clear the evidence that it was prompted by death motives.

Gifts in contemplation of death and the problems they present form the subject matter of chapter 12, to which the reader is referred for a more detailed discussion of this topic.

3.18 Life insurance

The proceeds of life insurance are includible in the estate of the deceased insured if:

1. He owned the policy or any incidents therein at the time of death or;
2. The policy was payable to his estate.

The premium payment test, which required the inclusion of the proceeds of all insurance purchased by the decedent on his life in his estate even though ownership was vested solely and exclusively in others, was happily discarded by the 1954 Code.

Policies on the lives of others, owned by the decedent, are includible at their terminal reserve or (in some cases) replacement value at the date of death.

Life insurance forms the subject matter of chapter 15, to which the reader is referred for a detailed discussion of this subject.

3.19 Annuities

The 1954 Code contains a specific provision for the taxability of survivorship annuities. Prior to this amendment there was considerable uncertainty as to the basis of the inclusion of the value of these future payments. Assume the husband purchased a joint and survivorship annuity for his life and the life of his wife. Upon his death payments of $5,000 a year were to be continued to his wife, who had an expectancy of ten years. The case law tended to include the present value of these future payments on the theory that the husband had made a transfer with income reserved for life. More difficulty was encountered in cases where an employer, under a deferred compensation arrangement, agreed to pay stated sums on retirement to the husband with continued payments to the wife, if she survived. Here there was difficulty in finding that any "transfer" had ever been made by the husband, as required by the Code.

The new provision applies to all payments made following the death of the primary annuitant, under contracts (other than insurance) where the payments may be regarded as a transfer from him. Thus, it applies to survivorship annuities purchased from insurance companies, private annuities, and contracts between employer and employee. It does not matter whether the payments are for a fixed number of years or for life. The amount to be included in the gross estate will be based upon the value, as of the date of the decedent's death, of the payments that are to be made following his death. The portion of the value to be included, however, is only the percentage of the purchase price paid by the decedent. Thus, if he paid the full price the full value is included; if he paid only half the cost only half the value of the future payments is included. Contributions made by an employer are attributed to an employee except those made to qualified pensions, stock bonus, profit-sharing, or retirement plans. Thus the Code excludes from the taxable estate a portion at least and in many cases the full amount of annuities under qualified employee pension and profit-sharing plans.[1] This exemption applies to estates of decedents dying after December 31, 1953.

3.20   Retained life estates

The value of the gross estate includes the full value of all property transferred during life, by gift, after March 3, 1931, if the donor retains for his life or for a period not ascertainable without reference to his death or for a period which does not in fact end before his death, either:

1. The possession and enjoyment of, or the right to the income from the property; or

2. The right alone or in conjunction with any other person to designate who shall possess or enjoy the property or the income therefrom.

Reserved life estates and the problems they present form the subject matter of chapter 14, to which the reader is referred for a detailed discussion of this topic.

3.21   Possibilities of reverter

The full value of all property transferred by gift during life, wherein the donor reserves a possibility of reverter, will be included as part of his tax estate, if possession and enjoyment by the donee may be obtained only by surviving the donor,

---

[1] Note that HR 10 Plans do not enjoy this favored exclusion.

but only if the value of the reversionary interest immediately before the death of the decedent exceeds 5% of the value of such property. With respect to transfers made before October 8, 1949, the reversionary interest must arise by the express terms of the instrument of gift. Thus, Husband conveys Blackacre to Wife for life, remainder to Son, but if Wife predeceases Husband, Backacre to revert to Husband in fee. Here the reversion is express and assuming Wife is 50 and Husband is 55, the value of the chance that the property will return to Husband is undoubtedly worth more than 5%, i.e. he has more than 1 chance in 20 of regaining the full fee title. The full value of Blackacre, less the vested life estate in Wife, will be included in Husband's estate since his death is the event which first gives Son an indefeasible remainder.

Possibilities of reverter and the problems they present form the subject matter of chapter 14, to which the reader is referred for a detailed discussion of this topic.

3.22 *Retained powers*

The gross estate includes the value of all property transferred by gift where the enjoyment thereof is subject to any change through the exercise of a power by the decedent alone, or in conjunction with any other person, to alter, amend, revoke, or change the terms of the gift. The most limited retained powers may cause the gift to be incomplete for estate tax purposes under this section, whereas only the very broadest powers will attract estate tax where the powers are vested in one other than a grantor. These latter powers are discussed in chapter 5.

Revocable transfers and the problems they present form the subject matter of chapter 14, to which the reader is referred for a detailed discussion of this topic.

3.23 *Powers of appointment*

Powers represent, perhaps, the most useful tool in the estate planner's kit. Chapter 5 is devoted to this topic. Suffice it to say here, in this summary of the federal estate tax law, that a general power is defined as a power, by will or deed, to appoint property to any person or persons, including the holder of the power, his creditors, his estate, or the creditors of his estate. Unless the holder (donee) of the power can appoint the property for his own benefit it is a special power. Neither the existence nor the exercise of a special power will attract estate tax. With respect to general powers created before October 21, 1942, the property over which the power exists will be subjected to estate tax only if the power is exercised. But the mere existence of a general power created on or after October 21, 1942, will result in the inclusion of the property in the taxable estate whether exercised or not. There are many refinements to the above summary, and the reader is referred to chapter 5 for a detailed treatment of this subject.

Valuation

3.24 *Valuation*

For purposes of estimating probable death costs it is enough for the estate planner to make rough approximations of values. In the larger estates it may be advisable to list a possible high and low value for particular assets, making two alternative tax computations.

Securities traded on recognized exchanges present no problems generally in preparing the estate tax return. Where, however, this is a large block and the market is "thin" a substantial reduction under the market quotation may be proper under the blockage rule. Disputes may arise as to values of real estate, mortgages, notes, etc. The submission of careful and detailed appraisals by qualified persons will prove most helpful.

In the valuation of business interests, stock in close corporations, doubtful claims, other assets for which no ready market exists, the criteria are extremely vague and wide differences of opinion between the taxpayer and the examining agent will almost certainly develop. It may be said that there are as many valuation problems as there are different types of property and the issues can be resolved only by a good deal of give and take on both sides. The problem should be recognized for what it is, a horse trade, and an executor and his advisers would do well to remember that the figure suggested by the agent does not necessarily fix the top amount the Commissioner may seek if the matter goes to litigation. In Estate of Eugene H. Kelly the return submitted a value of $54,709.78 for 106 shares of stock. The investigating agent determined a value of $106,000. The Commissioner later increased this value to $424,000 and the Tax Court finally fixed a value of $233,000.

It should also be noted here that particularly in the more modest estates the lowest possible value may not always be the least costly. Assume an estate with net assets of $60,000 plus Blackacre, with a value variously estimated at between $30,000 and $40,000. The estate tax on $90,000 is $3,000; on $100,000 it is $4,800. Thus the lower value will save $1,800 but if the property is later sold for $40,000 a possible $2,500 capital gains tax may be incurred. If the property is held and is depreciable the extra $10,000 may be worth $4,000 or $5,000 or more in income tax deductions, depending on the legatee's top brackets.[2] While the estate tax value does not necessarily fix the income tax cost basis, it is so generally accepted as doing so that, except in the most unusual cases, it may safely be assumed to have this result.

3.25   Optional valuation date

The executor may, at his election, value the estate assets for federal tax purposes at their values at the date of death or six months from the date of death. The election must be made at the time of filing a timely return, i.e. nine months after the date of death or within any later date if the time is extended by the Commissioner. This option came into the law during the depression as a result of the hardships caused by sharp declines in values. There were said to have been hundreds of estates of persons who died in 1929 whose gross asset value in 1930 was less than the federal tax due.

---

[2] There may, of course, in some cases be some depreciation recapture but if this occurs it merely reduces to some extent the advantage.

If the executor elects the six months from date of death value, all assets disposed of during the period are valued as of the date of sale, exchange, or distribution. Thus if some General Motors stock was sold to raise cash, some Standard Oil distributed to a legatee, these two items would be included at their values at the dates of disposal by the executor.

Any property whose value is affected by mere lapse of time is to be valued as of the date of death with an adjustment for any difference in value due to factors other than lapse of time. This exception refers to depreciable items.

Suppose the decedent owned a patent. At the time of his death it had a life of seven years and a value of $70,000. With no change whatever in economic conditions it would be worth $65,000 six months later. If, in fact, it is worth, due to a slight recession, $45,000 at the later date, $50,000 is to be reported. This is obviously proper in view of the policy behind the option.

The Commissioner originally took the position that if the later date valuation was elected all interest and dividends received during the period must be included in the tax estate. The regulation was held invalid in *Maas* v. *Higgins*.[3] However, any extraordinary dividend will not be recognized as reducing the worth since this would open the door to avoidance and violate the basic objectives of the legislation.

Deductions

3.26   Deductions in general

Again, for the purpose of estimating probable death taxes, deductions may be approximated. These will vary widely with the individual estate owners, depending on likely liabilities at death. Costs of administration, including executor's commis-

---

[3] Note that if A owns an insurance policy on B's life and A dies the value of the unmatured policy is part of A's estate. Suppose B then dies within six months of A and A's executor elects the alternate valuation date. Rev. Rul 63–52 holds the increase to face value is not income and hence is not excluded property. Hence the full proceeds are includible in A's estate *if* the alternate valuation date is elected.

sions and attorney's fees, differ greatly in different sections of the country and for estates of different sizes.

Deductions are limited to the extent allowed "by the laws of the jurisdiction . . . under which the estate is being administered." If a state court approves a claim, after a hearing on the merits, the Commissioner is bound by such determination. Of course, there is no requirement that claims be litigated. Most claims will be recognized as indisputable by the executor, paid and allowed without question.

The 1954 Code made an important change with respect to deductions. Under the old Code allowable deductions could not exceed the value of the property included in the gross estate and which under local law was subject to the claims against the estate. Thus, if the decedent left $100,000 of life insurance and $100,000 of jointly owned property and his family paid funeral expenses, debts, etc., of $25,000, no deductions were allowable since the property was not liable under state law for these obligations. It is now provided that if such items are in fact paid prior to the time of filing the estate tax return they shall be allowed.

3.27 Funeral expenses

Burial expenses are deductible. The Regulations limit the expenditures "for a tombstone, monument, mausoleum, or for a burial lot, either for the decedent or his family, to a reasonable amount." The cost of transportation of the person bringing the body to the place of burial is also deductible. While there are a few cases to the contrary, the cost of perpetual care is generally disallowed.

3.28 Administration expenses

Expenses in connection with the collection of assets, the payment of debts, and the distribution of estate property are deductible. Thus, court costs, accounting fees, necessary travel, clerk hire, appraiser's fees, cost of maintaining estate assets, brokerage fees, etc. are all deductible. Expenses, uncertain as to amount, at the filing of the return, such as attorney's fees, may be estimated.

Perhaps the most frequently litigated issue involves the executor's commissions. A bequest or devise to an executor may be a gift or it may be compensation for his services. If the latter it is deductible by the estate and constitutes taxable income to the executor. On the other hand, a bequest to which he becomes entitled merely by qualifying and which is not conditioned on the performance of any service is not deductible and is received free of income tax. Whether a particular bequest is a gift or compensation depends on the intent of the testator as determined by construing the terms of the will. Even where intended as compensation the executor may avoid the income tax by promptly waiving any commissions but at a sacrifice of the estate tax deduction. Where he is a high bracket taxpayer and a substantial beneficiary, the family as a whole may be better off if he agrees to undertake the task without compensation.

Costs of administration such as attorneys' fees and executors' commissions may at the option of the executor be deducted from the estate's income tax return rather than from the estate tax return. Generally, because income tax rates are higher, using these deductions for income tax purposes will result in an overall saving.

3.29 Claims against the estate

All legally enforceable obligations existing at the time of death are deductible except that where the obligation is founded upon a promise or agreement it must be supported by an adequate and full consideration in money or money's worth. Further the relinquishment of marital rights is not considered to any extent a consideration in money or money's worth. Thus where a wife was entitled to a $50,000 bequest under a prenuptial agreement, the court held nothing was deductible in the estate of the husband on account of this obligation in spite of its enforceability under state law.

The Regulations state that liabilities imposed by law or arising out of torts are deductible. Such claims need not be supported by full and adequate consideration. In *Commission* v. *Maresi* the court held a claim under a divorce decree was not a claim based upon a promise or agreement and therefore need not be supported by full and adequate consideration. It would appear, however, that if there was merely an agreement, not incorporated in a decree of divorce or separation, then the claim would not be deductible. Congress in 1954 amended the gift tax sections of the Code to make clear that any agreement relative to marital and property rights incident to a divorce, if the divorce occurs within two years thereafter, shall, for gift tax purposes, be deemed to be for a full and adequate consideration. Unfortunately no corresponding amendment was made to the estate tax sections. The deductibility may, therefore, depend on whether the agreement is incorporated in the decree.

3.30   Unpaid mortgages and suretyship arrangements

For an unpaid mortgage to be deductible the value of the property must be includible in the estate. Where the decedent owns only a half interest in mortgaged property, only half the indebtedness may be deducted, even though he is jointly and severally liable. This is sound since the decedent's estate, if it paid the mortgage, would have a right over by the rules of subrogation. Thus, in *Duval* v. *Commissioner,* the decedent had guaranteed a $200,000 obligation of a corporation, in which he had a substantial interest. At his death the corporation was perfectly solvent and able to pay the debt. The executor paid it, however, and claimed a deduction. This was disallowed on the theory that the estate immediately on payment became entitled to reimbursement from the corporation and if the deduction were to be allowed, a corresponding asset, i.e. the right of reimbursement, should be included in the estate return. From what has been said above as to mortgages it should not be assumed that the value of the property limits the deduction. If the value of the included property is $20,000 but the mortgages is $30,000, the full $30,000 is deductible, assuming the decedent to have been personally liable for the mortgage debt.

3.31   Community property

All claims and expenses which are the personal obligations of the decedent may be deducted in full. Any obligation which is attributable to the marital estate is deductible only to the extent of one half, since only one half of the marital estate is includible. What claims are allocable to the personal estate and what to the marital is a matter of local state law. In most community-property states the executor administers the whole estate, though only half is included in the decedent's tax estate. Since commissions are therefore incurred on behalf of the entire community property, only one half are deductible. If, however, a particular item of expense can be attributed to the decedent's interest solely, as fees in the settlement of the estate tax, they are deductible in full.

3.32   Marital deduction

The marital deduction forms the subject matter of chapter 4, to which the reader is referred for a discussion of this topic.

3.33   Losses

Under Code Section 2054 the estate may, at the option of the executor, deduct either from the estate tax return or from the income tax return, but not from both, any losses sustained (after the decedent's death) from "fires, storms, shipwrecks, or other casualties or from theft," provided the losses are not compensated for by insurance or otherwise.[4] Sometimes it will be to the advantage of the estate to take the deduction from the estate return, in other instances the saving will be greater

---

[4] Under the 1964 Code amendments the first $100 of any casualty loss is not deductible for income tax purposes.

if it is used to reduce the income tax payable. No generalization is possible here.

It should also be noted that, both here and in the election provided by the optional valuation date, see section 3.25, as well as in the election to deduct administration expenses from either return, the executor may under the typical marital deduction formula clause, increase or decrease the marital deduction bequest by the choice he makes.

3.34   Charitable bequests

The amount of all bequests for public, charitable, and religious uses are deductible. The requirement that deductions for claims be limited to the extent they were contracted for a full and adequate consideration in money or money's worth does not apply to enforceable pledges to charitable organizations. This was not always true. In *Taft* v. *Commissioner* the court held that an amount paid by an executor on a charitable subscription made by a decedent was not deductible even though the estate was legally liable for the payment. This result was changed by what is now section 2053(c) which makes enforceable pledges deductible as if they were charitable bequests.

See discussion in section 7.10 of Charitable Remainder Trusts.

Exemption, rates, credits

3.35   Exemptions

There is a specific exemption of $60,000. A return must be filed in every case where the gross estate exceeds $60,000, even though, because of deductions, no tax is payable.

3.36   Rates

Section 2001 provides as follows:

Section 2001.   *Rate of tax*   A tax computed in accordance with the following table is hereby imposed on the transfer of the taxable estate, determined as provided in Section 2051, of every decedent, citizen, or resident of the United States, dying after the date of enactment of this title:

If the taxable estate is:	The tax shall be:
Not over $5,000............................	3% of the taxable estate.
Over $5,000 but not over $10,000..............	$150, plus 7% of excess over $5,000.
Over $10,000 but not over $20,000.............	$500, plus 11% of excess over $10,000.
Over $20,000 but not over $30,000.............	$1,600, plus 14% of excess over $20,000.
Over $30,000 but not over $40,000.............	$3,000, plus 18% of excess over $30,000.
Over $40,000 but not over $50,000.............	$4,800, plus 22% of excess over $40,000.
Over $50,000 but not over $60,000.............	$7,000, plus 25% of excess over $50,000.
Over $60,000 but not over $100,000............	$9,500, plus 28% of excess over $60,000.
Over $100,000 but not over $250,000...........	$20,700, plus 30% of excess over $100,000.
Over $250,000 but not over $500,000...........	$65,700, plus 32% of excess over $250,000.
Over $500,000 but not over $750,000...........	$145,700, plus 35% of excess over $500,000.
Over $750,000 but not over $1,000,000.........	$233,200, plus 37% of excess over $750,000.
Over $1,000,000 but not over $1,250,000........	$325,700, plus 39% of excess over $1,000,000.
Over $1,250,000 but not over $1,500,000........	$423,200, plus 42% of excess over $1,250,000.
Over $1,500,000 but not over $2,000,000........	$528,200, plus 45% of excess over $1,500,000.
Over $2,000,000 but not over $2,500,000........	$753,200, plus 49% of excess over $2,000,000.
Over $2,500,000 but not over $3,000,000........	$998,200, plus 53% of excess over $2,500,000.
Over $3,000,000 but not over $3,500,000........	$1,263,200, plus 56% of excess over $3,000,000.
Over $3,500,000 but not over $4,000,000........	$1,543,200, plus 59% of excess over $3,500,000.
Over $4,000,000 but not over $5,000,000........	$1,838,200, plus 63% of excess over $4,000,000.
Over $5,000,000 but not over $6,000,000........	$2,468,200, plus 67% of excess over $5,000,000.
Over $6,000,000 but not over $7,000,000........	$3,138,200, plus 70% of excess over $6,000,000.
Over $7,000,000 but not over $8,000,000........	$3,838,200, plus 73% of excess over $7,000,000.
Over $8,000,000 but not over $10,000,000.......	$4,568,200, plus 76% of excess over $8,000,000.
Over $10,000,000............................	$6,088,200, plus 77% of excess over $10,000,000.

3.37 *Credit for state death taxes*[5]

The amount of any state death taxes paid may be subtracted from the tax as determined under the preceding table, provided, however, that the maximum to be subtracted may not exceed the maximum determined under the following table, set out in section 2001:

If the taxable estate is:	The maximum tax credit shall be:
Not over $90,000	$\frac{8}{10}$ths of 1% of the amount by which the taxable estate exceeds $40,000.
Over $90,000 but not over $140,000	$400 plus 1.6% of the excess over $90,000.
Over $140,000 but not over $240,000	$1,200 plus 2.4% of the excess over $140,000.
Over $240,000 but not over $440,000	$3,600 plus 3.2% of the excess over $240,000.
Over $440,000 but not over $640,000	$10,000 plus 4% of the excess over $440,000.
Over $640,000 but not over $840,000	$18,000 plus 4.8% of the excess over $640,000.
Over $840,000 but not over $1,040,000	$27,600 plus 5.6% of the excess over $840,000.
Over $1,040,000 but not over $1,540,000	$38,800 plus 6.4% of the excess over $1,040,000.
Over $1,540,000 but not over $2,040,000	$70,800 plus 7.2% of the excess over $1,540,000.
Over $2,040,000 but not over $2,540,000	$106,800 plus 8% of the excess over $2,040,000.
Over $2,540,000 but not over $3,040,000	$146,800 plus 8.8% of the excess over $2,540,000.
Over $3,040,000 but not over $3,540,000	$190,800 plus 9.6% of the excess over $3,040,000.
Over $3,540,000 but not over $4,040,000	$238,800 plus 10.4% of the excess over $3,540,000.
Over $4,040,000 but not over $5,040,000	$290,800 plus 11.2% of the excess over $4,040,000.
Over $5,040,000 but not over $6,040,000	$402,800 plus 12% of the excess over $5,040,000.
Over $6,040,000 but not over $7,040,000	$522,800 plus 12.8% of the excess over $6,040,000.
Over $7,040,000 but not over $8,040,000	$650,800 plus 13.6% of the excess over $7,040,000.
Over $8,040,000 but not over $9,040,000	$786,800 plus 14.4% of the excess over $8,040,000.
Over $9,040,000 but not over $10,040,000	$930,800 plus 15.2% of the excess over $9,040,000.
Over $10,040,000	$1,082,800 plus 16% of the excess over $10,040,000.

---

[5] No reference is made in the text to the credit for foreign taxes since this credit occurs only in rare cases. Its existence should, however, be noted.

Assume the taxable estate is $240,000. The maximum credit is $3,600. If the state tax amounts to $6,000 the credit is limited to $3,600. If, however, the state tax is $1,500, then the credit is limited to $1,500. It should be noted that in almost all cases the full credit will be available, since in all states except Nevada, there is in addition to the regular succession tax, if any, an additional estate tax[6] designed solely to take up the difference between the regular death tax and the maximum allowable credit. Thus, if the tax, as assumed above, were $1,500, the state estate tax would automatically be the difference between $1,500 and $3,600, or $2,100.

3.38 Credit for gift taxes

There is a credit for gift taxes paid on transfers subsequently included in the taxable estate, with the limitation that it may not exceed the proportion of the total estate tax which the property given away bears to the entire gross estate.

It generally comes as a shock to students to learn that a transfer may be subject to both gift and estate taxes. However, a little reflection will indicate that such a possibility is inevitable in some situations. Perhaps the most obvious illustration is a gift in contemplation of death. Assume an estate owner, in contemplation of death to avoid estate taxes and for no other reason, gives away $100,000. It is necessary to impose a gift tax on the transfer (1) because it shifts the income tax on the future income, and (2) it cannot at that time be known with any degree of certainty whether the transfer will incur estate tax since the donor may live for more than three years after the transfer. The double tax where it occurs is generally not a hardship since the allowance of a credit against the estate tax for the amount of the gift tax paid is, in most cases, a full or substantially full credit.

3.39 Credit for tax on prior transfers

The 1954 Code eliminated the deduction for previously taxed property and substituted a credit for the previous taxes

---

[6] Florida, Alabama, Georgia and Arkansas impose an estate tax measured solely by the amount of the federal credit.

paid. Under the old deduction taxpayers often ran into insuperable tracing difficulties resulting in the denial of the deduction solely because of a failure of proof.

The credit, however, may not exceed the lower of (1) the estate tax paid on the property, or (2) the amount by which the present decedent's estate tax would be increased if the value of the transferred assets were included in his estate and the relief under this section was not available. In addition, the figure obtained as the lower of (1) or (2) must be reduced 20 percent for each two-year period following the death of the transferor. Thus, the credit is 100 percent of the amount so computed if the first decedent died within two years of the present decedent, 80 percent if within three or four years, 60 percent if within five or six years, 40 percent if within seven or eight years, 20 percent if within nine or ten years.

3.40 Payment of the tax

The tax is due with the filing of the return, i.e. nine months after the date of death. Code Sections 2006 and 2007 require the recipients of life insurance and property which was subject to a general power of appointment to bear their proportionate shares of the tax. Other than that, the burden of the tax is left to state law. Since the tax is an estate tax, one on giving, rather than an inheritance tax, one on receiving, the courts generally imposed the burden on the residue. Because of the hardships this rule created, many states now have apportionment statutes which require that the tax be borne equitably among the beneficiaries. It is clear that the will may override both state and federal statutes and that the testator may charge the taxes where he will. Because of the heavy impact of death taxes, wills generally contain such tax clauses to avoid doing violence to the testator's general plan. See section 7.19.

In any case where it is found that payment on the due date would cause undue hardship, the Commissioner may extend the time for payment for a period or periods not to exceed one year for any one period and for all periods not to exceed ten years.

Where a large portion of the decedent's estate consists of a closely held business, the executor may, as a matter of right, pay the tax in installments. In general, when the value of the interest in such a closely held business exceeds 35 percent of the gross estate or 50 percent of the taxable estate, the executor may elect to pay all or a part of the tax attributable to the decedent's interest in the business in not more than ten equal annual installments. The interest is an attractive 4 percent.

4

Marital deduction bequests

In general

4.1 Introduction

The marital deduction in the Code is comparatively new. It is extremely important and the estate planner should have an intimate knowledge of the way in which it operates. It offers opportunities in some cases for tremendous tax savings. Its use, in other cases, may prove very costly. Further the courts have construed the marital deduction provisions most strictly. Slight variations from the precise requirements of the Code sections have frequently resulted in unnecessary increases in taxes. Since the deduction is still in its infancy a familiarity with the historical background that prompted Congress to allow the deduction is important in understanding the Code section.

4.2 Historical background

As noted in section 3.14 the residents of community property states enjoyed a tremendous tax advantage (income, gift, and estate) over residents, similarly situated, in common law jurisdictions. Thus, the Texan, who, during his married life, amassed a fortune of $200,000 paid on death an estate tax of $4,800. The New Yorker, who had the identical good fortune, paid $31,500. The Texan could give $66,000 free of gift taxes, the New Yorker only $33,000. On a $50,000 income the New Yorker paid twice the income tax of the Texan. The reason for this was that under community property law one half of the earnings of either spouse automatically became the property of the other and the Supreme Court in *Poe* v. *Seaborn* recognized this property division concept as a limitation on the taxing authorities.

4.3 The 1942 solution

In 1941 and 1942 efforts were made to eliminate this discrimination. The efforts failed in Congress insofar as they were directed at income tax equalization but resulted in estate and gift tax amendments, which treated the spouse to whose efforts the community property was attributable as the owner for tax purposes. This partial equality did not satisfy the taxpayers in the common law states who resented the serious income tax discrimination. Indeed a number of jurisdictions, Hawaii, Michigan, Nebraska, Oklahoma, and Oregon, substituted the community property system for their traditional property law in order to gain the income tax advantage.

At the same time the community property residents objected vigorously to the change which they claimed placed them at a distinct disadvantage. The New Yorker and the Texan were now being taxed the same amount on the assumed $200,000 estate accumulated through the husband's efforts, but the New Yorker could arrange to avoid any estate tax on his wife's later death by giving her a life interest only in his estate. The Texan, however, since he could control the disposition of only half the wealth, could eliminate only half from the later tax. Further, the presumption in favor of community property cast a heavy burden of proof on the survivor in cases where inadequate records had been kept. When the Supreme Court sustained the constitutionality of the 1942 amendments to the estate tax, the community property taxpayers joined the common law taxpayers in seeking a new solution.

4.4 The 1948 solution

The 1942 amendments were repealed. The now familiar income tax splitting was introduced. In addition common law taxpayers were permitted to split gifts and, in effect, split the estate into taxable and nontaxable halves, if they desired. Thus, instead of forcing the common law system on community owners, common law residents were permitted for tax purposes to elect to obtain the community property advantages. This was accomplished in the estate tax field by freeing one half of the gross estate from tax if it were left to a spouse in substantially the same way that the law of Texas, for example, vests it in a spouse. The Congressional objective was, speaking generally, to permit these tax-free bequests to a surviving spouse, provided the amount given would be subject to tax on the subsequent death of the survivor. Unfortunately, the Code, instead of setting forth this general principle, states in considerable detail, the requirements for a marital deduction bequest, with the result that many bequests to spouses may fail to obtain the deduction even though it is clear the assets given will form part of their taxable estates on their later deaths. It is for this reason that the statute must be carefully studied and strictly adhered to even though certain of the more glaring pitfalls were eliminated in 1954.

Estates and transfers which qualify

4.5 *Estates which may qualify for the marital deduction*

The deduction is available to the estates of citizens and residents of the United States. It applies to intestate as well as testate transfers, but the property must pass at death or have passed during life, from the decedent to his spouse. The questions of survivorship and of lifetime transfers are reserved for the immediately following sections. It should be noted here, however, that property interests assigned or surrendered to a spouse as a result of a will contest or the settlement thereof will be regarded as having passed to the spouse from the decedent only if the assignment or surrender was a bona fide recognition of legally enforceable rights. In *Estate of Barrett* the decedent and her husband were parties to an antenuptial agreement in which each waived all rights in the other's property. The wife died and the husband claimed one third of her estate, which amounted to about $400,000. After considerable negotiation he accepted $10,500 in settlement of his claim. Since the court found the compromise was the result of arm's length bargaining, it allowed the deduction for this sum as passing from the decedent to her spouse.

4.6   *Renunciations*

Renunciations make possible some post mortem planning. Property passing to a wife outright under a will or by intestacy will qualify, of course, for the marital deduction. Further, in most jurisdictions the wife may claim against the will. Thus if the will leaves the entire estate to the children, the wife may claim her intestate share and this will form the basis for a marital deduction. What about cases where the will leaves the entire estate to the son and he refuses to accept? If, as a result of his refusal, the property or a part of it passes to the wife, it will, since 1966, qualify for the marital deduction. Similar renunciations of life insurance proceeds or other inter vivos gifts to third persons may result in property passing to a spouse. If this is the effect of such a renunciation it may increase the marital deduction.

The law prior to 1966 did not permit renunciations to have this effect.

4.7   *Survivorship*

To qualify, the bequest must pass to a person who is the "surviving spouse." Generally this will not cause any problems since all that need be shown is that the parties were married and not divorced: Apparently bequests to a spouse from whom the decedent was legally separated will qualify.

Problems will arise, however, where deaths result from a common accident and it is not possible to establish the order of deaths. Under these circumstances the Regulations provide that if it is impossible to determine who died first, any presumption, whether established by local law or the decedent's will, shall govern. To the extent that such presumption results in the inclusion of a bequest in the taxable estate of the spouse deemed to have survived, the marital deduction will be allowed in the estate of the other spouse. While the risk of the deaths occurring under circumstances where there is no evidence as to the order of deaths may be slight, wills frequently contain a simultaneous death clause, wherever it is important to obtain the marital deduction. And it will be important to obtain it in all those cases where one of the spouses owns the bulk of the family wealth. Assume Husband has $200,000, and Wife's assets are nominal. If Wife survives Husband, or if Wife is presumed to have survived Husband, the tax on his estate will be $4,800. The tax on her estate may be limited to $4,800. But if she predeceases him, or is presumed to have predeceased him, the tax on his estate will be $31,500, with no tax on her estate. In the absence of any reference to the matter of survivorship in the will, if the order of deaths cannot be determined, both the common law rule and the rule under the Uniform Simultaneous Death Act (law in practically all states) distributes the estate of each as though he were the survivor. Thus, in the absence of any clause in the will, the marital deduction will be lost at a cost, in the example above, of $21,900.

Prior to the marital deduction it was customary to provide that if any legatee failed to survive the testator for some appreciable time, he should be deemed to have predeceased him. This avoided passage of the property through the estate of a legatee who failed to survive long enough to enjoy the bequest and thereby saved considerable administration expenses and taxes. It still represents a desirable clause for other than marital deduction bequests. But with respect to bequests to spouses, lawyers frequently (but not always)[1] find it advisable to reverse the usual presumption and provide that the spouse legatee shall be deemed to have survived. Thus in the example above, the will of the husband would contain a clause creating a presumption that his wife survived him.

The type of clause used is vitally important, if the deduction is desired in all possible contingencies under which it may be obtained. There are three general types of clauses:

1. *Common disaster*   "In the event my wife and I die as a result of a common accident she shall be presumed to have survived me."

----
[1] See 7.16.

2. *Time*   "In the event my wife survives me by 60 days, she shall be" presumed to have survived me.

3. *Simultaneous death*   "In the event that my wife and I die under such circumstances that it is not possible to determine who predeceased the other she shall be deemed to have survived me."

Clause 1 is not satisfactory. The objective has nothing to do with a common disaster but rather with the question of proof of the order of deaths. Probably the deduction would be available if both spouses died as a result of a common disaster and under circumstances that were such that the order of deaths could not be determined. But it is the latter condition that is solely important, not the element of a common disaster. Further, suppose Wife demonstrably died two days before Husband. Here the deduction would be denied, because Wife did not, in fact, survive but under the clause she would receive the bequest which would pass through her estate with unnecessary administration expenses, state taxes, and possible federal estate taxes because the credit for previously taxed property would be less than complete if Wife individually owned any assets at the time of her death.

Clause 2 will not achieve the desired result if the deaths are simultaneous since she must survive by 60 days in order to take. Since nothing would pass to her there would be no deduction.

The clause lawyers generally recommend is as follows:

"In the event my wife and I die under such circumstances that there is no sufficient evidence to establish who survived the other, I hereby declare that my wife shall be deemed to have survived me and this will and all its provisions shall be construed upon that assumption and basis."

It should be noted that this clause is not used indiscriminately, since in many circumstances the marital deduction is desired only on the assumption that the surviving spouse is likely to survive for a substantial number of years. This will be true wherever both spouses have substantial estates. For the type of recommended clause in these cases, see section 4.19.

4.8   Amount of marital deduction

The amount of the marital deduction is limited to 50 percent of the "adjusted gross estate." This is a new concept created by the 1948 Act and is important only for purposes of computing the deduction. The "adjusted gross estate" is defined by Section 2056(c)(2) as equal to the amount of the decedent's gross estate less the deductions allowed by Code Sections 2053 and 2054. These are funeral expenses, administration expenses, debts, and claims against the estate and losses incurred during settlement of the estate arising from fires, storms, shipwrecks, or other casualties, or from theft, when not compensated for by insurance or otherwise. It will be remembered that the losses specified above may be deducted, at the option of the executor, either from the income tax return or from the estate tax return.[2] They affect the marital deduction only if deducted from the estate tax return. Thus at times it may be possible to increase the amount of the allowable marital deduction by electing to take these items against the income tax rather than the estate tax. Neither the $60,000 exemption nor charitable bequests are deducted in determining the adjusted gross estate.

In order not to permit the deduction with respect to community property all community property interests included in the estate and the percentage of deductions allocable thereto are subtracted. In addition, if the decedent and his spouse have at any time converted community into separate property after December 31, 1941, the separate property so acquired and any property received in exchange therefor is treated as if it were community. Thus once community, always community, for tax purposes. Any other rule might permit three-fourths of the estate instead of one-half to escape gift and estate taxes. Thus, assume Husband and Wife own a community estate of $400,000. They convert it to separate property. Each now has $200,000 and no taxable gift has been made by either to the other. Husband dies, leaving his estate to Wife. If he were

---

[2] See 3.32.

allowed a marital deduction, $300,000 of the $400,000 would escape tax.

The computation of the maximum allowable marital deduction may be illustrated by an extremely simple example. Assume Husband owns stocks, bonds, cash in bank, etc., worth $200,000. No lifetime gifts have been made. There is no insurance, no jointly owned property, no property over which he has a power of appointment. Debts, including unpaid income taxes, current bills, etc. total $13,000. Funeral and administration expenses amount to $12,000. He leaves $25,000 to charity, residue equally to his wife and two children, with a tax clause charging all death taxes to the shares passing to the children.

Gross estate.....................................	$200,000
Less debts and administrative expenses..........	25,000
Adjusted gross estate....................	$175,000
Maximum allowable marital deduction.......................	$87,500

Something less than the maximum is allowable in this case, however, since the deduction may not exceed the amount actually passing to the wife. Under the will her share of the residue will amount to $50,000 (gross $200,000 less $25,000 charitable bequest and $25,000 administration expenses and debts leaves $150,000; ⅓ of $150,000 equals $50,000).

The computation of the taxable estate will be as follows:

Gross estate...		$200,000
Less debts and adm. exp......................	$25,000	
Charitable bequest........................	25,000	
Marital deduction........................	50,000	100,000
Net estate..		$100,000
Less specific exemption............................		60,000
Taxable estate..		$ 40,000

4.9 Transfers qualifying for the marital deductions

The property interest must be one which "passes or has passed to the surviving spouse." Passing includes all methods by which property may be transferred during life or at death to the extent such transfers are included in the tax estate. Thus, the proceeds of life insurance, jointly owned property, gifts in contemplation of death, etc., may enter into the computation of the maximum allowable marital deduction and also into the computation of the amount actually allowed. Assume a decedent's estate consisted of the following:

Cash...	$ 5,000
Life insurance, owned by him, payable to wife...................	50,000
Residence, paid for by him, owned jointly with wife.............	25,000
Gift to son in contemplation of death...........................	50,000
Revocable trust, with corpus distributable at his death in equal shares to wife and son..	50,000
Miscellaneous..	5,000
Gross estate..	$185,000

Under the will everything is left to the son. Assume debts and administration expenses total $15,000 and that all death taxes are to be paid from the residuary estate.

The adjusted gross estate would be $170,000 and the maximum allowable marital deduction $85,000. Actually passing to the wife are the following:

Insurance...	$ 50,000
Residence...	25,000
Her share of revocable trust...................................	25,000
	$100,000

Since $100,000 exceeds the maximum allowable deduction, the deduction would be limited to $85,000.

4.10 Transfers which do not qualify for the marital deduction

Not every interest given to a spouse will qualify. In order to achieve the basic objective that any property received tax-free by the spouse, because of the deduction, will be taxed as part of her estate, unless given away or consumed, Section 2056(*b*)(1) disqualifies those interests (subject to certain exceptions) which may fail upon the lapse of time or the occurrence of an event or contingency, if it is possible that a third party may enjoy the property upon the termination of the wife's interest. Thus, "to my wife for 10 years, remainder to

X," "to my wife during widowhood," "to my wife for life" are all illustrations of what are called terminable interests. "To my wife in fee but if she fail to survive my brother, then over etc.," would also be a terminable interest. In order to avoid the terminable interest classification the property must vest in the surviving spouse and no other person may have any interest therein, vested or contingent, which may follow the interest of the spouse. There are three exceptions to the rule that a terminable interest will disqualify the property.

1. The bequest to the spouse may be conditioned upon survivorship for six months or upon the deaths occurring other than as a result of a common disaster.

2. Bequest of a life interest, coupled with a general power of appointment.

3. Life insurance proceeds paid under settlement options, provided the spouse is given the equivalent of a general power of appointment. These exceptions will be discussed in subsequent sections.

The terminable interest rule disqualifies what are called "tainted assets." Suppose Father transfers, by gift, Blackacre to Son, reserving the rents for 20 years. At death he leaves the term for years to Mother. Standing alone this bequest does not look like a terminable interest since Mother has the entire property rights in the bequest. However, it will not qualify since the property passed to Son without adequate consideration and by reason of such passing, Son may enjoy it on the termination of Mother's interest. Rarely will an estate contain a tainted interest, such as the above, but if it does, the executor may not marshal assets by allocating it to another legatee. Unless tainted assets are specifically given to others, or excluded from the wife's bequest, there is a kind of conclusive presumption, for the purposes of computing the deduction, that they will be given to the wife. For this reason lawyers generally include in the marital deduction bequest a provision like the following:

"Notwithstanding anything to the contrary contained in this my will, I direct that in establishing the marital deduction share for my wife there shall not be allocated to that share any property or the proceeds of any property which would not qualify for the marital deduction allowable in determining the federal estate tax on my estate."

Further, if the decedent directs his executor to acquire a terminable interest for the surviving spouse, that interest will not qualify even though it should come within one of the exceptions, noted below. Thus, a direction to purchase a nonrefund annuity would disqualify the bequest of the purchse price.

4.11 Transfers which qualify but diminish the marital deduction

Even if the bequest qualifies, the deduction may be diminished by:

1. Amounts payable therefrom, as a gift of Blackacre subject to a mortgage;

2. Amounts which pass to the wife in satisfaction of deductible claims;

3. Amounts subject to death taxes payable by the wife.

The reason is that the deduction is limited to the amount actually passing to the wife as a bequest. The above rules are necessary to avoid double deductions (in items 1 and 2) or the allowance of a deduction for an amount not actually passing to the wife (item 3). The will may avoid the effect of item 1 by requiring the executor to discharge the mortgage and the effect of item 3 by charging all death taxes to that portion of the residuary estate passing to legatees other than the spouse.

Types of qualifying bequests

4.12 Summary of bequests which qualify for the marital deduction

1. A bequest in fee; see section 4.13.

2. A bequest of an indefeasibly vested remainder; see section 4.14.

3. A bequest of a life estate with a general power of appointment; see section 4.15.

4. A bequest of a life estate with remainder to the estate of the spouse; see section 4.16.

5. A power of appointment trust; see section 4.17.

6. An estate trust; see section 4.18.

7. A bequest conditioned on survivorship for not more than six months or by death of the spouse occurring other than as a result of a common disaster; see section 4.19.

In addition to the bequests listed above various non-testamentary transfers may be qualified for the marital deduction such as jointly owned property, life insurance proceeds, revocable trusts, and other gifts to a spouse that may form part of the tax estate. These will be discussed in a subsequent chapter.

4.13   Bequests in fee

Obviously the outright bequest qualifies. This is the only form of bequest that precisely corresponds to the type of ownership that the community property system vests in the surviving spouse by operation of law. The others are permissible, however, since they assure taxation of the property on the death of the wife, unless given away or consumed during her life.

4.14   Bequests of indefeasibly vested remainders

Where Wife has adequate income from other sources, Husband may leave his estate to his Mother for life, remainder to Wife, her heirs and assigns forever. The value of the remainder qualifies for the marital deduction since no interest follows that of the Wife.

4.15   Bequests for life with unrestricted power to invade

This technique is new with the 1954 Code. A bequest to the Wife, under the 1939 Code, for life with power to sell, consume, and give was held not to qualify for the deduction despite the fact that the full value of the property would be includible in the estate of the wife on her later death because she had the equivalent of a general power of appointment. The courts, however, had strictly construed the statute. Her interest was a terminable one and since no trust was created the transfer was technically outside the exception for power of appointment trusts. These rulings created hardships in those areas of the country where legal life estates were commonly preferred to trusts. The 1954 Code now provides that a life estate with a general power of appointment will qualify the property. See section 4.17.

Care must be taken to bring the gift within the terms of the statute. It is clear that a power to invade the corpus for the widow's needs or for her support will not achieve the desired result since her rights are limited by objective standards. A power to sell and consume may or may not include a power to give. Difficult questions of construction will arise wherever the language used creates any uncertainty. For this reason lawyers generally follow the language of the Code rather than traditional phraseology of "consume" or "invade." Thus "to my wife for life, with a general power to appoint the property to any person or persons including herself or her estate." It is not necessary that she be given the power by both deed and will. It is enough that she may appoint the property either during her life or at her death.

4.16 Bequest of life estate, remainder to estate of the spouse

A bequest to "my wife for life, remainder to her estate" will qualify. Such an interest is said not to be terminable since no other person has any interest in the property.

4.17 Power of appointment trusts

Perhaps the most widely used method of qualifying property is the trust with a general power of appointment. Under the

1948 Act, the wife must have been entitled to all the income from the trust estate and her general power must have extended to all the trust property. This resulted in a number of unhappy decisions denying the deduction in cases where a single trust was created under which the wife was to receive half the income and was given a general power over half the corpus. To obtain the deduction it was necessary prior to 1954 to create two trusts, one of which would be solely and exclusively for the benefit of the wife. This was known as the marital deduction trust. As appears from the discussion in section 6.18, whether separate trusts or partial interests in a single trust are created depends to a considerable extent on the phraseology used. Thus, the will may direct the trustee to hold the estate in trust, paying the spouse one half of the income or it may direct the trustee to divide the estate into two separate trusts, and to hold one such trust for the wife, paying her the annual income, etc. Only in the latter case was it possible to obtain the deduction. Happily, this trap has been eliminated by the 1954 Code which requires that the wife need only be given the income from a specific portion of the trust and that the general power need only extend to that specific portion.

For such a power of appointment trust or marital deduction share therein to qualify five conditions must be met:

1. The wife must be entitled to all the income;
2. It must be payable at least annually;
3. The wife must have a general power of appointment exercisable in favor of herself or her estate;
4. The power must be exercisable in all events;
5. No other person may have any power to appoint any part to any person other than the wife.

Powers of appointment are discussed in chapter 5. Suffice it to say here that a general power of appointment is a power given to the wife to either withdraw the property at her pleasure from the trust at any time and for any reason or to direct at her death that the property become a part of her estate or be used to satisfy her creditors. It is sufficient to qualify a trust for the marital deduction if the spouse is given the power to appoint by will alone. She need not be given the power to withdraw the principal during her life.

The income requirement may be satisfied if the wife has the right to demand the trust be made income producing. Thus unless a trust has a specific provision authorizing investment in unproductive property or permitting the retention of unproductive assets, this requirement will be satisfied.

4.18   Estate trusts

It is permissible to create a trust for the wife for life, remainder to her estate. Such a trust, income to wife for life, remainder to her estate, falls outside the terminable interest rules as no interest will pass to anyone other than the spouse and her estate. Therefore this type trust is free of the requirements of the power of appointment trust. It may on occasion be a useful device if it is desired to accumulate income or to invest in nonproductive property.

Income tax savings may be realized through the power to accumulate. Against this must be weighed the certainty that the accumulations will be taxed as part of the wife's estate at her death, along with the original corpus.

The wife has in substance a general power of appointment by will since she can freely dispose of the property at her death to anyone she desires. However, the estate trust has the disadvantage that the corpus will form part of the probate estate of the wife, resulting in increased executor's commissions, will be subject to the claims of her creditors, and will attract state inheritance tax whereas the power of appointment trust is not part of her probate estate and may escape death taxes in those jurisdictions that tax only exercised powers.

4.19   Bequests conditioned on survivorship

Where both spouses have substantial estates it may, nevertheless, be advisable to provide for the marital deduction in the wills of both Husband and Wife, on the assumption that, while this will increase the overall tax bill, the surviving spouse may live for many years after the first death. Assume Husband and Wife are each about 45 years of age. Each has an estate of about $600,000. They are residents of Illinois.

A computation of their death taxes, with and without the marital deduction, would show:

Estate of $600,000, without marital deduction, on first death.

Federal tax...	$145,000
Illinois tax..	42,000
Combined tax...	$187,000
On second death..	$187,000
Combined taxes on both deaths.................................	$374,000

Estate of $600,000, with marital deduction, on first death.

Federal tax...		$ 59,000
Illinois tax..		42,000
Combined tax...		$101,000
On second death, estate of $900,000.		
Federal tax....................................	$238,000	
Illinois tax.....................................	89,000	327,000
Combined taxes on both deaths............................		$428,000

The overall taxes are increased here by use of the marital deduction somewhat more than $50,000. But if one of the spouses should die while the other is still in his or her late forties or early fifties, it may be well to incur the increased taxes, getting the bulk of the tax delayed for many years. As Trachtman puts it, there is much to be said for "taking the cash and letting the credit go."

1. The survivor will enjoy a larger capital sum for his or her life;

2. The increased taxes may be avoided through gifts which to a considerable extent may come within his or her exemption and annual exclusions;

3. The reduced tax in the first estate may be vitally important to avoid sacrifice sales, if the estates are not particularly liquid.

But these advantages are predicated upon the assumption that the second death will occur years after the first. The use of the marital deduction would be disastrous if the deaths occurred within a few weeks of each other. It is possible to provide that the gift to the surviving spouse shall be conditioned upon six months' survivorship and its not occurring as a result of a common disaster.

There are practical objections to the use of common disaster clauses. Husband and Wife may be involved in an automobile accident. Wife may not die for several years thereafter. Who, assuming any one of several fact situations, is to say in the meantime that her later death may not have a causal connection with the accident. Meanwhile it will not be safe for the executor to distribute anything to her. Only on her death may it be established whether or not she was entitled to any share in his estate. Further the marital deduction may be lost, even though she becomes entitled to the bequest, since the Regulations provide that the marital deduction will not be allowed if, on the final audit of the return, it is still possible that the property may not pass to the surviving spouse.

Lawyers usually use a time clause, which will, in fact, cover practically all common disaster cases.

"If my wife fails to survive me by six months, this will and all its provisions shall be construed upon the assumption and basis that she predeceased me."

Where it is desired to obtain the deduction in all possible events, i.e. where one spouse has the bulk of the family wealth, the clause used is the simultaneous death clause (see section 4.7). Where it is desired to obtain the deduction only because of the likelihood that the surviving spouse will live for many years after the first death (this will be true where both spouses have substantial estates) the clause used is the time clause, noted above.

When and how lawyers use the deduction

4.20   *When to use the deduction*

Wherever one spouse has the bulk of the family wealth it will be desirable to provide for the marital deduction in the will of the propertied spouse. Conversely, the will of the other should exclude the spouse or limit any interest given to a life estate. Careful investigation of all the facts should be made before reaching a decision, even in what on the surface seems the obvious case. Many husbands have assigned their insurance policies to their wives in order to remove the proceeds from their estates under Code Section 2042. Assume Husband has $100,000 of assets and $100,000 of life insurance, the policy being owned by Wife. The fact that Wife owns the insurance and that, on his death, it will create in her a substantial estate is sometimes overlooked. Here it may be preferable not to use the marital deduction in Husband's will. Its use would save $4,800 in federal taxes on his death but will swell Wife's estate at her later death, putting the property bequeathed into higher brackets than were avoided. If her estate becomes $150,000, the tax will be $17,900, whereas if Husband left her only a life estate it would be limited to $4,800.

In many cases both spouses will have substantial estates. Here tentative tax computations (1) assuming the use of the deduction, and (2) assuming no deduction, will be found useful. The effect of state inheritance taxes should be carefully considered. No rule of thumb is possible, particularly because many state death taxes do not include all the items that are in the federal gross estate. But the mere fact that larger taxes will be incurred on the later death should not necessarily be determinative for the reasons set forth in section 4.19.

Where doubt exists many lawyers think it wise to provide for the deduction relying upon the widow's right to renounce the bequest if, at that time, the factors creating the uncertainty have been resolved and such action then seems desirable.

4.21   How lawyers use the marital deduction

It can be just as costly to qualify an excess amount of property as not to use the deduction at all. Thus, assume Husband leaves his entire estate of $200,000 to Wife. His estate tax, because of the deduction, is only $4,800 but on the subsequent death of Wife, her estate will pay a tax of $31,500, less a credit which cannot exceed $4,800 and may be considerably less if Wife survives for several years. Here he ought to qualify only one half. Then the tax on his death will be $4,800 with a later tax of $4,800 on her death, instead of the combined taxes of $36,300.

4.22 Dollar amount bequests

It is obviously not possible, in cases where it is desired to obtain the maximum marital deduction, to arrive at a dollar amount with any degree of accuracy. The date of death, the value assets now owned will have at that time, the likely conversions that will take place, what future gifts may be made, what losses will occur, what inheritances will be received, all make even the roughest approximations wild guesses at best. For this reason a bequest of $100,000 or any other fixed amount will not give any assurance that the maximum marital deduction or anything close to it is likely to be obtained. And if obtained, it is probable that an excess of qualified property may result in unnecessary taxes on the death of the surviving wife.

4.23 Bequests of one half of the residue

Like dollar amount bequests, bequests of one half of the residuary estate are quite as likely to miss the desired amount by a wide margin. The reason for this is that the tax estate and the probate estate will rarely be the same. The will operates on the probate estate only, which will frequently be a relatively small portion of the tax estate. Assume X has:

Cash in bank (individual account)	$ 5,000
Residence, owned jointly with wife	30,000
Life insurance, payable to wife	60,000
U.S. "E" bonds, payable on death to wife	10,000
Business interest	80,000
Miscellaneous	5,000
Total	$190,000

His tax estate will total $190,000. His probate estate will only total $90,000. (Cash, business interests, miscellaneous.)

If his will leaves one half of his estate to his wife in such a way as to qualify for the marital deduction, this bequest will amount to $45,000, if we ignore debts and administration expenses. How much property qualifies for the marital deduction will depend on the nonprobate items. If the wife is lump sum beneficiary of the insurance, then the residence, the insurance, the bonds, and the legacy will all qualify. Here $145,000 qualifies for the deduction but the maximum deduction will only be $95,000. Such a clause unnecessarily qualifies an additional $50,000 and exposes it to tax upon the wife's death.

On the facts assumed nothing should have been left to the wife under the will in such a way as to qualify for the deduction. But the difficulty with so drafting the will is that assets do not remain static. Assume X sells the residence on retirement and redeems the bonds on maturity. He then invests the proceeds in securities in his own name. Further, assume he changes the insurance designation in such a way as to disqualify the insurance proceeds. Now nothing outside the will qualifies, and, if the will qualified nothing, the deduction would be wholly lost.

4.24 *Formula amount bequests*

What is needed is a clause keyed to the marital deduction provisions of the Code.

Where the testator wants his widow to receive a fixed dollar amount, i.e. give her a general legacy, the clause should read somewhat as follows:

"If my wife, Mary, survives me, I give, devise and bequeath to her a sum of money which shall be equal to (*a*) one half of the value of my adjusted gross estate as finally determined for federal estate tax purposes, less (*b*) the value of all interests in property, if any, which pass or have passed to my wife under other items of this my will or otherwise than under this will but only to the extent that such interests are for the purposes of the federal estate tax law included in determining my gross taxable estate and allowed as a marital deduction. In fixing the dollar amount of this bequest all values shall be those finally determined for federal estate tax purposes. This legacy may be paid to her in cash or in kind. To the extent property, rather than money, is used to satisfy this legacy the fair market value of such property at the date of distribution (rather than its estate tax value) shall be credited against the dollar amount due her."

4.25 *Fractional share bequests*

Where the testator desires his widow to have as a marital deduction bequest a share the amount of which may fluctuate after his death, i.e. a share in the residue, the clause should read somewhat as follows:

"If my wife, Mary, survives me, I direct my executors to set aside that fractional share of my estate which is equal to (*a*) one half of the value of my adjusted gross estate as finally determined for federal estate tax purposes, less (*b*) the value of all interests in property, if any, which pass or have passed to my wife under other items of this my will or otherwise than under this will but only to the extent that such interests are for the purposes of the federal state tax law included in determining my gross taxable estate and allowed as a marital deduction. In determining what this fractional share of my estate is, the values finally determined for estate tax purposes shall be used.

"I give, devise, and bequeath this said fractional share of my estate to my wife, as a marital deduction bequest. In allocating assets between this marital deduction bequest and the residuary bequest made in item of this my will my executor shall, consistent with equitable principles requiring impartiality as between legatees, act impartially in such allocation so that the marital deduction share and the residuary share shall share ratably in any changes in value of assets between the valuation dated used for estate tax purposes and the date of distribution."

In the dollar amount bequest a capital gains tax may be

incurred since values at date of distribution, where the distribution is in kind, may be greater than those on the estate tax valuation date. On the other hand where the fractional share type formula is used the wife shares in all increases in value and this may have the adverse effect in a rising market of subjecting a larger dollar amount of the first estate to estate tax on her later death.

Which type of formula is preferable will depend on the fact situation in each case and the general objectives of the estate owner.

4.26   Pitfalls in formula clauses

Since the executor has the option to take date of death values or six months from death values, he may by his decision increase or decrease the bequest to the wife under a formula clause. Thus, assume the decedent had created a revocable trust for his daughter, which on the date of his death had assets worth $100,000. His probate estate consisted of bonds worth $200,000. Under a formula clause the wife's bequest would amount to $150,000, if we ignore debts and administration expenses. If six months from the date of death the value of the assets in the revocable trust is $200,000, and if the executor elects the later date, the marital deduction bequest will amount in value to $200,000. The same possibility exists for increasing or decreasing the deduction if casualty losses occur, since these are deductible at the option of the executor on either the estate tax return or the income tax return.[3] To avoid this difficulty wills sometimes direct that the executor shall elect the estate tax valuation date that will produce the lesser estate tax and that any deductible losses shall be deductible from the income tax or the estate tax, whichever produces the greater tax reduction.

A word of warning about the indiscriminate use of these formula clauses may be appropriate. They have been criticized and they can cause real trouble in a limited class of cases.

---

[3] See note 1, page 57.

Assume a second wife who is not on speaking terms with the children of the first marriage. The husband's probate estate consists of $150,000. To placate the children who resented the second marriage he had given them $50,000 two years before his death. The Commissioner suggests this may have been in contemplation of death. He also suggests that the husband's business interest may be worth $50,000 more than the executor concedes. Under the clause suggested the widow is on the Commissioner's side. Her bequest under the will, if the gift is determined to be in contemplation of death will be increased by $25,000. If the Commissioner's valuation of the business is finally sustained, her bequest will further be increased by another $25,000. But this is the unusual situation. In most cases family harmony exists and all can be counted on to assume a properly adverse position to the tax gatherer.

5

Estate tax savings through use of testamentary trusts

In general

5.1 Introduction

Bequests to persons in substantial amounts, or bequests to persons of substantial means, whether they be specific, general or residuary, should generally be in the form of life estates rather than fee interests, absent other considerations that make limiting such gifts undesirable. An outright bequest of $200,000 to a legatee with nominal assets will be subjected to state inheritance and federal estate taxes on the subsequent death of the legatee, with constantly decreasing credits for the earlier taxes paid. Thus, if such a legatee dies ten years after his benefactor, the federal tax will amount to $31,500 and the state tax, while it will vary widely, may run as high as $15,000 or $16,000. In addition, unnecessary attorney's and executor's fees of $6,000 to $8,000 each may be incurred. Thus, the cost that creation of a life interest will avoid may be well in excess of $55,000 and probably would rarely be less than $40,000.

Where such bequests go to persons who already have considerable wealth the unnecessary taxes will be even greater since the assets given will be pushed into higher brackets. Thus, assume Sister A and Sister B each have estates of $100,000. Each leaves her estate to the other, with contingent gifts over to the family of a deceased brother, if the sister legatee predeceases the testatrix. Sister A dies first. The federal tax on her estate will be $4,800. This will be true whether the bequest to B is outright or for life. But on Sister B's later death, if the gift is outright, her federal tax may be $31,500, whereas it need be only $4,800. Of course a gift of a life estate is not the same as absolute ownership. If it were, the tax saving would not be possible. However, to a very considerable extent, the benefits of outright ownership may be given to the life tenant without the tax burdens. It will be the purpose of this chapter to explore the techniques available for assuring to the life tenant the economic advantages of the capital without its disadvantages.

5.2 Successive life estates and the rule against perpetuities

Generally testators will be satisfied to "skip" the tax on the death of the primary beneficiary, with a distribution of principal at his death. Thus Sister A may give Sister B a life estate, remainder to her brother's children then surviving, the issue of any deceased child to take his parent's share. Here there are no perpetuity problems, since all interests will vest indefeasibly at the expiration of a life in being (B) at the creation of the interest (the death of A). The same will be true where the nonmarital trust is for the spouse for life, remainder to the children, etc., or to a son for life, remainder to his children.

In the larger estates it may well be desired to skip as many successive death taxes as permitted by law. Here the disposition may be "income to my wife for life, and, upon her death, to my then surviving children and the issue of any deceased children, per stirpes, until 21 years after the death of the last survivor of my wife, my children, and my grandchildren in being at the date of my death" at which time the principal shall be distributed to, etc.

Many wills and trusts contain a clause substantially as follows, in order to eliminate any possible risk of a violation of the Rule.

"Notwithstanding the directions heretofore given my trustee as to the distribution of income and principal, every trust established by this Will shall terminate, if it has not previously terminated, 21 years after the death of the last survivor of my wife, my children, and any grandchildren of mine in being at the date of my death.

"Upon such termination, my Trustee shall immediately transfer, convey and pay over the principal of each of the trusts to the lineal descendants then living of the child of mine on whose account the trust was established, per stirpes, and if none, to my lineal descendants then living, per stirpes, and if none, to the Regents of the University of Colorado."

5.3 Provisions for minors on termination

Since it is possible and frequently quite likely that minors will become entitled to principal distributions from long-term trusts, lawyers frequently avoid the rigidity of the guardianship laws of most states by providing that such interests shall vest absolutely in the minors but that their shares shall continue in trust during minority. It is settled that such a trust may continue beyond the period of vesting permitted by the rule against perpetuities.

5.4   Legal life estates vs. trusts

While the tax savings noted earlier may be obtained through use of either a legal life estate or a trust, the trust, while it appears, at first glance to be the more complex, is actually the simpler device to adopt. There is an amazing paucity of law in most jurisdictions on the rights, privileges, and obligations of life tenants and remaindermen, particularly if the remainder interests are contingent.

"I give, devise, and bequeath my entire estate to my sister Kate. If, however, Kate dies without issue, then the estate is to go over to my brother Henry, or if he be dead, to his lineal descendants, if any, per stirpes."

Does Kate have a legal life estate or a fee?

May Kate mortgage the property?

May she sell it?

Assuming she has a fee subject to the executory interests, she cannot convey or mortgage a good title without Henry's consent. But is that enough? What of the interests of whoever his heirs may happen to be at some uncertain time in the future?

May she tear down or make alterations of any existing structures?

Can she consume the capital?

Who can enforce whatever duties she may be under?

These and other difficult questions are unanswered in many jurisdictions. And where answered, the answers have not always been too satisfactory. Income tax problems may also raise their ugly heads. Does the sale of a life estate result in the entire amount being taxed as ordinary income? Does a life tenant have a cost basis, separate from the remainderman?

The Tax Reform Act of 1969 specially provides that on the sale of a life estate the seller's basis shall be zero.

Who pays the tax, if there is a tax, on the sale of the property?[1] Frequently the remainderman is as yet unborn or unascertained.

The above is not to say that a legal life estate should never be created. Valuable art objects, family paintings of great value, expensive jewelry, perhaps the family residence, may not be suitable trust assets. Where personal use only, rather than sale or conversion, is contemplated, the legal life estate may serve ideally but in general the trust will be found to be the more flexible medium and will present, over the years, fewer legal problems.

Powers of appointment

5.5 *Flexibility through powers*

If the choice were between a bare life estate and absolute ownership, testators might well decide it preferable to give the fee to the immediate and primary objects of their bounty, even at the substantially increased tax cost, noted in section 5.1. But the life estate can be made extremely attractive through the use of powers, some of which may be given to the life tenant, some may be vested in other persons, such as the trustee.

5.6 *Terminology and definitions of powers*

Powers have been used by estate planners for over 500 years. Prior to 1540, when it was not possible to devise land by will in England, the estate owner would convey Backacre to a "feoffee to uses" (the counterpart of the modern trustee) to hold the title "for the use of the grantor for life and then for such person or persons as the grantor might at any time designate in writing." He would then prepare a writing instructing the feoffee, on the grantor's death, to hold the land for the use of his daughter for her life and then for such children of

---

[1] The cases tend to indicate that the life tenant will be treated as a trustee.

hers as she might designate, and if she failed to designate the takers, then equally to all her children.

The estate owner was and is called the *Donor* of the power. His daughter, under the last designation, was and is called the *Donee* of the power. Her children were the possible *Appointees*. Here the children are also the *Takers in Default*. Under the power, the estate owner reserved for himself a power by which he could appoint to anyone without limitation, including himself or his estate. This was known as a *General Power;* and since it was exercisable during life or at death, it would today be called a *General Power by Deed or by Will*. If the Power is exercisable only at death, it is known as a *General Power by Will*. If it is exercisable only during life, it is a *General Power by Deed*. The power given to the daughter is called a *Special or Limited Power* because the class of appointees is restricted to her children.

It is customary in creating trusts today to give Trustees special powers over the distribution of income and corpus. These are known as *Powers in Trust,* since the donee of such a power has a fiduciary obligation in deciding whether or not to exercise it. On the other hand, the nontrust powers may be exercised arbitrarily by the donee except that the donee of a special power may not exercise it in such a way as to benefit anyone outside the class of appointees.

5.7 Taxation of powers

It should be noted that the powers discussed in this chapter are limited to powers conferred on persons other than the donor of the power. Chapter 14 deals with the taxation of reserved powers. This distinction must be constantly kept in mind. Where a power is given to a person other than the grantor the power may be quite broad without attracting any tax consequences. On the other hand, powers reserved by a grantor, even of the most restrictive character, will have adverse tax consequences.

Prior to 1942 only exercised general powers attracted estate taxes. Property subject to a general power, if the donee refrained from exercising the power, passed without tax to the default takers. And, of course, special powers, whether exercised or not, were tax free.

In 1942 Congress was persuaded that taxpayers were avoiding estate taxes through the use of such broad special powers that they were in substance general powers. Thus the Board of Tax Appeals had indicated that a power to appoint to any one except Brother Walter and his descendants was not a general power, if Walter or any of his descendants survived the donee. One estate planning wag is said to have excluded only Adolf Hitler from the class of possible appointees.

The common law has always recognized that a general power by will and by deed was for many purposes the equivalent of outright ownership, which economically, of course, it is. All the donee need do is call upon the trustee for a conveyance of the title to him. Thus, the period of the rule against perpetuities does not begin to run from the creation of an interest, if any person has a general power by deed and by will to appoint the property. A general power by will alone was not in most jurisdictions regarded as the equivalent of ownership. Only if the donee exercised the latter power was he treated as owner under property law. It was these common law concepts that determined estate tax liability prior to 1942.

Congress, in 1942, subjected the property under the donee's control to tax under every power except (1) a power to appoint within a class which included no others than the spouse of the donee, spouse of the donor, descendants of the donor (other than the donee), descendants of the donee or of his spouse, spouses of such descendants and charitable organizations, and (2) a power to appoint to a "restricted" class if the donee had no beneficial interest in the property. This latter exception was primarily designed to permit the usual discretionary powers in trust that are customarily given to trustees.

While the pre-1942 rules may have offered too many tax avoidance opportunities, the 1942 rules were found too rigid and were said to be unduly burdensome and restrictive of usual family dispositions that were in no sense tax motivated. As a result Congress enacted the Powers of Appointment Act of

1951, which was carried over without change in the 1954 Code.

Pre-1942 powers

5.8 *General powers*

Because many taxpayers had relied on the rules as they existed before 1942, Congress provided that only exercised general powers created before October 21, 1942 would subject the property to estate taxes. It also provided that the lifetime exercise of such a general power would incur gift tax. Pre-1942 powers include:

1. Powers created by persons who died prior to October 21, 1942;

2. Powers created by persons dying before July 1, 1949, if the will was executed before October 21, 1942, and not thereafter republished. The 1949 date was adopted because under the 1942 legislation, Congress had given taxpayers an opportunity to change their wills, by delaying the effectiveness of the 1942 legislation for a year. The time was extended each year until 1949.

3. Powers created by deed executed before October 21, 1942.

General powers are defined as powers exercisable in favor of the donee of the power, his creditors, his estate, or the creditors of his estate. A power to withdraw corpus is thus a general power unless limited by an external standard relating to the donee's health, education, support, or maintenance. Thus, a power permitting the widow to withdraw all or part of the corpus at any time for any reason is a general power, whereas, a power to encroach upon the corpus to the extent necessary to enable her to maintain her accustomed standard of living is not. Further if a pre-1942 power can be exercised only with the consent of another, it is not a general power and its exercise will not incur gift or estate tax.

Thus, with respect to pre-1942 powers, the property subject to the power will be taxed as part of the estate of the donee only if he exercises it by will or during his life by a disposition that runs afoul one of the other Code Sections. Obviously the exercise of a power during life may be in contemplation of death, or the power may be exercised in such a way as to retain a life estate, or a possibility of reverter, or a power to amend or revoke. This is likely to occur where the donee appoints the property to a trust, and, of course, it could occur in an outright transfer.

5.9 Special powers

Neither the existence nor the exercise of pre-1942 special powers, i.e., any power not falling within the above definition of a general power, will give rise to either gift or estate taxes.

Post-1942 powers

5.10 Special powers

The rules are the same as for pre-1942 special powers. They may be freely retained and freely exercised without tax consequences.

5.11 General powers

The mere possession of a general power created after October 21, 1942, will result in the inclusion of the property in the estate of the donee, whether he exercises the power or not. If the power is exercised or completely released during life, gift tax will be incurred. Further, if the exercise or release results in a disposition includible under Sections 2035 to 2038 (contemplation of death, reserved life estate, possibility of reverter, and retained powers to alter, amend, revoke, or terminate), the fund will be subjected to estate tax, with credit for the gift tax paid. Thus assume Wife is entitled to the income for life with a general testatmentary power. She releases the power. The effect of this is equivalent to a transfer to the takers in default with a right to the income reserved for life. A reduction of the power so that it is for the future only exercisable in favor of the children avoids gift tax because it is incomplete, but the later release or exercise in favor of the children will give rise to gift tax. If not completely released the fund over which the power exists will be part of the wife's estate.

The definition of a post-1942 general power is the same as the pre-1942 general power except for joint powers.

A general power is a power which is exercisable in favor of the donee, his creditors, his estate, or the creditors of his estate except that a power to invade is not a general power if limited by an ascertainable standard relating to the donee's health, education, maintenance or support.

A general power, as above defined, if created after October 21, 1942, will still be treated as general even though the consent of another person is required unless:

1. The consent of the donor is required.

2. The consent of a person having a substantial adverse interest is required.

3. The consent of a person in whose favor the power may be exercised is required. In this last classification, the power is treated as general only in part.

In the first group above, nothing is to be included in the estate of the donee, since for estate tax purposes the donor is treated as the taxable owner.

In the second group the power is in no sense the near equivalent of ownership because of the substantial adverse interest. Thus, "to my wife for life, remainder to my son, with power in my wife to appoint the fund to herself, but only with the consent of my son." If the son consents, it is he who is making a gift of the remainder, not his mother.

In the third group the power is general in part only. Assume Son and Daughter are given a power to jointly appoint to any person or persons, including themselves. On any appointment each is really making a gift of one-half. It seems not unfair to treat each as having a general power over one-half which is what the estate and gift tax sections do in effect.

5.12   Successive powers

The common law rule against perpetuities measured the time for required vesting in the case of a special power from the date of its creation. For this reason it was possible to skip the estate tax only for one or two generations. Delaware law, however, was changed to provide that the time should be measured from the date of exercise. This made it possible, in Delaware, through a series of special powers to transmit estates tax free indefinitely. Congress quickly passed what is now Section 2041(a) to close this loophole by providing that the exercise of any power, whether general or special, is taxable if it is exercised in such a way as to create another power that under local law validly postpones the vesting of any interest for a period ascertainable without regard to the date of the creation of the first power.

5.13   Lapse of powers

The lapse of a power is considered the release of the power, with gift and possible estate tax consequences. This treatment seems sound, since a lapse is the substantial equivalent of a release. Assume Wife, the income beneficiary of a trust, has a power to withdraw corpus in whole or in part at any time prior to her 60th birthday. This is her only power. The fund amounts to $100,000. Wife celebrates her 60th birthday without exercising her withdrawal privilege. Clearly she has made a gift to the remainderman. The day before her birthday the fund was hers for the asking, the day after, the remainderman was richer in the fact that for the first time he had an indefeasible interest of substantial value. Her inaction rather than her action brought about the result.

This particular problem of lapse caused considerable difficulty in cases where a life tenant of a trust was given a noncumulative right to withdraw $10,000 a year, for example. Assume the fund amounts to $100,000. Ten years pass without a withdrawal. In each of these years a gift was made, not, however, in the amount of $10,000, since it was only a gift of the remainder interest. Depending on the life expectancy of the life tenant, the value might vary anywhere from a few hundred dollars to several thousand. But the real difficulty was that each of these gifts was treated as a transfer with the income retained for life. Thus at the end of the tenth year, the mere permitting of the powers to lapse would cause the inclusion of the entire property in the estate of the life tenant. This is still true as to the portion of any withdrawal privilege in excess of 5 percent of the corpus or $5,000, whichever is greater.

Since it is frequently highly desirable, particularly in the more modest trusts, to grant withdrawal privileges, the Code now provides that the lapse of a power shall be considered a release and therefore a gift only to the extent that the property which could have been appointed exceeds the higher of $5,000 or 5 percent of the assets subject to appointment.

5.14 How lawyers use powers in estate planning

Powers are extremely useful estate planning tools, wholly apart from taxation. They enable estate owners to control the devolution of their property through two or more generations without having to set the pattern with too much rigidity. It is not possible to foresee all the possible contingencies over a 100-year period. Births and deaths, commercial success, interests and capacities of children yet unborn, fluctuations in income yields, all make it undesirable to tie up property too tightly. The special power is the most efficient tool yet devised to enable the estate owner to set out the general purposes and leave to succeeding generations the filling in of the details as to the objectives to which his property is to be devoted. Father may leave his property to Son for life and then to Son's children as Son shall appoint. This enables Son 25 or 35 years later to determine the distribution among his children in the light of events occurring long after Father's death. One daughter may have married a wealthy man, another a commercially unsuccessful artist, one son may have physical or mental handicaps that call for special considerations, another may have ample funds and few responsibilities. As the *Restatement of Property* puts it: "In a sense the power of appointment extends the personality of A (Father) through the balance of the life of B (Son)."

In addition, the use of special powers offers tremendous estate tax saving opportunities. Assume Mother has $200,000 she inherited from her husband. Son, their only child, is married and has three children. He is modestly successful. His salary is $20,000. He owns his own home, worth $25,000; has about $15,000 in stocks and bonds; $40,000 of company furnished insurance and $20,000 purchased directly by him. Thus his estate, were he to die, would amount to $100,000.

If Mother leaves her estate outright to him (ignoring death costs, for ease of illustration) he will, on his later death, have an estate of $300,000. If he takes full advantage of the marital deduction, his estate tax on $150,000 will be $17,500 and, because of the marital deduction bequest, his wife's estate will incur a tax of $17,500, combined taxes of $35,000. Should his wife predecease him, or should he for some other reason not use the marital deduction, the federal tax on his estate would amount to $59,100. On the other hand, if his mother leaves him a life interest only in her estate, there will be no federal tax on his death, assuming he takes advantage of the marital deduction; if he foregoes it, the tax will only amount to $4,800. Thus, the possible tax savings range from $35,000 to $55,000.

Of course, a bequest in trust for life is not the same as an outright bequest. If it were, the taxes could not be saved. To what extent may the capital be made available to the son, if he ever needs it, without losing the tax advantage? The rules discussed in this chapter furnish the answer and, it is believed, in most cases, permit sufficient flexibility to make the creation of a trust advisable.

1. Under the lapse provisions of the Code (see section 5.11), the Son, in addition to all the income from the trust, may be given the right in any year or years that he may desire, to withdraw $5,000 or 5 percent of the value of the then corpus

whichever is greater. He may do this at his mere whim and pleasure, without any explanation to the trustee and for any purpose. The result of this power will be to cause the inclusion in his taxable estate of only the amount he could have withdrawn and had not withdrawn, in the year of his death.

2. If, in order to maintain his accustomed standard of living or to meet extraordinary medical expenses, he needs funds in addition to the income and $5,000 or 5 percent of capital, he may be given the right to demand such additional amounts from the trustee. Because of the objective standard, he would have an enforceable right against the trustee.

3. The trustee may be given a power in his sole and absolute discretion to distribute principal to the son for any reason satisfactory to the trustee. Here, he must persuade the trustee. He has no right. Suppose he wants to go into a business. He must persuade the trustee to advance a substantial amount of capital to him. But this limitation on his control may prove beneficial, since two heads are better than one where large investments are contemplated. The trustee's consent may be more readily obtained if the clause granting this power reminds the trustee that the trust was created primarily for the benefit of the son.

4. He may be given a special power by deed to appoint principal to his wife and children.

The possession of the power will enable him to make, to a considerable extent, tax-free gifts to his children.[2] Thus, if a daughter is about to marry he may appoint a sum to her for the purchase of a home, or if a son is about to enter business he may appoint to him whatever initial investment the son may be required to make.

5. Lastly, he may be given a special power to appoint the principal by will to and among his family, just as though he owned it. Of course, he must be deprived of the doubtful privilege of being able to appoint it to his creditors and, because the rule against perpetuities runs from the date of the creation of the power, he may not tie up the fund for as long a period as if he had outright ownership.

---

[2] Whether cutting short the income interest constitutes a gift to the extent of the value of the future income is an unsettled question.

In many cases the fullest possible use of powers will not be taken advantage of. Thus, in the usual case the primary beneficiary will be given the income with a discretionary power in the trustee to distribute principal during life. Frequently, there will be added a special testamentary power of appointment. Particularly in small estates the $5,000 withdrawal privilege will appeal to testators and, occasionally, there will be added the privilege of withdrawal measured by an objective standard such as maintenance of the accustomed standard of living. The important thing to recognize is that the use of these powers can make the principal available to the life tenant without the tax burdens placed upon outright ownership.

6

Income tax savings through use of testamentary trusts

6.1   Introduction

Since the trust is a separate tax-paying entity and since trustees may be given discretionary powers to distribute or accumulate income, and to the extent distributed, to sprinkle it among several taxpayers within the family group, considerable income may be kept within the lower tax brackets. The chapter will concern itself with the taxation of testamentary trusts. The subject of inter vivos trusts, particularly those the income from which may be taxed back to the grantor, is reserved for chapter 14.

6.2   The taxation of trust income in general

The basic objective of the Revenue Acts from the beginning of our modern income tax system has been clear—to tax trust income once, either to the beneficiary or to the trustee. In the typical trust, the trustee will be directed to distribute the entire income annually. It should and will be taxed to the beneficiary or beneficiaries who receive it. However, many trusts, particularly for minors, authorize the accumulation, in the discretion of the trustee, of all or part of the income. In these cases it would be unfair to tax the prospective beneficiaries on amounts not yet received and which may, in fact, never be received by any presently identifiable person as one or more may predecease the date of payment. Such income, however, ought not to escape tax. For this reason the general scheme has been to tax to the trustee income accumulated for later distribution, and to the beneficiary income actually paid out. To prevent too easy tax avoidance the beneficiary is taxed on the amount distributable to him, rather than on the amount actually paid to him. This obviously prevents the trustee from arbitrarily delaying payments in order to keep the income in lower brackets.

6.3   Background of the present law

During the 30s the rules for taxing trust income offered tremendous tax avoiding possibilities. One extremely popular plan was the annuity. In *Burnet* v. *Whitehouse*, the will provided an annuity of $5,000 to be paid out of income or capital, if necessary. The income was adequate to meet the charge and it was, in fact, paid from income, but the Supreme Court held the beneficiary was not taxable on the income received since the gift did not depend upon income. It was a charge on principal "to be satisfied like any ordinary bequest" and therefore fell within the income tax exclusion for "gifts and inheritances." *Helvering* v. *Pardee* held the trustee taxable on income used to satisfy an annuity payment. Thus the coast was clear. Instead of giving the income to A, B, and C and subjecting it to tax at their top brackets, it became necessary only to estimate the probable annual yield and provide for annuities. Assume the fund that was to go into trust for A, B, and C amounted to approximately $300,000. The draftsman could with considerable safety give each of them a $4,000 annuity, with little risk of corpus encroachments.

Another popular device was known as the Dean trust. This type derived its name from the case which sustained its validity as a tax minimization device. The trustee would be directed to distribute each year's trust income on the following January third, to the beneficiary, if he were alive on that date; otherwise, the income was to be paid to a successor beneficiary. The income was held taxable to the trustee since it was not distributable within the tax year of the trustee. The tax having been paid upon it, it was received three days later by the beneficiary as a capital distribution.

In an effort to deal with these problems Congress in 1942 added some extremely complex and never well understood provisions to the 1939 Code. In general they attempted to tax the beneficiary (1) on all trust income of the prior year received by him within the first 65 days of the following year, as though he had received it on the last day of the preceding year (to overcome the Dean case), and (2) on all distributions of the taxable year to the extent of the trust income for the preceding 12 months (to overcome the annuity device).

The solution was not particularly satisfactory to the Treasury. All that estate owners needed to do was to arrange to delay distribution for two years. The first year's income was then taxable to the trustee, the second year's income to the beneficiary. Indeed, under the 65-day rule the beneficiary could be put substantially on an annual receipt basis by alter-nating the payment dates between March 3 of even years and March 8 of odd years. Further, the very complexity of the statute brought forth so much criticism that it was obviously doomed. It is said to have been ignored in large areas of the country simply because it was not understood by either Trea-sury agents or trust administrators.

In addition, there were several inequities in the general rules relating to the taxation of trust income that called for correc-tion, such as the wastage of deductions and the hardship result-ing from taxing beneficiaries on otherwise nontaxable receipts, because they were classified as income under local trust law. For this reason the sections taxing trust income were com-pletely overhauled in the 1954 Code.

Simple trusts

6.4 Trust income, local law and tax law

While the Code itself does not classify trusts as "simple" and "complex," Part B of subchapter J deals with the rela-tively uncomplicated type that have come to be called "simple trusts," a phrase used to describe them in the Committee Re-ports. All other trusts are commonly classified as "complex trusts." The simple trust, to which we shall first direct our attention, is any trust whose provisions require the distribution of the entire net income, with no charitable beneficiaries, and no capital distributions. There may be a power to distribute capital but if no distribution is, in fact, made during the tax year the trust remains a simple trust for that year.

From the above definition it will be seen that the simple trust classification includes the great majority of trusts in oper-ation: income to the wife for life, remainder to the children, or income to be distributed to and among the wife and children in such amounts and proportions as the trustee may determine. Generally speaking, the complex trust is one that permits ac-cumulations of income for later distribution.

Because income in the trust sense may be very different from income in the tax sense, the trustee of a simple trust, even though he is required to distribute all the income (local law sense) may be taxable on part of the income (tax sense). For example, capital gains under local laws are generally treated as additions to corpus and not as income to be distributed to the current income beneficiaries. The same may be true of extraordinary cash dividends, particularly where the trustee is authorized to make an allocation between income and principal. Further, profit realized on lapsed options are capital in the trust law sense. But each of the above enumerated items constitutes income in the tax sense. Thus, a simple trust may be taxed on a considerable amount of tax-income even though it is required to distribute all its income (trust law sense) to the beneficiary, and still retain its classification.

Many trust instruments authorize the trustee in his discretion to allocate receipts and disbursements to income or capital or partly to each. The allocation made by the trustee will generally be determinative of the tax question. But where a trustee allocated all ordinary cash dividends to capital the court held that the beneficiary was taxable on the dividends because it determined that, under local law, this was an abuse of the power of the trustee; that the beneficiary could have demanded the dividends; and that, therefore, they constituted distributable income.

6.5 *Distributable net income*

As noted above, in the simple trust the beneficiary will pay tax on the ordinary income items distributed to him, the trustee will pay tax on the capital gains. Thus the trust is a conduit. This result is reached through the concept of "distributable net income" introduced in the Code for the first time in 1954—though the conduit principle, with some exceptions, prevailed under the 1939 Code. The present Code provides that the beneficiary shall not be taxed on more than the distributable net income and that the trustee's deduction may not exceed distributable net income. Distributable net income means, in general, taxable income before the deduction for distributions and before the $300 personal exemption for simple trusts ($100 for complex trusts), but after exclusion of capital gains and losses, and in the case of simple trusts only, extraordinary cash dividends and taxable stock dividends which the trustee in good faith allocates to corpus.

Assume the trustee receives $6,000 in ordinary dividends, $4,000 in interest, has a long-term capital gain of $2,500 and receives an extraordinary cash dividend, which he allocates to capital, of $5,000. Distributable net income amounts to $10,000. This is the maximum amount on which the beneficiary may be taxed and represents the maximum amount of the trustee's deduction for distributions. The trustee will pay tax on the capital gain and the extraordinary cash dividend.

Further, the beneficiary may not be taxed on more than the taxable income of the trust. This corrects certain inequities which existed under prior law. *In Johnston* v. *Helvering,* the trustee invested in a mortgage. Assume the investment to have been $600,000. The mortgagor defaulted. No interest was paid for several years. The mortgagee, having taken over the property, sold it for $450,000. In accordance with the applicable state law, he paid a portion of the proceeds, assume $60,000, to the life tenant to make up for income not received while the mortgage was in default. Although the trust obviously had a loss and no income to distribute, the court held the amount paid to the beneficiary taxable income, since it arose out of the beneficiary's claim to income. Happily the 1954 Code makes this result impossible, since the beneficiary's taxable income cannot exceed the trustee's taxable income.

Even where gross income and trust income (local law) are the same, the taxable income may be less than trust income due to the different treatment of deductible expenses. Assume trust income of $10,000, with $1,500 of commissions, chargeable $1,000 to capital and $500 to income. Here trust income, the amount actually distributed to the beneficiary, will amount to $9,500. But the taxable income of the trust, because the entire $1,500 is deductible under Code Section 212, amounts to $8,500. Under the 1939 Code the beneficiary was taxable on $9,500; under the 1954 Code on $8,500. This prevents wasting deductions, which formerly occurred when the trust had no taxable income, in a year when it had deductions.

6.6 Capital gains

As noted, capital gains are excluded from the concept of distributable net income, except for the unusual case where the terms of the trust allocate them to income. Capital losses enter into the concept only when they offset gains required to be distributed. In the usual case, where gains are allocated to corpus, the income beneficiary gets the benefit of the other corpus deductions. Thus, if the trust has a $10,000 capital gain, $12,000 of distributable income, and a $1,000 commission charge against principal, distributable net income is $11,000.

6.7 Tax exempt interest and dividends

Since the trust is treated as a conduit, tax exempt income maintains its tax exempt status in the hands of the beneficiary. This result is achieved mechanically by including it in distributable net income but according it the same preferred status after distribution. Dividends also retain their same character. Thus if the trust has $2,000 tax exempt interest, $4,000 taxable interest, $6,000 dividend income, distributable income amounts to $12,000. But the $12,000 is treated as it was in the hands of the trustee, to wit: $2,000 of the interest is exempt, $5,900 of the dividend income taxable (because of the $100 dividend exclusion).

If, in the above example, we assume commissions of $1,200 and a $250 deductible attorney's fee incurred in connection with the taxable interest item, $200 of the commissions would be apportioned to the tax exempt interest and, therefore, not deductible. Hence distributable net income would amount to:

1. Tax exempt interest		$ 1,800
2. Taxable interest		4,000
3. Dividends		6,000
		$11,800
Less commissions	$1,000	
Fees	250	
Net distributable income		$10,550

6.8 *Depreciation*

The depreciation deduction for trust assets is apportioned between beneficiary and trustee in accordance with the terms of the trust instrument or, if no provision is made, in accordance with allocations of the trust income. Under trust law generally, the trustee is not required to retain any income to offset depreciation with respect to items originally transferred to the trust, but must set up a depreciation reserve for assets subsequently acquired. Assume a trust whose sole asset is an apartment home received on the creation of the trust. If the trust instrument is silent as to the duty of the trustee to maintain a depreciation reserve, and the income after expenses is $10,000 with depreciation of $3,000, the income under both trust law and under tax law is $10,000. This is distributable to the beneficiary but he is' allowed a $3,000 depreciation deduction. Even if there were no income, he would be entitled to the depreciation deduction. This is the same as prior law. If the trustee, pursuant to the instrument, or because he had purchased the apartment house as a trust investment, retained the $3,000 in a reserve, then the trustee, rather than the beneficiary, would be entitled to the deduction.

6.9 *Several beneficiaries*

Where there are several beneficiaries, each is taxed on his share of distributable net income. If this exceeds taxable income, he is taxable on his proportionate share. In the distribution of special items such as tax exempt interest, dividends, etc., he is regarded as receiving his proportionate share, unless the instrument earmarks a particular type of income for a particular beneficiary. This offers the opportunity of providing that tax exempt income shall be payable to Mother, for example, with other income to the lower income bracket members of the family providing the distribution provisions have some significance, apart from their tax significance. Thus a provision that A shall be entitled to one half of the trust income and that it shall consist first of the trust's tax exempt income, the balance, if any, to be made up from taxable income, would not satisfy this requirement. On the other hand, a provision that 40 percent of the trust corpus shall be invested in tax exempt securities (with annual adjustments to reflex changes in market values) and that A shall be entitled to all of the tax exempt income, should achieve the result since these provisions have significance quite apart from their tax significance.

6.10   Failure to distribute taxable income

The law of constructive receipt or of accounting principles does not apply. It is the amount distributable, not the amount actually received that is important. This can occasionally cause hardship, where the trustee wrongfully withholds income, but is necessary to prevent avoidance. Otherwise, the trustee might delay payments until a year when the beneficiary had large deductions.

Complex trusts

6.11   Accumulation trusts

Generally a complex trust is one wherein the trustee has the power to accumulate income. These trusts formerly offered tremendous tax avoidance possibilities, as noted in section 6.3.

6.12   Throwback rule

To meet this problem, in 1954 the five-year throwback rule was introduced. Under this rule any distributions from accumulations within the prior five years were retaxed to the beneficiary as though distributed in the years earned by the trust. But because of the many exceptions to the rule it proved wholly inadequate. Thus, distributions at majority, on termination of a trust in existence for more than nine years, distributions for emergency purposes, and distributions of less than $2,000 in excess of current income all escaped its rigors.

Under the new law an unlimited throwback is required. It includes capital gains as well as ordinary income and all of the helpful exceptions have disappeared.

As in the past, the trustee will initially pay the tax on accumulated income. Except for a simple trust, i.e., one that is required to distribute all of its income or a discretionary trust that has in fact never accumulated income, whenever a distribution is made, even on final termination, the beneficiary must again report the income and capital gains and recompute his tax as though he had received such income in the years earned by the trust.

A simple example will illustrate how the rule is expected to operate. Assume a trust produces $1,300 a year income and that the trustee's fee chargeable against income is $100. Further assume a tax of $200 with the balance of $1,000 being accumulated and that this is repeated for each of ten years. In the eleventh year the trust distributes its $1,200 of net current income and $10,000 of principal. Obviously this is inaccurate, as trust income would have increased over the years since the accumulations would themselves produce income. Also, there could be varying amounts each year and there would be an occasional capital gain. But for simplicity these factors are ignored.

The beneficiary in the year of distribution will report the current $1,200 with his other income and compute a partial tax. He will then recompute his tax for each of the prior ten years as though he had received $1,200 in each of those years (each year's accumulation plus the tax paid by the trustee). These increases will be added to the partial tax and, generally, he will be allowed a credit for the taxes paid by the trust.

The above procedure is called the "exact method." Obviously there will be many cases where the beneficiary's records are not available or are incomplete. To provide for such cases (but available for use in all cases at his election) the beneficiary may use what is called the "shortcut" method. Here he takes the total accumulations plus the taxes paid on them, $12,000 in our example, divided by ten (the number of years to which the distributions relate) to obtain the average distribution, i.e., $1,200. He then obtains an average increase in tax by recomputing his taxes for each of the immediately preceding three years as though he had received $1,200 in each year. If in one year the increase would have been $250, in a second, $300, and in the third, $350, the average increase is $300. He then multiplies this average by ten to obtain the tax on the total accumulations. Again he is entitled to a credit for the taxes paid by the trustee.

Obviously a beneficiary will elect the exact method if he was in low brackets during several of the earlier years involved. On the other hand, the shortcut method will be preferable if he was in lower brackets during the last three years.

All distributions are deemed to come from the earliest accumulations. This is the reverse of the old five-year throwback and is designed to ease some of the record-keeping problems. Also, all distributions come first from ordinary income and only when all accumulated ordinary income has been exhausted will any amounts be deemed to come from accumulated capital gain.

There are certain exceptions to these basic rules.

1. The shortcut method may not be used where there have been throwback distributions to the same beneficiary from two or more other trusts in earlier years. This prevents using multiple trusts with staggered payouts.

2. Where in some years there were only nominal accumulations (less than 25 percent of the average), these are to be excluded from the averaging computations. Thus, if $5,000 is accumulated in each of eight years and $250 in each of two years, the average income is determined (where all of it is distributed in one year) by dividing by 8 instead of 10. Here, $41,000 would be divided by 8 giving average income of $5,125. The average increase in tax for the last three years would then be determined by adding $5,125 to each of those years and the average increase in tax would be multiplied by 8 to determine the total increase in taxes, again with credit for taxes paid by the trustee.

3. Where a beneficiary has received other accumulations, he must include these in his income in the years deemed dis-

tributed in determining his current increase in tax. If the short-cut method is available, this would apply only to increase his basic income for the last three years to which the average imputed income is to be added.

4. If the amounts deemed distributed include years before the beneficiary was born, he will for those years be treated as single and having no other income.

5. If he uses the exact method, then, for any years before he was born that enter into the computation, he is denied any credit for the taxes paid by the trustee. The Committee reports fail to explain the reason for this but it may represent a good compromise to prevent the obtaining of what may be regarded as undeserved refunds.

These bewildering and frightening rules may not always operate to the disadvantage of taxpayers. For example, practically every 2503(c) trust (gift to minors section) will run afoul of the new provisions since they contemplate accumulating income. Assume that over 20 years $40,000 is accumulated less the taxes paid by the trustee. At 21 the trust terminates and on final distribution the beneficiary is deemed to have received $40,000 of accumulations. In many cases he will be entitled to a refund.

However, if the same minor were beneficiary of six like trusts, two created by his grandfather, two by his grandmother, one by his uncle, and another by his father, then he would have to increase his tax for the pertinent years by $12,000 instead of $2,000 and this would obviously put him in higher brackets than each of the several trusts. Hence, the unlimited throwback rule effectively prevents the abuses that multiple trusts permitted.

Refunds may also be available where there are discretionary trusts for several beneficiaries. Many trusts provide for distribution "to my son John or to any one or more or all of John's children." Under such trusts in making accumulation distributions the trustee may divide the fund among three or four children whose combined taxes may be lower than those paid by the trustee. No general rule can be laid down nor can one predict with any certainty what ultimate tax the accumulations may bear. But if the trustee has broad discretionary powers to pay out or to accumulate income and to sprinkle income and principal among a group he may be relied upon to watch for appropriate years and appropriate beneficiaries.

6.13 Several beneficiaries

Where there are several beneficiaries, to whom distributions are required to be made, the items of income are apportioned pro rata, as in the simple trusts. Where, however, some of the payments are mandatory and some discretionary, the mandatory distributees are treated as having received the distributable income, and only if payments to them amount to less than the full amount of such income, will the discretionary beneficiaries be treated as receiving taxable income. Assume $25,000 of current income, of which $10,000 is accumulated, the remaining $15,000 is required to be and is distributed to A, $10,000 of prior accumulations are distributed to B, a discretionary income beneficiary, and $10,000 of corpus is paid to C, a discretionary corpus beneficiary. Here A, a mandatory beneficiary, has $15,000 taxable income, B and C each have $5,000 since the payments to them are discretionary.

6.14 Separate shares

There are two situations where these rules would operate unfairly: (1) where each beneficiary's interest is in a separate share, and (2) where a capital bequest is paid out in a year when income is accumulated. Suppose a trust for the benefit of two children, A and B; income may be paid to them or accumulated. But if accumulated, it is to be added to the share of the child to whom it might have been paid and is to be held for his benefit. If the trust had $10,000 of income and retained A's share of the income but paid to B his share, $5,000, plus $5,000 of his share of the capital, B would be taxed under the above rules on $10,000 as income, $5,000 of which would never be available to him. To avoid this the Code provides that each share shall, for this purpose, be treated as though it were a separate and distinct trust. Thus in the case supposed, the tax treatment would be based on the assumption that there were two trusts, one for A and one for B. See section 6.16 discussing multiple or separate trusts.

6.15   Bequests

Further, if under the terms of the trust an amount is to be paid as a gift or bequest of a sum of money or of specific property and it is paid all in one year or in not more than three installments, it is to be considered as a payment from corpus, even if trust income is accumulated in the year or years of payment.

Trust income tax saving possibilities

6.16   Separate or multiple trusts

In drafting a trust bequest for several beneficiaries the draftsman has two alternative techniques. He may create one trust for each beneficiary or class of beneficiaries or he may create a single trust in which each beneficiary is given a fractional interest. Thus, the will may provide that the residue is to be held in trust and that each of the testator's four children is to receive one-fourth of the income each year, with a one-fourth share of principal on termination. Here there is a single trust with four beneficiaries. Assume that securities with a cost to the trustee of $20,000 are sold several years later for $40,000. The trustee has a long-term gain of $20,000, 50 percent of which is taxable at the ordinary progressive rates or, at the election of the trustee, at the alternative 25 percent rate upon the full amount of the gain. Since the tax on $10,000 (after deducting the $300 simple trust exemption) is $2,640, the trustee will undoubtedly elect this in preference to the alternative tax of $5,000.

The draftsman of the above trust might have directed the trustee to divide the fund into four equal shares and to hold one share, as a separate and distinct trust, for each child. In this case there would be four separate trusts, each with its own exemption and each subject to the beginning rates. Here, instead of one gain of $20,000, there would be four gains, each in the amount of $5,000, 50 percent of which is $2,500. The tax on $2,500, after allowance for the $300 exemption, amounts to $444. Multiplied by 4, the combined taxes would amount to $1,776 or a difference of $864.

6.17   Accumulation trusts

In many cases it is desirable to give the trustee a discretionary power to pay over the income or to accumulate it. Where a beneficiary has income in excess of his needs, it is a tax waste to require distribution, since the income, if distributable, will be taxed to the beneficiary whether he draws it out or not. On the other hand, if the power is vested in the trustee, he may pay it out if needed, if not, he may retain it and initially pay tax at the lower rate. Here a number of separate trusts will prove particularly valuable. Nor should the unlimited throwback rule cause hesitancy in using this device, since even if paid out in later years, the tax cost will be at least postponed and may, in some cases, as noted in section 6.12, even result in refunds.

6.18   Family residence in trust

If the family residence is left to the residuary trust with right in the wife to occupy it rent-free, trust income used to maintain the property will be taxed to the trustee, since it is nondistributable. The wife's occupancy is not a taxable benefit to her. Of course, the expenses must be limited to those incurred in the preservation of the property, insurance, repairs, mortgage interest, etc. Expenses incurred for the wife's personal enjoyment, light, heat, telephone, etc., would be taxable to her if the trust paid them, on the theory that they were paid for her benefit.

6.19 Authorizing trustee to purchase life insurance

The trustee of a testamentary trust may be authorized to purchase life insurance on the lives of the beneficiaries, if local trust law does not prohibit such use of income as an indirect form of accumulation. Since the income so used is nondistributable it will be taxed to the trustee. Assume Son has $20,000 of taxable income, aside from his trust. If the trustee distributed $4,000, his aditional income tax, even if he were married, would amount to $1,280, leaving $2,720 for premiums. On the other hand, if the trust purchased the insurance only $3,372 of gross trust income would be needed to pay the same premium, since the income tax would only be $552. Further, all estate tax is eliminated on the proceeds as Son does not own the policy. The insurance proceeds may, nevertheless, be used for normal insurance purposes, i.e., the making of cash funds available to the family at death, through an authorization to the trustee to purchase nonliquid assets from the estates of any beneficiary.

6.20 Sprinkle clauses

Even if all the income is needed, it may prove very costly to have it all taxed to the high bracket family member. Thus assume Son has three children and an income of $32,000 as a corporate executive. Father leaves one-half his estate in trust with Son as income beneficiary. This produces $10,000 a year. This additional $10,000 only nets Son $5,860. If the $10,000 could be spread among the three children, for tax purposes, it would net each child, almost twice as much. This would reduce annual income taxes by as much as $3,000.

The tax saving may be accomplished if the trustee, instead of being directed to pay the income to Son, is authorized to pay it in whole or in part to either Son or to any one or more of Son's issue. The trustee may then give it to Son or divide it among the children or make any other allocation that seems desirable in each tax year. Presumably the trustee in exercising his discretion will be guided by the ultimate use and the tax burden.

These discretionary income trusts are not merely tax avoidance devices, but useful estate planning tools. They have been used by English lawyers for hundreds of years, in large part, as a method of protecting beneficiaries against creditors. They are extremely useful apart from tax considerations where it is desired to take care of the family of a deceased child. The testator may worry about paying the income to his son's spouse, since she may remarry. On the other hand, he may worry about its going directly to the grandchildren. Here the sprinkle trust is an ideal device since the trustee will presumably pay it to the spouse, so long as the children are young, have unequal needs, and the spouse is without the obligations and temptations that a second marriage may entail. It is in essence a power of appointment over income. Testators rarely balk at giving a trustee a power of appointment over corpus: Query— why there should be any hesitancy about the lesser power over income?

The Revenue Service has recently ruled the trust income used for the support of a dependent will be taxed to the person upon whom rests the support obligation. Thus, in a sprinkle trust, if the trustee applies income for the support of a minor the Service may attempt to tax this income to the parent. The issuance of these regulations has caused considerable concern but properly understood and applied they do not seem likely to unduly curtail the use of the sprinkle device.

The Regulations make it clear that the obligation to support is limited to the duty imposed by local law. They state: "The term 'legal obligation' includes a legal obligation to support another person, if and only if, the obligation is not affected by the adequacy of the dependent's own resources. For example, a parent has an obligation, within the meaning of the preceding sentence, to support his minor child if property or income from property owned by the child cannot be used for his support so long as his parent is able to support him."

In the great majority of cases the income will not be used for the discharge of the obligation.

1. Frequently the beneficiaries will be over 21 and no obligation will exist.

2. Where minors are involved, the trustee will generally accumulate the income.

3. Where the parent's financial means are limited, income applied by the trustee for support will be demonstrably over and above the parent's obligation.

4. In the more doubtful cases as to the extent of the obligation, difficult and unsettled questions as to the measure of the parent's obligation will arise.

Perhaps it will be advisable to include in these trusts a provision that the income may be used only if the parent's funds are inadequate for the desired purpose. This will satisfy the desires of most donors and should go far to avoid the effect of the regulations. The fact that income is used will not be determinative of its taxability to the parent. There will still be the question of his obligation. Within the widest limits, this is fixed by the parent. Only in the event of a divorce does a court interpose its judgment as to the extent of the obligation. Does a parent have an obligation to send his minor child to college? Certainly not, if his financial situation does not warrant such an expenditure. Even if it does, the parent should not be regarded as violating any duty if he refuses to afford the child this opportunity. Extremely difficult and uncertain questions will arise where trust income is used in such cases, should the Treasury attempt to tax such income to the parent.

Assume a not unusual variation of the sprinkle device; the testamentary trust with income from the marital deduction trust going to the wife for her own benefit and the income from the nonmarital trust being payable to the wife "to be used by her for the benefit of the children." As to the latter income the wife is a subtrustee. She may use the income only for the benefit of the children. Assume each trust has a corpus of $100,000 and produces $4,000. The regulations state: "Normally, in the case of a parent's obligation to support his child, the extent of the parent's legal obligation of support, including education, will be determined by the family's station in life and by the means of the parent, without consideration of the trust income in question." Hence in the case suggested a considerable portion, if not all, of the children's $4,000 should escape inclusion in the mother's taxable income.

Thus while the new Regulation may go beyond existing case law, devices for spreading income among the family still offer substantial income tax saving opportunities.

7

Tax considerations in other will provisions

7.1   Introduction

There are tax pitfalls in some of the traditional ways in which estate owners have wished to take care of particular legatees which may be worth studying. Further survivorship and tax clauses have become increasingly important. What is said in this chapter with respect to these clauses has significance in the area of insurance beneficiary provisions. In the life insurance contract the usual survivorship provision is the 30-day clause. Many companies will permit a reverse simultaneous death clause. Lastly the fact that the federal tax is to be apportioned to insurance proceeds, unless the will otherwise provides, should not be overlooked.

General legacies

7.2 *Precatory bequests*

It is not uncommon to phrase bequests in absolute terms but to attach moral obligations thereto. This has long been a way of taking care of the erring son or vesting a discretionary power in a trusted legatee. Thus in *Mississippi Valley Trust Co.* v. *Commissioner,* a testator left his estate to his sons and in a subsequent paragraph provided: "I have heretofore expressed my wishes as to certain charitable gifts, and I therefore make no such bequests, preferring that my sons shall make such donations within their sole discretion as shall seem to them to be best." The sons gave $1,000,000 to the University of St. Louis. The estate was denied any charitable deduction since the gift to the sons was absolute. Undoubtedly the moral obligation was as real to the sons as if it had been legally imposed but the tax cost of the moral obligation was well in excess of $325,000. A bequest "of $1,000,000 to such charities as my sons may select" or, indeed, "$1,000,000 absolutely to my sons and if they disclaim, then to such charities as they may select," would have saved the tax money by obtaining the deduction for the gift actually made.

Sisters A and B each received $500,000 from the estate of their father. Sister A had a worthless son whose family she had supported for years. Sister B was unmarried. A's will left her entire estate to B "with the confident expectation, but without imposing any legal obligations that B will use it for the support of my son and his family." B did so use it for years until the youngest child reached 25. During this period heavy income taxes were incurred that were made higher because of her own income. She then distributed the fund equally among the son, his wife, and his children, fearful of the heavy estate shrinkage it would incur on her death. This cost better than $100,000 in gift taxes. Then she spent three years worrying that the transfers might be taxed as gifts in contemplation of death.

Both income and gift taxes could have been saved by the omission of the words "without imposing any legal obligation." Thus, "to B to be used by her for the education, support and maintenance of my son and his family, in such manner as she may determine," would have imposed a trust obligation on B. The income would not have been taxed to her when used for the benefit of the son's family. The distribution of the corpus would not have incurred gift tax. Nor would she have felt any compulsion to make the distribution since there would have been no potential estate tax liability. While the tax consequences would have been different, her control over the purse strings would have been the same, since to her, as to most people, the moral obligation was as binding as a legal one would have been.

7.3 Bequests as compensation

A sole proprietor died intestate without any immediate family. His key employee alleged the existence of a contract under which the decedent had agreed to leave him the business in exchange for his promise to continue in the decedent's employ throughout his life. The business was worth about $200,000. When the employee was told that the transfer of the business to him might well result in the receipt by him of $200,000 of income taxable in the year received, he immediately dropped his claim. All he wanted was some assurance that he could continue to have his job. Where could he find the tax money? Even with the new income averaging provisions of the Code the income tax could be well in excess of $100,000.

Bequests are specifically excluded, as are gifts during life, from the concept of gross income. But the bequest, like the gift, must not be for services rendered and therefore classifiable as compensation. The books are full of cases which raise the problem of gift or compensation. Employees' bonuses are taxable even though no contractual rights to them exist. Tips constitute taxable compensation. A company gave its president a yacht as a wedding present. Another gave a faithful employee $6,000 on his retirement at age 65. Both of these were held compensation as they were given in recognition of services rendered. On the other hand, in *Snyder and Berman, Inc.* v. *Commissioner,* a payment was made to a disabled officer of a family corporation. It was held not deductible since there was a finding that the "disbursement was made in the interests of the family rather than for the benefit of the business."

Whether a transfer is a gift or income depends on the motivation, not on the existence of a legal obligation. Was it designed to further compensate or was it motivated by love and affection? Gifts are made within the family. Rarely do transfers outside the family spring from gift motives.

The problem of the bequest is different in that gift motivation is more likely to be present in the will cases from the very nature of the situation, but a legacy is not, per se, tax free. In *McDonald* v. *Commissioner,* the decedent left the residue of his estate to his nurse and companion: "In appreciation of many years of loyal service and faithful care rendered me . . . . Miss McDonald has cheered, comforted and encouraged me through sickness, sorrows, disappointments and discouragements." The court held the bequest exempt but only because the evidence indicated that the legatee was more an intimate friend than a hired employee. The decedent had been divorced. Miss McDonald had lived and traveled with him for many years. Hence the relationship had more family flavor than business. But what of bequests to faithful servants, loyal employees? Here the motivation is mixed and probably they should be tax free. Draftsmen, however, will be wise not to unduly emphasize the services aspect as the controlling motive. This only raises a red flag. Caution would suggest that the bequest be made and the motives left unmentioned, lest a (generally) wrong impression be created.

There is, in these cases where no contract to further compensate by will exists, no advantage to the estate, in having the bequest classified as compensation, since no deduction will be allowed as, by our assumption, no enforceable obligation existed.

7.4   Bequests of income

Not infrequently there will be a number of bequests of a few hundred or a few thousand dollars to friends and distant relatives, with the residuary estate going to the high income tax bracket members of the immediate family. Frequently the overall income tax cost will be less if these miscellaneous legatees are given bequests from income from the residuary trust, so that all of the income for the first year or two goes to them. The delayed residuary legatee may be given an immediate bequest of capital to compensate him. Perhaps the smaller legatees should be given increased amounts to offset the income taxes on their bequests. The important point is that the income the estate produces will bear lesser income tax in their hands than in the hands of the residuary beneficiary.

7.5   Bequests of income items

Prior to 1934 much income earned but not collected prior to death escaped income tax. Thus if a cash basis lawyer died with receivables of $25,000, these items were included in his gross estate, received a cost basis of their far market value, and to the extent of this basis were later received tax free as capital by his legatee. To close this loophole the law was changed to require the inclusion in the year of death of all items that had accrued at the time of death. This put the cash basis taxpayer on an accrual basis for the last year of his life. But the Treasury gave this amendment a very broad interpretation, which the Supreme Court sustained, by requiring the inclusion of all payments that might later become due because of services performed by the taxpayer before his death, even though they could not be regarded as "accrued" in the usual meaning of that word. This proved ruinous to lawyers and other professional men by bunching several years' income into a single return and consequently pushing it into higher and higher brackets. Congress corrected this inequity by eliminating the accrual and making all income "in respect of a decedent" taxable to the actual recipient as and when received with a deduction for an estate tax paid with respect to such item. See section 3.10.

The estates of many persons will contain a substantial number of "income with respect to a decedent" items. Thus a life insurance agent will have several years of renewal commissions coming due after death. Business executives will have a number of years of deferred compensation payments guaranteed. Professional men and others whose businesses consist in large part of personal services will leave much "work in progress" that will later produce ordinary income. These items should receive particular attention. If $10,000 or $20,000 is to go to charity, these assets represent the cheapest source of payment, since the fact that they are taxable makes no difference to the tax-exempt organization. If there are no charitable bequests, then a number of accumulation trusts or low bracket taxpayers represent the ideal recipients of such items.

7.6 Gifts of fractional shares rather than stated amounts

A left securities in trust to pay the income to B and when he reached 40 to pay him $5,000,000 of corpus. The trustee, upon B's attaining 40, discharged $3,200,000 of this capital payment with stock that had a cost basis to the trust of $1,200,000. It was held the trust realized a taxable gain of $2,000,000 as a result of this transaction. The result seems sound and is in accord with the general capital gains law. The trustee was indebted to the beneficiary in the sum of $5,000,000. He discharged this debt with property that cost him considerably less. It is well settled that if a rent obligation or other debt is paid in property that has appreciated in value, a taxable exchange has occurred. On the other hand, if the bequest is of a fractional share, no dollar amount is owed. No gain or loss is recognized on the distribution of the residuary estate or the payment of a specific legacy. Here the tax could have been avoided by a direction that at 40, B would receive one fourth or other fractional share of the corpus. Of course B would in this latter case take the trustee's low cost basis but this would affect him adversely only if and when he sold the stock during life. If he retained it until death, the entire gain would escape tax, since his legatees who acquire a new basis, i.e., market value at date of death or six months from death, if the optional valuation date is selected. See section 3.24.

7.7   Bargain purchase bequests

Where son A is the only member of the family actively engaged in father's business, father's will frequently gives him an option to buy the business at two thirds or other percentage of its value. Here the disposition is part a bequest and part a sale. But *Mack* v. *Commissioner* held in this type bequest that A's cost basis was the amount he actually paid for the business. This, of course, would be most significant in the cases where father operated as a sole proprietor[1] and would always be significant on a later sale of the business or part interest therein by the legatee. While the law is still unsettled a later case has suggested that the basis of a bargain purchaser under a will ought to include the value of the option. This latter approach seems preferable.

7.8   Bequests to corporations

Occasionally a bequest will be made to a corporation. Three brothers and two sisters pooled a portion of their funds for investment in a family corporation. Brother A, a bachelor, died and left his individually owned properties to the corporation.

---

[1] The lower cost basis would affect each individual asset in the business, both those held for resale and those used in the trade or business.

Assume that the cost basis of the surviving brothers and sisters for their stock in the corporation was $100. It remained $100 after the receipt of the bequest, though the corporation was now considerably richer. Its stock prior to the bequest, let us assume for purposes of illustration, was worth on sale or dissolution $150. After the bequest the fair market value of each share jumped to $180. The gift to the corporation thus increased the potential capital gain liability needlessly. Had the individuals been given the properties their basis would have been current market (value at the date of death). If they individually contributed them to the corporation, the cost basis of each share would have been increased (on the values assumed) to $130. Absent other considerations bequests to corporations are not desirable from a tax standpoint.

7.9 Vested remainders

The creation of contingent remainders has caused trouble in the settlement of state inheritance taxes. Thus a gift to A for life, remainder to B if he survives, otherwise to X, a stranger to the blood, may result in the remainder interest being taxed at the higher rate applicable to X, with a possible refund if B ultimately comes into the property. To avoid this difficulty lawyers sometimes create indefeasibly vested remainders. But this may result in the incurring of much heavier death taxes than the inheritance tax problem avoided. Thus, if the bequest is "to A for life, remainder to B and his heirs," and B predeceases A, the value of B's remainder interest will be included in B's taxable estate (both state and federal) even though B never had the enjoyment of the property. Here the careful draftsman would have avoided any tax on B's death by phrasing the bequest "to A for life, remainder to B but if he predeceases A, then to B's children who survive A."

7.10 Family charitable trusts

A small family charitable trust may be advantageously created even in modest estates. Suppose a testator leaves $20,000 to his son and daughter as trustees, for the purpose of making such gifts to charities as they may, from time to time, determine. The principal amount will escape estate tax, the income will be free of income tax, and the children may use the income and principal to meet the constantly growing demands for charitable gifts to organized charities that they would otherwise feel obligated to make from their own funds.

Such a trust must under the Tax Reform Act of 1969 conform to the new requirement for charitable foundations, i.e., the instrument must require annual distributions of income and must *expressly* prohibit self-dealing, retaining excess business holdings, making speculative investments, and making any "taxable expenditures."

7.11   Charitable bequests

For the reasons stated in section 7.6 it may be preferable to provide for fractional share gifts to charities rather than stated amounts. Thus, instead of $5,000 to the X charity, a bequest of one one hundredth of the estate may result in the avoidance of a capital gains tax to the executor when and if he satisfies the bequest by the delivery of property to the charitable legatee.

Charitable remainder testamentary trusts have also been popular particularly among childless couples. The typical plan was to leave one half of the estate to the survivor in such a way as to obtain the marital deduction and one half in trust, income to the survivor for life, remainder to charity. Prior to the Tax Reform Act of 1969 it was possible to authorize the trustee to invade principal if ever needed by the surviving spouse to maintain her accustomed standard of living. An estate tax deduction was allowed for the value of the remainder interest if the chances of invasion were so remote that there was no appreciable risk that any portion of the principal would be so needed. But the Treasury became concerned that in fact some principal for which a deduction had been permitted might in fact be diverted from charity. There was the further risk that through investment manipulation the charity might suffer. Thus, the trustee might invest in high yield securities that would benefit the life tenant at the expense of the charity. To eliminate these possibilities the Tax Reform Act of 1969 provides that such charitable remainder trusts will be denied any estate tax deduction unless there is (1) no power of invasion and (2) the life tenant is given either an annuity in an amount not less than 5 percent of the initial value of the corpus or annual payments of a percentage (not less than 5 percent) of the value of the corpus each year. Thus, under the latter plan, if the initial corpus were $100,000 and the percentage 5 percent, the life tenant would be entitled to $5,000. If the next year the capital had increased to $120,000, the payment for that year would be $6,000. Such a trust (unitrust) may provide that in the event the trust income in any year is less than the required amount, only the trust income need be paid over and the deficit may be made good in a later year.

These trusts may continue for the lives of beneficiaries in being at the date of creation of the trust or for a fixed period of years not exceeding 20.

The new rules apply to trusts created after December 31, 1969, except as to testators dying before October 9, 1972, without having republished their wills. Thus a grace period is allowed for conforming existing wills to meet the new requirements.

7.12   Effect of charitable bequests on the marital deduction

A charitable bequest does not reduce the maximum allowable marital deduction whereas an inter vivos gift does. It would, therefore, appear at first glance that a testamentary bequest would be preferable to a gift during life. For example, if T, whose property is estimated at $500,000, were to leave one half of his estate to his wife and one half to charity, there would be no federal tax. The wife's share would qualify for the marital deduction. The half going to charity qualifies for the charitable deduction. On the other hand, were he to give to charity $250,000 prior to his death and leave his reduced estate to a widow, his estate tax would be $11,000. In this case only 50 percent of his estate at death, i.e., $125,000 will pass free under the marital deduction. But this tells only half the story. When the wife dies in case one, the full $250,000 will be subject to tax (otherwise it would not have qualified for the marital deduction). The tax thereon would be $47,000; whereas in case two, her tax need only be $11,000. Thus the inter vivos gift results in a decrease in overall taxes of $25,000.

Case One—Charitable Gift at Death

Death of Husband

Estate...		$500,000
Marital deduction (bequest to wife)............	$250,000	
Charitable deduction........................	$250,000	
		500,000
Taxable estate..............................		0

Death of wife

Gross estate (received from husband)....................		$250,000
Less specific exemption................................		60,000
Taxable estate..		$190,000
Federal estate tax..............................	$ 47,000	

Case Two—Inter Vivos Charitable Gift

Death of husband

Estate, after inter vivos gift to charity....................		$250,000
Less marital deduction.......................	$125,000	
Less specific exemption.......................	60,000	
		185,000
Taxable estate..............................		$ 65,000
Federal estate tax..............................	$ 11,000	

Death of wife

Gross estate (portion received from husband qualifying for marital deduction. It is assumed the balance was left in trust in such a way as to avoid any tax on wife's death)........................		$125,000
Less specific exemption................................		60,000
Taxable estate..		$ 65,000
Federal estate tax..............................	$ 11,000	

Summary

Combined taxes, case one.....................................	$ 47,000
Combined taxes, case two.....................................	$ 22,000
Difference..	$ 25,000

Common disaster and like clauses

7.13 Objectives of survivorship clauses

Too often a standardized common disaster clause is used for all wills without adequate consideration of the objectives for which such clauses are designed.

Objectives:

1. Perhaps foremost in the minds of most estate owners is the fear of double death taxes.[2]

2. To those who have had experience in the handling of estates the avoidance of successive administration expenses, particularly lawyer's and executor's fees, measured, as they generally are, by the value of the estate, will loom large.

3. There will be times when unnecessarily exposing the property to possible creditors of a legatee's estate may worry testators.

4. More frequently the thought that a legatee's widow may have her share of the legatee's estate enlarged at the expense of the legatee's children will trouble even those who highly regard the daughter-in-law but are not unmindful of the possibilities of remarriage.

5. A childless husband may not relish the thought of his wife's family enjoying his wealth shortly after his death.

6. Many legacies are purely personal in character. A testator wants his friend to benefit by the bequest but he has no interest at all in the objects of the friend's bounty.

7. In addition to one or more of the above, testators may want to avoid the litigation that may result from uncertainty as to the time of deaths.

8. In many situations the marital deduction is desired only if the spouse is likely to outlive the testator by many years.

9. Perhaps more frequently the marital deduction is desired even if the spouse survives for but a moment.

---

[2] The credit on the tax for prior transfers will frequently prove inadequate.

7.14 Typical clauses

Typical clauses designed to accomplish one or more of these objectives fall into three types.

1. *Time clause* "For the purpose of this will a legatee or devisee shall not be deemed to have survived me if such legatee or devisee dies within 90 days after my death."

2. *Simultaneous death clause* "If any legatee or devisee dies simultaneously with me or under such circumstances as to render it difficult or impossible to determine who predeceased the other, I hereby declare that I shall be deemed to have survived such legatee or devisee and this will and all its provisions shall be construed upon that assumption and basis."

3. *Common disaster clause* "If any legatee or devisee and I die as a result of a common disaster, the said legatee or devisee shall be deemed to have predeceased me and this will and all its provisions shall be construed upon that assumption and basis."

Not infrequently two types will be combined. Thus the clause may read "if any legatee or devisee and I die in a common disaster or under such circumstances that it cannot be determined who died first, such legatee or devisee shall be presumed to have predeceased me."

It should be noted that in the absence of any clause, both at common law and under the Simultaneous Death Act, if the order of deaths cannot be established by proof, the testator's property is distributed as if he had survived the legatee.

7.15 Analysis of each type

Apart from the marital deduction, most of the objectives may be better achieved through use of a trust or legal life estate. In cases that otherwise lend themselves to the use of these devices the draftsman may well be advised to use one or the other in preference to a survivorship clause. A survivorship clause will be found satisfactory only where the objective is accomplished by delaying the gift for a relatively short time, or where because of the amount involved or the type of property, a trust is not indicated and a legal life estate not a desirable solution.

Simultaneous death clause   This type of clause fixes the order of deaths only when there is insufficient evidence to establish who died first. Many variations of the clause merely substitute a new issue inviting litigation, i.e., where the circumstances are such that it is "difficult to determine" who died first. It fails to accomplish any of the desired objectives, apart from a marital deduction objective, because the testator is really not concerned with whether he and his beneficiary die at about the same time or under circumstances leaving the question doubtful. What he really wants to avoid is having his property pass through the estate of a legatee who will not live long to enjoy it.

This type is unsatisfactory in that:

1. It frequently fails to eliminate litigation.

2. It will bring about the very result the testator desired to avoid if his legatee survives him by five minutes.

Common disaster clause   This type may be even more unsatisfactory.

1. It frequently gives rise to litigation as to whether the accident or peril or disaster was the cause of both deaths.

2. It fails to cover the rather rare case where the deaths occur at about the same time from unrelated causes.

3. It may result in leaving titles unsettled for years. H and W are in a motor accident. H dies shortly thereafter. W, badly crippled, lives on for years without recovering. When, if ever, during her life, may H's executor safely pay over her bequest? How can he be certain her later death may not have a causal connection with the earlier accident?

Note from the objectives listed above that the testator is never really concerned with deaths from a common cause but rather with deaths that occur within a relatively short time of each other.

Time clause   The time clause will almost always avoid litigation except for the rare case where the bodies are found after a considerable period of time and hence the date of the testator's death cannot be determined. It will solve all the simultaneous death cases and practically all the common disaster cases.

1. Clauses such as "to those of my nephews who survive to the date of the distribution of my estate" should be avoided. Aside from the power they give the executor to decide who shall take by hastening or delaying distribution, such clauses in many jurisdictions may be void as violating the rule against perpetuities since there are no measuring lives and it is possible that distribution of the estate may be delayed beyond 21 years. This is silly, but is probably the law in a number of jurisdictions.

2. If the postponement is for too long a time it may create undesirable uncertainty in titles.

7.16   Recommended clause for a nonmarital deduction bequest

The time clause is the recommended clause for other than marital deduction bequests. Whether to use 60 days, 6 months, or a year will depend on the circumstances of each case. Testators generally desire prompt distribution of their estates, particularly as to small legacies. Titles are left uncertain during the intervening period and executors may be in doubt as to some of their duties. Generally 30 to 60 days should appear adequate, since deaths from common causes are most likely to occur within a relatively short time.

7.17   Recommended clauses, marital deduction bequests

Where the deduction is desired in all events, i.e., where one spouse has the bulk of the family wealth, the reverse simultaneous death clause should be used. See discussion and form at section 4.7. Where the deduction is desired, in spite of a possible heavier tax burden, on the assumption that the surviving spouse will live for many years to enjoy the bequest, the time clause should be used. See discussion and form at section 4.19.

Tax clauses

7.18   Income and gift tax clauses

Wills generally authorize the executor to file joint income and gift tax returns with the surviving spouse; otherwise he may hesitate to assume the liabilities involved. By filing a joint return without such authorization the executor becomes individually liable for the full amount of the tax, including any later assessments and penalties, and may not seek reimbursement from the estate. An innocent spouse and presumably her personal representative may be relieved of liability for tax, interest, and penalties if an omission from gross income amounts to more than 25 percent of gross income, the spouse had no reason to know of the omission, the spouse did not significantly benefit from the items omitted, and other facts and circumstances would make it inequitable to hold her liable.

7.19   Death tax clauses

A few examples will indicate the importance of a tax clause in a will. Testator's will left $500,000 to son A, $500,000 to son B, residue to X University. His estate amounted to approximately $1,500,000. In some jurisdictions the X University would receive practically nothing. In others, it would receive the full $500,000. Assume another decedent created a revocable trust during life of approximately $300,000 for the benefit of his children. His will, reciting that he had adequately taken care of his children by the trust, divided his estate (of about $60,000) among friends and faithful employees. The federal estate tax (amounting to about $60,000 on a taxable estate of $360,000) must be paid but if it comes from his probate estate, his will will be an empty shell.

Except for the proceeds of life insurance and property over which the decedent had a general power of appointment, the Code is silent as to the source from which the tax money shall ultimately come. Local law determines on whom the burden falls, except for insurance proceeds and funds subject to a general power of appointment. But in all jurisdictions it is clear that the will may override both federal and state law by specifically providing the sources of payment.

The common law rule charges the taxes against the residue. Thus, in the first case suggested above, the charity would take practically nothing since federal estate taxes would amount to approximately $500,000. This might have been what the testator intended. He may have felt, as many do, that he wanted his sons to receive a fixed amount and he was not concerned whether charity or the Government took the lion's share of what remained. But he may have been interested in the X University. If the taxes were chargeable against the individual legatees, the total tax burden would have been $150,000 less, since the taxable estate would have been $1,000,000 rather than $1,500,000. In case two, if the common law rule applies the legatees will get nothing and the testator could hardly have intended this.

Because the common law rule worked so many hardships, many states have adopted apportionment statutes under which the tax is equitably apportioned among the beneficiaries. Under such a statute the University would receive $500,000. Its share would not be burdened with any part of the tax since it was not responsible to any extent for the imposition of the tax. But there is no particular reason for believing that the testator wanted this result. Also, if one of his friends in case two was given a $500 legacy, it may be questioned whether the decedent intended this to be reduced by 30 percent for his share of the federal tax.

Because the tax burden is so great there is always a real risk that the estate owner's plan may be completely upset by having the tax burden fall where he never intended it to fall. For this reason wills should and generally do contain a clause that clearly expresses his intent.

8

Jointly owned property

8.1   The estate tax statute

Code Section 2040 requires that there be included in the tax estate of the decedent the full value of all property, in which he had an interest at the time of his death, jointly with another, with right of survivorship except to the extent that the survivor can affirmatively demonstrate the proportion, if any, that funds belonging to him and never received from the decedent by way of gift, were used to acquire the property. This includes tenancies by the entireties, joint tenancies of both real and personal property, joint bank accounts, government bonds registered in the name of A, payable on death to B, Totten-type savings accounts and all like interests in property.[1]

---

[1] Reg. Sec. 20.2040–1 states: "Joint interests—(a) **In general.** A decedent's gross estate includes under Section 2040 the value of property held jointly at the time of the decedent's death by the decedent and another person or persons with right of survivorship, as follows:

"(1) To the extent that the property was acquired by the decedent and

Here the test of inclusion is not who owned the asset but who paid for it. If the jointly owned property was acquired by the owners through gift or inheritance, then only the proportionate share of the decedent becomes part of his taxable estate. Where the property is held by owners as tenants in common, only the decedent's fractional interest is included.

Thus, if Husband purchased Blackacre for $40,000 and took title in his name and Wife, as joint tenants or as tenants by the entireties, the full value of Blackacre, as of the date of his death, or six months later if the optional valuation date is used, will be taxed as part of his estate. If Wife, instead of Husband, were the first to die, nothing would be included in her estate, always assuming Husband could establish that he furnished the entire purchase price. If, however, Father had devised the property to them, then only half the value would be included in the estate of the first dying spouse.

---

the other joint owner or owners by gift, devise, bequest, or inheritance, the decedent's fractional share of the property is included.

"(2) In all other cases, the entire value of the property is included except such part of the entire value as is attributable to the amount of the consideration in money or money's worth furnished by the other joint owner or owners. See Section 20.2043–1 with respect to adequacy of consideration. Such part of the entire value is that portion of the entire value of the property at the decedent's death (or at the alternate valuation date described in Section 2032) which the consideration in money or money's worth furnished by the other joint owner or owners bears to the total cost of acquisition and capital additions. In determining the consideration furnished by the other joint owner or owners, there is taken into account only that portion of such consideration which is shown not to be attributable to money or other property acquired by the other joint owner or owners from the decedent for less than a full and adequate consideration in money or money's worth. Property will not be treated as having been acquired from the decedent for less than adequate and full consideration in money or money's worth if it represents income from property acquired from the decedent. For this purpose, gain (whether realized or unrealized) resulting from appreciation in the value of property is not 'income' from property. The entire value of jointly held property is included in a decedent's gross estate unless the executor submits facts sufficient to show that property was not acquired entirely with consideration furnished by the decedent, or was acquired by the decedent and the other joint owner or owners by gift, bequest, devise, or inheritance.

"(b) **Meaning of 'property held jointly.'** Section 2040 specifically covers property held jointly by the decedent and any other person (or persons), property held by the decedent and spouse as tenants by the entirety, and a deposit of money, or a bond or other instrument, in the name of the decedent and any other person and payable to either or the survivor. The Section applies to all classes of property, whether real or personal, and regardless of when the joint interests were created. Furthermore, it makes no difference that the

8.2 Constitutionality

The constitutionality of this section of the Code was sustained in *United States* v. *Jacobs,* even though the joint tenancy had been created in 1909, long before the estate tax was in effect.

8.3 Marital deduction

Jointly owned property, to the extent that it is included in the gross taxable estate and passes by survivorship to a spouse,

---

survivor takes the entire interest in the property by right of survivorship and that no interest therein forms a part of the decedent's estate for purposes of administration. The Section has no application to property held by the decedent and any other person (or persons) as tenants in common.

"(*c*) **Examples.** The application of this Section may be explained in the following examples in each of which it is assumed that the other joint owner or owners survived the decedent:

"(1) If the decedent furnished the entire purchase price of the jointly held property, the value of the entire property is included in his gross estate;

"(2) If the decedent furnished a part only of the purchase price, only a corresponding portion of the value of the property is so included;

"(3) If the decedent furnished no part of the purchase price, no part of the value of the property is so included;

"(4) If the decedent, before the acquisition of the property by himself and the other joint owner, gave the latter a sum of money or other property which thereafter became the other joint owner's entire contribution to the purchase price, then the value of the entire property is so included, notwithstanding the fact that the other property may have appreciated in value due to market conditions between the time of the gift and the time of the acquisition of the jointly held property;

"(5) If the decedent, before the acquisition of the property by himself and the other joint owner, transferred to the latter for less than an adequate and full consideration in money or money's worth other income-producing property, the income from which belonged to and became the other joint owner's entire contribution to the purchase price, then the value of the jointly held property less that portion attributable to the income which the other joint owner did furnish is included in the decedent's gross estate;

"(6) If the property originally belonged to the other joint owner and the decedent purchased his interest from the other joint owner, only that portion of the value of the property attributable to the consideration paid by the decedent is included;

"(7) If the decedent and his spouse acquired the property by will or gift as tenants by the entirety, half of the value of the property is included in the decedent's gross estate; and

"(8) If the decedent and his two brothers acquired the property by will or gift as joint tenants, a third of the value of the property is so included."

will qualify for the marital deduction. Hence a limited amount of jointly owned property with a spouse will not have adverse estate tax consequences, if the decedent's will uses a formula clause or otherwise arranges the bequests in his will so as to obtain the maximum marital deduction, without qualifying an excessive amount of property. Without a formula clause this is difficult as what may be held jointly today, may be held separately tomorrow.

It is generally undesirable in the larger estates to hold the bulk of the family property in joint ownership, where one of the spouses is the major contributor. Thus assume Husband purchased Blackacre, an apartment house, for $200,000. Title is taken in the joint names of Husband and Wife, with right of survivorship. This is their sole substantial asset. On Husband's death there will be a relatively small ($4,800) federal estate tax since Blackacre qualifies for the marital deduction. But on Wife's later death, her estate tax will be $31,500 since her estate will be valued at $200,000. Here the joint ownership results in the overqualification of property for the marital deduction. If Husband had taken the title in his own name and by will created a marital deduction and a nonmarital deduction trust along the lines suggested in chapters 4 and 5, his federal estate tax would be $4,800 and Wife's later federal estate tax would be limited to $4,800. Or, if Husband had taken title in their names as tenants in common and then in his will left his interest to Wife for her life, the same reduced federal estate taxes would be payable.

Aside from the family residence, joint tenancies may be undesirable. Nothing is gained from an estate tax standpoint and much can be lost, either through unnecessarily increasing the tax estate of the donee survivor or because the survivor, though not, in fact, a donee, cannot prove the extent of his contributions.

8.4   Tracing the contribution of joint owners

Where both spouses, and what is said here is equally applicable where the joint owners are other than Husband and

Wife, have independent estates or earnings the difficulties of tracing the source of the contributions frequently result in the imposition of taxes solely because of a lack of affirmative proof. Thus, assume Husband and Wife over a period of 25 years deposit whatever dividend and salary income each has in a joint account. From this account each draws at his pleasure for living expenses, personal items, gifts, contributions to the support of relatives, vacations, etc. At intervals, as the bank deposit increases, withdrawals are made for the purchase of securities, in their joint names. Whose money purchased what? How can the surviving wife show that her funds were used to purchase, in whole or in part, any particular shares of stock? Many a case has floundered through lack of adequate record keeping.

The statute requires that the contribution of the survivor must not be originally traceable back to the decedent. Thus, if Husband gave Wife $10,000 which she later contributes as her share to the joint purchase of X stock, this will be treated as his contribution, since it originally belonged to him. Suppose, however, in addition to the $10,000 from Husband, she had inherited $9,000 from Aunt Nellie prior to the purchase of the stock. Was it his money or Aunt Nellie's that she contributed?

There is one limitation on this rule that traces the original source of the contribution which may occasionally be useful. Contributions that come from the income from gift property are not charged back to the donor. Thus, in *Harvey* v. *United States* the court found as a fact that the Wife's contributions to the jointly owned property came, not from the property given to her by husband (even though she had no other assets or earnings) nor from that property in a converted form, but was "traceable to (1) profits made through sales of the original gift property and successive reinvestments of the proceeds of such sales,[2] or (2) rents, interests, and divi-

---

[2] The Treasury does not agree that profits from jointly owned property are not to be treated as attributable to the original contributor. Note the Regulations quoted at page 140 that "gain whether realized or unrealized resulting from appreciation is not 'income' for property."

dends produced by such property in its original or converted form while title thereto was in the wife." The opinion in part states: "It seems clear that none of the cases cited contains any support for the novel proposition that income produced by gift property, after the gift has been completed, belongs to the donor and is property received or acquired from him by the donee; nor is there, in these cases, anything to impeach the conclusion of the trial court, or that of the Tax Court in the *Howard* case, that the income produced by property of any kind belongs to the person who owns the property at the time it produces such income and does not originate with a donor who has made a completed gift of that property prior to its production of the income. Similarly, they fail to sustain the contention that the statute should be interpreted as excepting from inclusion in the gross estate such part of the jointly held property 'as may be shown to have originally belonged to such other person and never to have been received or acquired *or produced by property which was received or acquired* by the latter from the decedent for less than an adequate and full consideration in money or money's worth.' "

8.5   Services as contributions

When the funds used to purchase the jointly owned property come from a family business or family investments, the services of the wife may be recognized as responsible for a part of the purchase price if, but only if, it can be shown that there was an agreement that she was to participate in profits. Not only must the wife have been active in the business but there must be a showing of a contractual right to a share of the earnings. Thus, in *Bushman* v. *United States* the wife rendered services to the husband in the management of family real estate and in his law practice which the court found were of "inestimable value." Nevertheless, the full value of the jointly owned property was included in the husband's estate as the services were held to have been rendered "out of love and affection" and never valued by them so as to provide a basis for showing the amount of her contribution. A major difficulty to be overcome in these cases, in the absence of a formal partnership agreement, is that generally the husband has a right to the services of the wife under state law, with no obligation to compensate her.

8.6 Transfers of jointly owned property in contemplation of death

What are the tax consequences when gifts of jointly owned property are made shortly before death and are found to have been made in contemplation of death. Will the full value of the property be included in the taxable estate of the deceased owner on a showing that he contributed the entire purchase price? The difficulty is that he only transferred half the property since that is all he owned. On the other hand, it is arguable, the policy behind the Code would seem to suggest full inclusion. *Sullivan's Estate* v. *Commissioner,* and *Don Murillow Broackway* v. *Commissioner,* are authority for the inclusion of only half, the Court in the latter case saying, "If this result is contrary to the basic purpose of the estate tax statute and there is a loophole . . . the remedy lies with Congress."

This rule makes jointly owned property attractive for gift tax purposes. Thus if husband and wife own as joint tenants real estate worth $100,000, all paid for by the husband, the full $100,000 will be included in his gross taxable estate at death. Suppose a few months before his death and because he is suffering from an incurable disease, he and his wife transfer the land to their son. If the transfer is held to be a gift in contemplation of death, only one half or $50,000 may be included under these cases.

8.7 Creation of joint tenancy as a taxable gift

The creation of a joint tenancy, where one owner contributes all or more than his proportionate share of the purchase price, may attract gift tax. This is true wherever the transfer is irrevocable, except for the special statutory exception relating to spouses, noted below. Since the funds in joint checking accounts, savings accounts, government bonds, etc. may be recaptured the gift is revocable and therefore without gift tax consequences. On the other hand, if 100 shares of General Motors is purchased by Husband in the joint names of Husband and Wife, Wife acquires indefeasibly vested rights in the share of which Husband may not by later action deprive her, without her consent, and a gift tax is therefore incurred.

8.8   Valuation of interests

The tenancy by the entirety differs from a joint tenancy in that it is not destructible by one of the parties. If A and B own Blackacre as joint tenants, A may sell his interest to C and thereafter B and C hold as tenants in common. Or, A's creditors may levy upon and have his interest sold, again destroying the survivorship feature. For this reason the value of the individual interest of each of two joint tenants is always 50 percent of the full value, even if A is 30 and B is 70 years of age. But in many states neither the Husband nor the Wife can deal with their individual interests in a tenancy by the entirety in such a way as to destroy the survivorship rights of the other. Thus, if Husband sells his interest in the tenancy by the entirety property, and he subsequently dies while Wife is still alive, the entire estate vests in Wife. The same is true if his creditors levy upon and have his interest sold. All the Buyer acquires is the possibility of having the fee, if Husband survives. For this reason, if Husband is 70 and Wife is 30, the value of Wife's interest in the property, because of her longer life expectancy, is much greater than that of Husband. Thus, in jurisdictions where tenancies by the entirety are still recognized, the gift tax liability of Husband on the creation of such a tenancy, assuming he pays the full purchase price, is generally greater than half. Also, if Husband and Wife convert such a tenancy to a tenancy in common, the Wife may have made a taxable transfer.

8.9   Creation of interest without gift tax

Because spouses commonly take title to the family residence in their joint names without any thought of gift tax consequences and naturally, therefore, fail to file returns, Congress was persuaded in 1954 to permit the creation of joint estates by husbands and wives in real property without its being considered a gift at that time. The gift will occur on any later sale of the property if the proceeds are divided in a percentage different from the original contribution. Thus, if Husband paid 90 percent of the purchase price of $25,000 and Wife paid 10 percent and there was a later sale at $40,000, with the proceeds divided, all the Wife received in excess of $4,000 (i.e. $16,000) would be treated as a gift. This initial gift tax liability may be avoided at the election of the taxpayer. If he fails to file a return he is treated as having so elected. In order to have the creation of the tenancy treated as the taxable event a gift tax return must be filed. Again, it should be noted that this optional treatment is available only as to spouses and, as to them, only with respect to real estate.

8.10   Advantages of joint tenancies

Such property is generally free from the claims of creditors of the deceased owner. In some jurisdictions, inheritance taxes may be saved, since not all states follow the federal rules of inclusion but tax only the interest of the decedent. Further, it will avoid probate delays. For estates under $60,000 these advantages may make it attractive. For the larger estates some joint ownership may be desirable, particularly for the family residence. Joint ownership tends toward family solidarity. Prior to the 1954 Code there was a very distinct tax disadvantage, even for very small estates, in that the income tax cost basis of the property did not change at death. Assume Husband purchased the residence for $20,000 in 1935 taking title in his name and that of Wife. He died in 1950, with an estate, including the jointly owned residence, of $55,000, of which the residence accounted for $45,000. Wife sold the property a year later for $48,000. Under the 1939 Code, she had a long-term capital gain of $28,000, because her tax cost was $20,000. The technical reason was that the date of death value applied only to property acquired "by devise, bequest or inheritance" and the Courts had quite properly held that she had not so acquired the property. She had received it in a lifetime gift transaction and, therefore, took her donor's cost. On the other hand, if Husband had taken the title in his own name and left it to Wife she would have acquired it by inheritance and hence her cost would have been $45,000 and her gain $3,000. Happily, this inequity has been removed by the 1954 Code which gives the date-of-death value to all property includible in the gross tax estate.

8.11   Advantages of electing to have the gift tax deferred

The option to defer the taxable event would seem to offer some tax avoiding opportunities. Assume an apartment house produces a net of $40,000 a year. If transferred by Husband to Husband and Wife, jointly, and if under local law, Wife is entitled to half the rent, Husband can make the transfer of the apartment house tax free and, thereafter, there will be siphoned off, without any gift consequence, $20,000 a year to the Wife, which property will be hers absolutely and will not be included in Husband's taxable estate at death.

On the other hand, there will be times when Husband should elect to have the transfer taxable on creation. Assume Husband buys Blackacre for $60,000, $12,000 cash, $48,000 mortgage. He reduces the mortgage $12,000 a year. When the land is free and clear, five years later, it is sold for $100,000. If the title is in the joint names of Husband and Wife and no gift tax return was filed, and the proceeds are divided, $50,000 going to Wife, there will be a taxable gift, with, of course, the gift tax marital deduction available. If the facts were the same, except that Husband had elected to treat the creation as the taxable event, no gift taxes whatever would have been incurred at any time because one half of the $12,000 yearly payments, i.e., $6,000, were gifts to the wife, and obviously never exceeded in any year the gift tax marital deduction of $3,000 on each gift and the annual yearly exclusion of $3,000.

9

Revocable trusts and beneficiary designations

Revocable trusts

9.1   Advantages of revocable trusts

The revocable trust, as a will substitute is and always has been an extremely useful estate planning tool. For any one of a variety of reasons, it may be adopted as the vehicle for the transmission of part or substantially all of an estate at death.

1. It assures a continuity of investment management and flow of income.

2. It avoids the publicity attendant on probate.

3. It eliminates, in most cases, court supervision.

4. It reduces the likelihood of attacks on the ground of fraud and undue influence by dissatisfied heirs.

5. It may, in many cases, be a less expensive means of transmitting the estate.

6. It offers a choice of law, where the law of the domicile prohibits the accomplishment of particular objectives.

7. In many states it offers immunity from the claims of creditors of the estate.

8. It may be used to avoid statutory restrictions on charitable gifts.

9. In some jurisdictions it permits avoidance of the widow's "forced share," a result the testator may desire in order to protect rather than to deprive his spouse.

10. It offers opportunities for the creation of additional income tax entities.

In most cases the selection of a revocable trust as the medium for transmitting property at death[1] will be dictated by one or two of the above reasons. In all cases, where the nature of the estate owner's assets do not make a living revocable trust undesirable, it may be a useful planning tool.

---

[1] Another advantage is that a trust may avoid the necessity of incompetency proceedings if the estate owner becomes senile.

9.2 Continuity of management and flow of income

There are frequently delays in getting administration under way. Individual executors may be in distant parts of the world on business or vacation trips at the date of death. Weeks and occasionally a month or more may elapse in forwarding and getting back their oaths and consents to serve. Witnesses may be hard to locate. Occasionally the will itself may be difficult to find. Will contests can cause long delays. In all these cases, of course, a temporary administrator may be appointed. But his actions will be limited to the immediate necessities; he will not be guided by any long-range program. Thus favorable opportunities calling for prompt action may be lost. In addition, world affairs may suddenly affect stock market prices in such a way as to call for immediate liquidation of certain assets.

The revocable trust meets these problems and many more that arise in the day-to-day administration of property. Death causes no interruption in the investment program or in the collection and disbursement of income.

Income, distributable on the first of each month, goes to the grantor, if alive, otherwise to the next taker. Compare this with the interruption that death causes because of (1) the delay in probate, (2) the appointment of a new estate manager unfamiliar with the estate holdings and liabilities, and (3) the period required before any steady flow of income can be made available to the family.

9.3 Avoidance of publicity

The trust instrument and inventory of assets will be buried deep in the vaults of the trustee, free from the scrutiny of newsmen and the curious in the community. To some testators this is a weighty consideration.

9.4 Avoidance of court supervision

Many, if not most, living trusts are created, administered and terminated without ever coming under the supervision of a court, with a considerable saving in expense. On the other hand, the testamentary trust has its origin in court, with the court formally appointing the trustee. He, of course, will be the one designated by the decedent, but he comes under the eye of the court, to whom he is accountable and whose permission he must seek to resign or to distribute and be discharged. The extent of court supervision will vary widely in different states, but the noncourt trust is generally regarded as less costly to administer and terminate.

9.5 Protection against attacks

Where the estate is left by will, attack on its validity is, in a very real sense, invited. This is particularly true in jurisdictions which require probate in solemn form. Here the heirs are cited by formal subpoena to now raise any objections to the probate or "forever hold their peace." Even where probate is in common form, death raises the hopes and expectations of heirs and others that causes them to anxiously await the filing of the will. Their disappointed expectations are not always easily banished. On the other hand, the mere passage of time and the fact of a completed transaction throw a protection around the revocable trust. Its creation is not publicized and so it may operate for months or years unquestioned. Being an accomplished fact, disappointed heirs are less likely to attack it for lack of the settlor's capacity, or for fraud, or undue influence. For whatever reason, only rarely is the inter vivos trust upset, whereas the probate courts are sometimes thought of as a happy hunting ground.

9.6 Costs

Executors' and trustees' fees vary widely throughout the country. In many states, on an estate of $100,000 to $200,000 the executor's fees may amount to 3 percent or 4 percent of principal. There will also be counsel fees of at least a like amount. Frequently, trustees' fees are based on income, with no principal fee on the creation of the trust. Thus, 7 percent of income is not unusual. Obviously no executor's commissions are incurred with respect to a revocable trust and attorney fees are limited to a few hundred dollars. If a testator leaves his $100,000 estate to a testamentary trustee, executor and attorney's fees of $6,000 we may assume, for illustration, will result, with 7 percent income fees to the testamentary trustee thereafter. If the same testator had created a revocable trust during life and lived 5 years thereafter, fees prior to death on yearly income of $4,000 at 7 percent would amount to $280 a year.[2] However, since this is an income tax deductible item, the net cost might be considerably less than $200. Thus, the cost of a living trust up to the date when his post-death beneficiaries enjoy his bounty would be $1,000, whereas under a testamentary trust it would be $6,000 gross and, after allowing for the estate tax deduction, in excess of $5,000 net. To have the revocable trust cost as much, he would have to survive for 25 years, and if he did he would have had the benefit of the investment, caretaking, and bookkeeping services of the trustee throughout the long period.

To partially offset this advantage many trustees are beginning to impose a 1 percent death fee on the death of the grantor of a revocable trust because of the additional tax work involved.

9.7 Choice of law

One of the most important uses of the revocable trust is the opportunity it offers as to choice of governing law. In some jurisdictions, it is not possible to take full advantage of the tax savings available through use of accumulation trusts, since only accumulations during minority are permitted. Accumulation trusts may still be used in spite of the unlimited throwback rule. See section 6.12.

An estate owner who desires to authorize discretionary ac-

---

[2] Trustees almost universally waive any "receiving fee" on creation of a revocable trust.

cumulation, see section 6.19, may create a revocable trust in an adjoining state, with the desired provisions, to be effective as to the beneficiaries who succeed him at his death.

9.8 Immunity from creditors

By the law of many jurisdictions estate creditors may not get at funds in revocable trusts created by him during life. This probably is rarely a major consideration.

9.9 Charitable bequests

In many jurisdictions bequests to charity may not exceed a stated percentage of the estate or may be wholly void if the will was executed within 90 days or 6 months of the date of death. Revocable trusts have been held not to come within the ban of these statutes.

9.10 Forced share of the spouse

In some states the revocable trust has been used successfully to defeat the statutory share of a surviving spouse. Under these statutes the surviving spouse is permitted to elect to take one half or other percentage of the estate rather than accept the provisions made for her in the will. Many husbands prefer to leave the spouse's share in trust to protect her against herself. Suppose Husband leaves the estate in trust, income to Wife, with a discretionary power in trustee to invade corpus for her benefit. Wife falls prey to a dealer in uranium stocks who squires her about town to soothe her anguish. He may well persuade her that one half of a bird in hand is better than the whole bird on the bush, particularly when uranium stocks are available at bargain prices. She may well elect to take her statutory share outright, rather than be limited to the income from the entire estate.

In some jurisdictions the purely revocable trust will effectively accomplish his objective. Even in jurisdictions whose courts may strike down the trust as a sham insofar as she is concerned, draftsmen may learn much from the tax cases discussed in chapter 14, dealing with retained powers that may be exercised only with the consent of others. Thus, the widow's share may, in the writer's opinion, with reasonable assurance of freedom from attack, be put into a trust which may be disregarded for tax purposes only because of the specific statutory provisions as, for example, one in which the consent of one or two persons with nonadverse interests is required for revocation; probably with complete assurance, if the trust is irrevocable except for a retained special power of appointment. The retention of such a power would avoid any immediate gift tax, since the gift would be incomplete for gift tax purposes, and it would, nevertheless, be complete against interference of creditors or a surviving spouse.

9.11   Multiple trusts

The advantages of multiple trusts are discussed at section 6.18. The cautious draftsman is always troubled by the creation of several trusts for the same beneficiary where the differences are formal only. Thus, if there are three children, three testamentary trusts are indicated. It may be difficult to find a rational purpose for six. But if the fund is split half to a revocable lifetime trust and half reserved for testamentary disposition, six, not three, trusts will be the natural normal result, and contentions that there are only formal differences may confidently be expected never to arise.

9.12   Marital deduction

No difficulty is encountered in qualifying such a trust for the marital deduction, if this is desired. All that is needed is that the widow be given the requisite rights as to the date of the grantor's death. Thus, the trust may provide for the power of revocation during life with all the income going to the grantor followed by a dispositive paragraph giving the wife at his death all of the income from the trust for her life and the power to appoint the property at her death to any person or persons including her estate or the creditors of her estate. This gives her the requisite general power of appointment.

9.13 Tax clause

Since the revocable trust will form part of the tax estate of the grantor some provision should be made for the payment of the tax attributable to the trust assets. Some grantors will want it to bear its share of the estate tax; others will prefer that the estate tax be paid from the residuary estate.

Life insurance

9.14 Methods of payment of the proceeds

This chapter is concerned only with life insurance owned by the decendent at the time of his death. For a general discussion of income, gift, and estate taxation of life insurance proceeds and the uses of insurance in estate planning, see chapter 15.

The proceeds under the standard life insurance contract may be payable:

1. In a lump sum to a designated beneficiary;

2. Retained by the company under a promise to pay guaranteed interest for the life of the first beneficiary, with the principal to be paid upon his death, to a second beneficiary;

3. Payable in installments.

a) for a single life, without refund. This means the company's obligation ceases upon the death of the beneficiary.

b) for a fixed number of years, such as 10 or 20. This means that if the first beneficiary dies within the period, the payments will be continued to a secondary beneficiary until the expiration of the fixed period.

c) for life with a fixed number of years guaranteed, such, for example, as 10 or 20. This means that if the first beneficiary dies within the period, the payments will be continued until the expiration of the fixed period. But if the first beneficiary survives the period, the payments will nevertheless continue for the duration of his life.

The choice will depend on the facts of the particular case. Some insurance will generally be paid in a lump sum to take care of death costs. Where the estate is sufficiently large, the interest option may be selected. In many cases one of the installment options may be preferred, the third perhaps, being the most popular. Installment payments to a spouse have the attractive income tax advantage of the special $1,000 interest element exclusion, see chapter 15, whereas the full interest paid under the interest option is taxable as ordinary income.

Many policy owners may prefer to have the proceeds paid to a trustee. This is accomplished, with some variations, through the creation of a revocable unfunded life insurance trust, where the sole asset in the trust during the life of the insured, is the policy. With his death the trust becomes irrevocable and the proceeds are administered as in any other trust. By statute in some states the proceeds may be made payable to the trustee named in the last will and testament of the insured. Where this is permitted no separate inter vivos trust is necessary.

9.15 *Trust versus options*

The trust offers some advantages. The options offer others. Under the options:

1. There is security of income and capital.

2. There is the special income tax interest element exclusion for a spouse.

3. The payments may be guaranteed for life.

4. Through a combination of withdrawal and commutation privileges a degree of flexibility may be introduced.

Under the trust plan:

1. Complete flexibility is obtainable. The trustee can be given discretionary powers to pay or accumulate income, to distribute corpus as needed, etc.

2. There is protection against inflation since the trustee may be given broad investment powers.

Thus, changing family needs, emergencies, changes in the purchasing power of the dollar may be better cared for under the trust arrangement. But guaranteed protection of fixed dollars for life is only available through the options. Whether to create a trust or select the option payments under the contract will depend on the particular facts of each case and the personal predilections of the particular client. The options frequently serve better for smaller amounts. Where larger sums are involved and complicated family settlements desired, the trust may be found a more useful vehicle. But even here, because of the income tax advantage to the surviving spouse and the security of income and capital, it may be desirable to put some of the insurance under one of the options.

9.16 Qualifying the insurance for the marital deduction

The proceeds may be qualified for the marital deduction, if the fact situation indicates the desirability for this.

1. The lump sum payment, of course, qualifies.

2. The revocable insurance trust will qualify if all the conditions with respect to the qualification of a trust are complied with.

3. The installment option without refund qualifies since there is no interest following that of the spouse.

4. For the same reason any optional settlement will qualify if the principal or any unpaid installments, at the surviving spouse's death, are payable to her estate.

5. If a secondary beneficiary is named to take any unpaid amounts on the death of the spouse, the proceeds may be qualified if conditions, substantially similar to those required in the case of a trust are met.

Reg. Sec. 20.2056(b)–6 provides:

a) In general   Section 2056(b)(6) provides that an interest in property passing from a decedent to his surviving spouse, which consists of proceeds held by an insurer under the terms of a life insurance, endowment, or annuity contract, is a "deductible interest" to the extent that it satisfies all five of the following conditions (see paragraph (*b*) of this section if one or more of the conditions is satisfied as to only a portion of the proceeds):

1. The proceeds, or a specific portion of the proceeds, must be held by the insurer subject to an agreement either to pay the entire proceeds or a specific portion thereof in installments, or to pay interest thereon, and all or a specific portion of the installments or interest payable during the life of the surviving spouse must be payable only to her.

2. The installments or interest payable to the surviving spouse must be payable annually, or more frequently, commencing not later than 13 months after the decedent's death.

3. The surviving spouse must have the power to appoint all or a specific portion of the amounts so held by the insurer to either herself or her estate.

4. The power in the surviving spouse must be exercisable by her alone and (whether exercisable by will or during life) must be exercisable in all events.

5. The amounts or the specific portion of the amounts payable under such contract must not be subject to a power in any other person to appoint any part thereof to any person other than the surviving spouse.

b) Specific portion; deductible interest   If the right to receive interest or installment payments or the power of appointment passing to the surviving spouse pertains only to a specific portion of the proceeds held by the insurer, the marital deduction is allowed only to the extent that the rights of the surviving spouse in the specific portion meet the five conditions described in paragraph (*a*) of this section above. While the rights to interest, or to receive payment in installments, and the power must coexist as to the proceeds of the same contract, it is not necessary that the rights to each be in the same proportion. If the rights to interest meeting the required conditions set forth in paragraph (*a*)(1) and (2) extend over a smaller share of the proceeds than the share with respect to which the power of appointment requirements set forth in paragraph (*a*)(3) through (5) are satisfied, the deductible interest is limited to the smaller share. Similarly, if the portion of the proceeds payable in installments is a smaller portion of the proceeds than the portion to which the power of appointment meeting such requirements relates, the deduction is limited to the smaller portion. In addition, if a power of appointment meeting all the requirements extends to a smaller portion of the proceeds than the portion over which the interest or installment rights pertain, the deductible interest cannot exceed the value of the portion to which such power of appointment applies. Thus, if the contract provides that the insurer is to retain the entire proceeds and pay all of the interest thereon annually to the surviving spouse and if the surviving spouse has a power of appointment meeting the specifications prescribed in paragraph (*a*) (3) through (5) above, as to only one half of the proceeds held, then only one-half of the proceeds may be treated as a deductible interest. Correspondingly, if the rights of the spouse to receive installment payments or interests satisfying the requirements extend to only one fourth of the proceeds and a testamentary power of appointment satisfying the requirements of paragraph (*a*) (3) through (5) extends to all of the proceeds, then only one fourth of the proceeds qualifies as a deductible interest. Further, if the surviving spouse has no right to installment payments (or interest) over any portion of the proceeds but a testamentary power of appointment which meets the necessary conditions over the entire remaining proceeds (exclusive of interest accumulation), then none of the proceeds qualifies for the deduction. In addition, if, from the time of the decedent's death, the surviving spouse has a power of appointment meeting all of the required conditions over three-fourths of the proceeds and the right to receive interest from the entire proceeds, but with a power in another person to appoint one-half of the entire proceeds, the value of the interest in the surviving spouse over only one half of the proceeds will qualify as a deductible interest.

c) *Applicable principles*   (1) The principles set forth in § 20.2056(b)–5(c) for determining what constitutes a 'specific portion of the entire interest' for the purpose of section 2056(b) (5) are applicable in determining what constitutes a 'specific portion of all such amounts' for the purpose of section 2056(b) (6). However, the interest in the proceeds passing to the surviving spouse will not be disqualified by the fact that the installment payments or interest to which the spouse is entitled or the amount of the proceeds over which the power of appointment is exercisable may be expressed in terms of a specific sum rather than a fraction or a percentage of the proceeds provided it is shown that such sums are a definite or fixed percentage or fraction of the total proceeds.

2. The provisions of paragraph (*a*) of this section are applicable with respect to a property interest which passed from the decedent in the form of proceeds of a policy of insurance upon the decedent's life, a policy of insurance upon the life of a person who predeceased the

decedent, a matured endowment policy, or an annuity contract, but only in case the proceeds are to be held by the insurer. With respect to proceeds under any such contract which are to be held by a trustee, with power of appointment in the surviving spouse, see Section 20.2056(b)–5. As to the treatment of proceeds not meeting the requirements of Section 20.2056(b)–5 or of this section, see Section 20.2056(a)–2.

3. In the case of a contract under which payments by the insurer commenced during the decedent's life, it is immaterial whether the conditions in subparagraphs (1) to (5) of paragraph (*a*) of this section were satisfied prior to the decedent's death.

d) *Payments of installments or interest*   The conditions in subparagraphs (1) and (2) of paragraph (*a*) of this section relative to the payments of installments or interest to the surviving spouse are satisfied if, under the terms of the contract, the spouse has the right exercisable annually (or more frequently) to require distribution to herself of installments of the proceeds or a specific portion thereof, as the case may be, and otherwise such proceeds or interest are to be accumulated and held by the insurer pursuant to the terms of the contract. A contract which otherwise requires the insurer to make annual or more frequent payments to the surviving spouse following the decedent's death, will not be disqualified merely because the surviving spouse must comply with certain formalities in order to obtain the first payment. For example, the contract may satisfy the conditions in subparagraphs (1) and (2) of paragraph (*a*) of this section even though it requires the surviving spouse to furnish proof of death before the first payment is made. The condition in paragraph (*a*) (1) of this section is satisfied where interest on the proceeds or a specific portion thereof is payable, annually or more frequently, for a term, or until the occurrence of a specified event following which the proceeds or a specific portion thereof are to be paid in annual or more frequent installments.

e) *Powers of appointment*   (1) In determining whether the terms of the contract satisfy the conditions in subparagraphs (3), (4), or (5) of paragraph (*a*) of this section relating to a power of appointment in the surviving spouse or any other person, the principles stated in Section 20.2056(b)–5 are applicable. As stated in Section 20.2056(b)–5, the surviving spouse's power to appoint is "exercisable in all events" only if it is in existence immediately following the decedent's death, subject, however, to the operation of Section 20.2056(b)–3 relating to interests conditioned on survival for a limited period.

2. For examples of formal limitations on the power which will not disqualify the contract, see Section 20.2056(b)–5 (g) (4). If the power is exercisable from the moment of the decedent's death the contract is not disqualified merely because the insurer may require proof of the decedent's death as a condition to making payment to the appointee.

If the submission of proof of the decedent's death is a condition to the exercise of the power, the power will not be considered "exercisable in all events" unless in the event the surviving spouse had died immediately following the decedent, her power to appoint would have been considered to exist at the time of her death, within the meaning of Section 2041(a)(2). See Section 20.2041–3(b).

3. It is sufficient for the purposes of the condition in paragraph (*a*) (3) of this section that the surviving spouse have the power to appoint amounts held by the insurer to herself or her estate if the surviving spouse has the unqualified power, exercisable in favor of herself or her estate, to appoint amounts held by the insurer which are payable after her death. Such power to appoint need not extend to installments or interest which will be paid to the spouse during her life. Further, the power to appoint need not be a power to require payment in a single sum. For example, if the proceeds of a policy are payable in installments, and if the surviving spouse has the power to direct that all installments payable after her death be paid to her estate, she has the requisite power.

4. It is not necessary that the phrase "power to appoint" be used in the contract. For example, the condition in paragraph (*a*)(3) of this section that the surviving spouse have the power to appoint amounts held by the insurer to herself or her estate is satisfied by terms of a contract which give the surviving spouse a right which is, in substance and effect, a power to appoint to herself or her estate, such as a right to withdraw the amount remaining in the fund held by the insurer, or a right to direct that any amount held by the insurer under the contract at her death shall be paid to her estate.

9.17 Survivorship clauses

Most insureds are concerned about the possibility of multiple deaths as a result of rail, plane, or car accidents. While such common disasters are relatively rare, their occurrence may cause unanticipated and unwanted property dispositions. Hence, prudence would dictate that provision be made in insurance policies to cover this contingency. In addition the marital deduction allowed by the federal estate tax has created problems in this area that may require the reexamination of existing policy provisions.

Actually the insured is not primarily concerned with the possibility that he and his beneficiary may die as a result of a common disaster, but, rather, with the fact that his beneficiary may die at or about the same time that he does. He wants the beneficiary to have the proceeds only if the latter is going to live long enough to enjoy them. For this reason the life insurance policy provision will generally take the form of a time clause rather than a common disaster or simultaneous death clause. For example, the following time clause may be used:

All provisions whatsoever of this settlement agreement are to be so read that any beneficiary who survives the insured but dies prior to the thirtieth day after the death of the insured will be considered as not having survived the insured.

This clause covers all truly simultaneous deaths, i.e., where there is no evidence as to who survived, insured or beneficiary. It covers practically all deaths from common accidents and takes care of the cases where the insured and his beneficiary die from unrelated causes but at or about the same time.

Prior to the introduction into the Internal Revenue Code of the marital deduction, the time clause was universally used. However, there are many cases where, because of the marital deduction, it is now desirable to reverse the usual presumption so that the proceeds will vest in the insured's spouse even though she may survive for but a few hours.

Suppose an individual has $150,000, largely in life insurance. His estate plan qualifies enough of his insurance to obtain the maximum marital deduction except that the policies contain either a 30-day time clause or no survivorship provision of any kind. He and his wife die in an accident and there is no evidence as to who died first. The marital deduction will be lost in this case, and the federal death taxes on his estate will be $17,900, whereas, with the clause suggested below, such taxes need be only $1,050, with an additional $1,050 being paid by the estate of his wife. This example assumes that the wife's assets are nominal.

The reason that almost $16,000 in taxes may be saved by the use of a proper clause is that the marital deduction regulations dealing with the survivorship problem provide that if it is impossible to determine in any given case who died first, any presumption applied by local law, the decedent's will, or otherwise, will govern. Assume that instead of requiring the beneficiary to survive for 30 days (the customary provision) the policy has the following clause:

> All provisions of this settlement agreement are to be so read that if the insured and his wife die under such circumstances that there is no sufficient evidence to establish who survived the other, the wife of the insured shall be considered to have survived the insured.

Under this clause the proceeds would qualify for the marital deduction and become a part of the taxable estate of the wife, achieving the saving in taxes noted above.

This type of provision, however, known as a reverse simultaneous death clause, should not be recommended in every case. Many insureds, because their wives have substantial estates, will wish the benefit of the marital deduction on their deaths only on the assumption that their wives will live for many years. If, in the case suggested, the insured's wife also had an estate of $150,000, use of the deduction would save almost $16,000 on the first death but increase taxes on the second death by $22,500, a net increase of more than $6,000. It would be unfortunate to incur that additional $6,000 in taxes if both died at the same time or if the wife survived but for a few hours or a few weeks. Here again the 30-day time clause represents the solution.

To recapitulate:

1. For beneficiaries other than a spouse the time clause is always desirable.

2. For spouse beneficiaries where both spouses have substantial estates but where it is nevertheless desired to qualify the insurance for the marital deduction, the time clause is again indicated.

3. Where the insured spouse owns the bulk of the family wealth the marital deduction will be desired in every conceivable contingency. Here the reverse simultaneous death clause should be suggested. The proceeds should be put under the interest option with unlimited right to withdraw the proceeds at any time and/or with a general power to designate the successor beneficiary. The proceeds should not be payable in a lump sum since difficult fact questions, resulting in litigation, may arise to determine whether "there is no sufficient evi-

dence." The life income option with a period certain should not be recommended since this may result in a substantial loss to the secondary beneficiaries. The reason for this loss is that company practice is to separate the proceeds into two funds, one to provide for the period certain, the other for the deferred contingent life annuity. In one case the policy had a total death benefit of $25,187.50. The insurer determined that $17,956.41 was necessary to fund the 20-year certain payments and $7,231.09 was necessary to fund the payments for so long as the wife might live after the 20-year period. Here under a reverse simultaneous death clause the $7,231.09 would be lost since the obligation of the insurer would be limited to the period certain.

Deferred compensation designations

9.18   Deferred compensation

Most business executives have deferred compensation contracts that call for annual payments to commence on retirement and to continue for a period that may extend beyond their deaths. The executive with a salary of $50,000 or $75,000 is no longer interested in a current increase, the major portion of which would be eaten up in taxes. He would rather have $10,000 a year after 65 than $15,000 right now. These contracts usually provide for a fixed amount during his life, a reduced amount for the period during which his wife survives, and for payments over a guaranteed minimum number of years should he and his wife fail to live for their expectancies.

If the payments are to a named beneficiary under a qualified pension or profit-sharing plan, only the portion of the value of the postdeath payments attributable to the employees' contributions are taxable as part of his estate. Thus, the full amount will escape federal estate tax under a qualified noncontributory plan. But most key employees have, in addition to participation in the regular company plan, special arrangements which, because of their discriminatory nature, do not qualify for these tax-exempt benefits.

Provision for the postdeath payments is usually made by filing a designation with the employer. Where this asset represents an important part of the estate it will be desirable to consider whether or not to qualify such payments for the marital deduction. If the payments are to continue for the life of the wife only, they clearly qualify. If, however, there is a minimum number of guaranteed payments, then the designation of a contingent beneficiary to receive any unpaid amounts on the wife's death will result in the wife's being given a terminable interest. This may be avoided by having any unpaid amounts paid to her estate or by designating a trustee, instead of the wife, to receive the payments and then qualifying the trust by giving the wife all of the income plus a general power of appointment.

Pour-over wills

9.19   Bequests to revocable trusts

It may be that a revocable trust, a life insurance trust, or a deferred compensation trust will hold the bulk of the estate assets and that there will be little left to pass under the will. In many jurisdictions it is possible to leave the entire residuary estate to the trustee of the inter vivos trust and have it become a part of the corpus thereof and be administered according to its terms as of the date of decedent's death. This is a very useful device in those states which recognize its validity.

10

The federal gift tax

10.1 Introduction

Congress first imposed a gift tax in 1924, but, as drawn, it proved completely inadequate. It was easily and effectively avoided by spreading a contemplated transfer over several years since there was a $50,000 annual exemption. The Act was repealed in 1926, and at the same time there was enacted a conclusive presumption that all gifts, within two years of the date of death, were made in contemplation of death. The Supreme Court promptly held this conclusive presumption unconstitutional, and shortly thereafter, in 1932, the present gift tax was enacted. To prevent avoidance through piecemeal gifts a single lifetime exemption was provided. The Act further required that all transfers of prior years be taken into consideration in determining the applicable rate for gifts of the current year. See section 10.6. The tax was designed to compensate for loss of both estate and income tax revenues and, for this reason, the courts, in construing the coverage of the statute, have, speaking generally, imposed a gift tax on all transfers that escape either estate tax or shift income tax.

Gifts made in the calendar year 1971 and thereafter must be reported on a quarterly basis. The returns are due on the 15th day of the second month following the end of the calendar quarter, i.e., May 15, August 15, November 15, and February 15 of the following year. The tax is computed on a cumulative basis on gifts made through the end of the quarter. Filing and payment are not required until a quarter where total gifts for the year exceed $3,000 to any one donee. The gift-splitting election is now available for each quarter rather than on an annual basis as formally.

A quarterly return is not required for charitable transfers. These are to be shown on the last quarterly return for the calendar year unless the donor is required to file an earlier return covering noncharitable gifts.

10.2 Constitutionality

The constitutionality of a tax on gratuitous lifetime transfers was attacked in *Bromley* v. *McCaughn* on the ground that it was a direct tax and not apportioned as required by the Constitution. The Supreme Court held, however, that it was not a tax on property as such, but rather a tax on the exercise of one of the privileges of ownership. It was an excise on the privilege of giving and therefore a proper occasion for the imposition of the tax. Since the tax is on the act of transferring ownership, rather than on the property transferred, it is clear that it may be imposed, for example, on gifts of state and municipal bonds. The tax applies to the transfer of real property situated outside the United States. Congress resolved any constitutional doubts in favor of its power to reach such transfers and, to date, no taxpayer has been successful in persuading a court otherwise. The estate tax law formerly excluded real property situated outside the United States but in 1962 the estate tax sections were brought into conformity with the gift tax law. See section 3.5.

There are still unresolved questions concerning the validity of retroactive tax legislation in this area. In *Untermeyer* v. *Anderson* the Government sought to tax transfers made during the period the bill, that was to tax gifts, was still pending in Congress. The Supreme Court held the Act unconstitutional in so far as it attempted to reach transfers completed before the bill became law. While doubt has since been cast upon the correctness of this decision, Congress has never specifically undertaken any retroactive gift tax amendments since the

Untermeyer case. It now seems unlikely that it will change its consistent policy of making all gift tax changes prospective only, from either the date of enactment of the change or the following January 1st.

Deductions and exclusions

10.3 Lifetime exemption

Every donor is allowed a specific exemption of $30,000. The exemption, at the option of the donor, may be taken in any one year or may be spread over several years. Once exhausted no further exemption is permitted. For this reason it is generally referred to as the lifetime exemption.

10.4 Annual exclusions

In addition to the exemption, donors may make annual gifts (other than gifts of future interests in property) of $3,000 each to any number of persons, without incurring any tax and without encroaching upon the lifetime exemption. For example, a donor may give $3,000 to each of ten or more donees without affecting his exemption. The following year he may repeat the process. This privilege is called the "annual per donee exclusion," since in computing gifts the first $3,000 given to each donee is disregarded. There is no requirement that any return be made concerning such gifts. The committee reports indicate the policy behind the annual exclusion was the desire to relieve taxpayers of keeping records of and reporting small gifts. This amount was fixed sufficiently large to cover in most cases "wedding and Christmas gifts and occasional gifts of relatively small amounts."

Gift tax returns must now be filed on a quarterly basis. See section 10.1. No return for any quarter need be made until gifts to an individual in any year exceed $3,000. Thus, if $2,000 is given to A in January, no return is due for the first quarter (January, February, and March). If in April another $2,000 is given, a return must be filed for the quarter, May, June, and July. The return is due a month and a half after the end of each quarter.

10.5 Charitable gifts

The Tax Reform Act of 1969 increased the deduction percentage from 30 percent to 50 percent for contributions to publicly supported organizations. It remains at 20 percent for nonoperating private foundations and for gifts "for the use of" rather than to charities.

Contributions of appreciated long-term capital gain property to 50 percent organizations are limited to 30 percent unless the donor elects to reduce the amount of his contributions by 50 percent of what would have been his gain if he had sold the property in a taxable transfer. Where the property given is short-term gain property or ordinary income property, i.e., inventory, accounts receivable, paintings in the hands of the creator, letters memoranda, all appreciation is eliminated. Thus, there frequently will be no deduction as, for example, for the gift of a work of art painted by the donor. Gifts of other personal property must be reduced by 50 percent of any appreciation unless the use of the property is directly related to the donee's charitable function, i.e., a painting to an art gallery. There are many other new restrictions. No deduction is allowed for a gift of a remainder interest with retained life estate except for a residence or farm. See also sections 7.11 and 13.13.

The five-year carry-over for unused charitable deductions is still available for excess gifts to 50 percent charities.

10.6 Computation of the tax on gifts

Assume a single donor in 1952 made outright gifts to A of $60,000, to B of $2,500 and to C of $4,000. The gift to B would have been ignored. $57,000 of the gift to A and $1,000 of the gift to C would have been reported as taxable but presumably the donor would have deducted therefrom his $30,000 lifetime exemption, paying a tax on $28,000. If, in 1956 he made an additional gift to A of $40,000 he would first exclude his $3,000 annual exclusion for A and compute his 1956 tax as follows:

1. Amount of net gifts for the year 1956............................. $37,000
2. Total amount of net gifts for preceding years..................... 28,000
3. Total net gifts.. 65,000
4. Tax computed on item 3 (current year's gifts plus all gifts made in
   prior years beginning with 1932)................................. 8,175
5. Tax computed on item 2 (gifts for preceding years)............... 2,040
6. Tax for year 1956 (item 4 minus item 5)......................... $ 6,135

This method imposes the tax on a cumulative basis. It was designed with the expectation that total gift taxes paid over the years would measurably approach the estate tax that would have been paid on the donor's death had the gifts not been made. In practice, however, it obviously falls far short of this objective.

10.7 Gifts by corporations

The gift tax is imposed on transfers by individuals. It is, however, possible that a corporation may make a gratuitous transfer, particularly closely held corporations that are controlled by one or two individuals. If such a transfer is made to a stockholder, it will be treated as an informal dividend, or a partial return of capital. The reason is that every corporate distribution to a shareholder is conclusively presumed to be a dividend to the extent of existing earnings or profits. If the transfer is to an employee it is likely to be held to be additional compensation. Hence neither of these transfers raises any gift tax problems. But suppose the transfer is to an individual who is neither stockholder nor employee. Here it cannot escape classification as a gift. However a corporation has no authority to give away assets. The regulations treat such a transfer as a gift by the stockholders, and the tax is imposed on them individually. But sometimes overlooked pitfalls exist. Suppose X owns all the corporate stock of X Inc. The corporation transfers Blackacre, worth $20,000 to X's daughter. It is not only clear that X has made a $20,000 gift to his daughter, but it is equally clear that he will be treated as having constructively received a $20,000 taxable dividend, assuming the corporation has earnings and profits of at least that amount.

Tax saving through gifts

10.8   *Relationship between estate and gift tax rates*

Gift tax rates are fixed at exactly three quarters of the estate tax rates. This does not mean, however, that gifts will eliminate only 25 percent of potential estate taxes. The savings will almost always be very much larger because of the lifetime exemption, the per donee exclusions, and the fact that the amount of the net gift is taxed at the lowest gift tax rates and at the same time the gross value of the property given is removed from the higher estate tax bracket. For example, a gift of $50,000 by an unmarried donor, with an estate of $200,000, will incur a gift tax of $943 and will eliminate a potential estate tax of $15,000. The reason for this is that only $17,000 is subject to the gift tax[1] at rates beginning at 2¼ percent whereas the entire $50,000 escapes the estate tax of 30 percent.

10.9   *Table of gift tax rates*

If the taxable gifts are:	The tax shall be:
Not over $5,000	2¼% of the taxable gifts.
Over $5,000 but not over $10,000	$112.50, plus 5¼% of excess over $5,000.
Over $10,000 but not over $20,000	$375, plus 8¼% of excess over $10,000.

---

[1] After deduction of the $30,000 exemption and $3,000 exclusion.

If the taxable gifts are:	The tax shall be:
Over $20,000 but not over $30,000	$1,200, plus $10\frac{1}{2}\%$ of excess over $20,000.
Over $30,000 but not over $40,000	$2,250, plus $13\frac{1}{2}\%$ of excess over $30,000.
Over $40,000 but not over $50,000	$3,600, plus $16\frac{1}{2}\%$ of excess over $40,000.
Over $50,000 but not over $60,000	$5,250, plus $18\frac{3}{4}\%$ of excess over $50,000.
Over $60,000 but not over $100,000	$7,125, plus 21% of excess over $60,000.
Over $100,000 but not over $250,000	$15,525, plus $22\frac{1}{2}\%$ of excess over $100,000.
Over $250,000 but not over $500,000	$49,275, plus 24% of excess over $250,000.
Over $500,000 but not over $750,000	$109,275, plus $26\frac{1}{4}\%$ of excess over $500,000.
Over $750,000 but not over $1,000,000	$174,900, plus $27\frac{3}{4}\%$ of excess over $750,000.
Over $1,000,000 but not over $1,250,000	$244,275, plus $29\frac{1}{4}\%$ of excess over $1,000,000.
Over $1,250,000 but not over $1,500,000	$317,400, plus $31\frac{1}{2}\%$ of excess over $1,250,000.
Over $1,500,000 but not over $2,000,000	$396,150, plus $33\frac{3}{4}\%$ of excess over 1,500,000.
Over $2,000,000 but not over $2,500,000	$564,900, plus $36\frac{3}{4}\%$ of excess over $2,000,000.
Over $2,500,000 but not over $3,000,000	$748,650, plus $39\frac{3}{4}\%$ of excess over $2,500,000.
Over $3,000,000 but not over $3,500,000	$947,400, plus 42% of excess over $3,000,000.
Over $3,500,000 but not over $4,000,000	$1,157,400, plus $44\frac{1}{4}\%$ of excess over $3,500,000.
Over $4,000,000 but not over $5,000,000	$1,378,650, plus $47\frac{1}{4}\%$ of excess over $4,000,000.
Over $5,000,000 but not over $6,000,000	$1,851,150, plus $50\frac{1}{4}\%$ of excess over $5,000,000.
Over $6,000,000 but not over $7,000,000	$2,353,650, plus $52\frac{1}{2}\%$ of excess over $6,000,000.
Over $7,000,000 but not over $8,000,000	$2,878,650, plus $54\frac{3}{4}\%$ of excess over $7,000,000.
Over $8,000,000 but not over $10,000,000	$3,426,150, plus 57% of excess over $8,000,000.
Over $10,000,000	$4,566,150, plus $57\frac{3}{4}\%$ of excess over $10,000,000.

10.10 Advantages of lifetime gifts

Gifts obviously represent a means of avoiding federal estate taxes. In addition, state inheritance taxes, administration expenses, and attorney's fees will be reduced. Thus many estate owners follow a practice of annual giving. Assume there are three children and eight grandchildren within the family group. As much as $33,000 may be given to them tax free each year, without encroaching upon the lifetime exemption. This figure may be doubled if the donor is married and his spouse consents to the use of her exclusions, see section 10.18. Over a 10-year period such a single person could thus transfer $330,000 to his family, or if married, $660,000, free of both gift and estate taxes. But there are pitfalls and restrictions that must be avoided if the annual exclusions are to be obtained.

Gifts of future interests

10.11 Outright gifts

To qualify for the annual exclusion a gift must create a present interest in the property transferred. The reason given in the Congressional Committee reports for excluding gifts of future interests was that in many instances the donees of future interests might not be ascertainable at the date of the transfer. Thus, "to A for life, remainder to A's children who survive him," there would be no possible way of determining, in the year of the transfer, how many, if any, of A's children might share the gift. There may also be the additional policy reason that such gifts fall outside the purpose of the exclusion.

In any event, no exclusion is allowed for gifts of future interests. An outright gift clearly qualifies since the donee has the right to the immediate possession and enjoyment of the property transferred. Thus assume a conveyance of Blackacre, "to A for life, remainder to B and his heirs." A's life estate is a present interest. Its value is determined by his life expectancy. If he is 80 it is worth very little; if he is 15 it is worth 75 percent of the total value of Blackacre. B's interest is a future interest since he is not entitled to the immediate possession of the property. It is true he has an indefeasibly vested remainder. This means he has present rights in the land. He may sell or mortgage his interest. He may transfer it by gift or by will. But the present ownership of a future interest is not enough. What is required is the right to immediate possession and enjoyment. The statute has been strictly construed. If a donee's enjoyment requires the consent of any other person, the exclusion is lost. This latter principle was applied in *Nashville Trust Co.* v. *Commissioner,* where insurance policies were transferred to three children. The court held that the gifts were future interests because the children had to agree among themselves before any rights under the policy could be exercised. No one of them had an absolute immediate right.

Thus any delay to the immediate possession will be fatal. For example, a conveyance to A from and after next January 1st would be a future interest even if the transfer was made in the late months of the preceding year.

10.12   Gifts in trust

The Supreme Court has held that the individual beneficiary, rather than the trust, is the donee to whom the exclusion applies. Thus if there are five beneficiaries of a single trust there will be five exclusions—assuming all are given present interests. Transfers in trust generally are partly present and partly future since there is a gift of the income and a gift of the corpus. It is not material that there is only one donee. Assume the following transfer in trust: "income to A until 40 with distribution to him at that time or, if he be dead, to his estate." Only the gift of the income constitutes a present interest. What it is worth depends on A's age at the date of the creation of the trust.

This rule separating a gift into one of income and one of corpus can lead to absurd results. Suppose a trust of $10,000, income to A for two years, at which time the principal is to be distributed to him. The present interest, the right to the income for two years, is worth $752. If he were to receive the income for 15 years and then the principal, the present interest would be worth $4,400. Obviously a gift with the right to corpus at the end of 2 years is worth much more to the donee than one with a right to corpus after 15 years, but the amount of the allowable exclusion for the former more valuable gifts will be very, very much less. The latter gift to A gets the full $3,000 exclusion, the former more valuable gift only 25 percent of the exclusion, ($752).

Prior to the 1954 Code even more absurd results were reached. For a trust with income to A for life with the sensible provision that the trustee in his absolute discretion may encroach upon the principal for the benefit of A, the case law denied the exclusion *in toto*. The trustee might have distributed corpus the day after the trust was established. Hence no certain value could be attributed to the life estate. It obviously would have none, if distribution were made the day after the gift. Of course, this would never happen, but the possibility of its happening existed. Since no certain value could be given the income interest, the full exclusion was forfeited. Happily Congress has overruled these cases by providing in Code Section 2503(b) that the possibility that the life interest may be diminished shall be disregarded, if the discretionary power can be exercised only in favor of the income beneficiary.

If the trustee is authorized to pay out or accumulate income in his discretion, apart from the special statute relating to minors, see section 10.16, the gift of income is a future interest since there is no immediate right to possess and enjoy. The beneficiary may enjoy only if the trustee shall decide to distribute income. Meanwhile he has no present rights. For the same reason no exclusion is permitted for the "sprinkle type" trusts, see section 6.22, wherein the trustee is authorized to pay the income in whole or in part to any one or more of the children of A. Here no child has any present right to anything.

As we have seen, a mandatory direction to pay income to A will constitute a present interest in the income. For this reason, any substantial gift in trust will obtain the exclusion if the donee is given the right to income for even a few years. Thus, $50,000 will produce $2,000 a year and if the income is to be paid to A for 2 years and thereafter accumulated, absolutely or in the discretion of the trustee, the exclusion will be assured.

But suppose a trust, requiring the payment of income, starts with $3,000, or $3,000 is added to an existing trust. The gift is partly present and partly future and the exclusion will be obtained only in part. To avoid this result, it is possible to provide that the beneficiary may withdraw the corpus at any time. This makes the full gift a present interest but, generally, would defeat the objective of the grantor. It would also expose the property to estate tax on the death of the donee. For these reasons, except in the case of gifts to minors, see section 10.15, this technique is not generally used.

10.13 Gifts to corporations

In *Heringer* v. *Commissioner,* a corporation was formed by two couples. In exchange for $50,000, 50,000 shares of stock were issued, 20 percent to each couple and 30 percent to the children of each. In all there were 11 children. The shares were separately purchased by each stockholder. Six days later, the two couples transferred one half interest in Blackacre, owned by them, to the corporation. Less than a month thereafter, but in the following tax year, they transferred the other half interest in Blackacre to the corporation. Their gift tax returns for the two years claimed 88 exclusions, and reported total combined gifts of only 60 percent of the value of the property. Each transferor claimed one exclusion for each of the two years and for each of the 11 children, or a total of 22 exclusions for each transferor, on the theory that the gifts were made to the children individually rather than to the corporation.

The Tax Court held that only 8 exclusions were allowable to them and that the full value of Blackacre measured the amount of the gift. This result was predicated on the theory that the corporation was the real donee. It had received the full value of Blackacre. Further each transferor was entitled to one exclusion for each year or a total of 2 per transferor, making 8 in all.

Assume Blackacre was worth $300,000. Since the transferors

owned 40 percent of Blackacre it is difficult to see how they could have made a gift of $300,000, since the transfer only decreased their individual net worths by 60 percent and enriched the other stockholders by only 60 percent. One cannot make a gift to himself. This argument appealed to the Circuit Court which limited the amount of the gift to 60 percent of the full value. The upper Court, however, refused to pass on the number of allowable exclusions because, it said, if the stockholders were the real donees, the gifts were gifts of future interests and therefore disqualified. It is difficult to rebut the contention that any transfer of assets to a corporation, if a gift to the stockholders, is a gift of a future interest, see section 10.11. No stockholder has any immediate right to possess or enjoy corporate property. Under the rationale of the case, no exclusions will be allowed for transfers to corporations. None for the corporation since it is not the donee. This would seem to follow from the modification that reduced the amount of the gift by 40 percent. None for the stockholders, since, as to them, the transfers are future interests.

If the couples had changed the sequence of events the tax results would have been totally different. Suppose they had formed the corporation, and thereafter transferred the land. No gift tax consequences would have resulted at the time of transfer, since they owned all the stock. Further, their cost basis for the shares would have increased by the amount of the contributions to capital. If they then transferred 60 percent of the stock, half in December and half in January, to the 11 children, the 88 exclusions would have been assured and their donees would have enjoyed a much higher cost basis for their shares.[2]

While this may look like a triumph of form over substance, it is simply another illustration of the absurd results that the future interest exception sometimes brings about.

---

[2] It is possible that the exclusions claimed by family A for transfers to the children of B might have been denied on the theory that they were not gifts but transfers in consideration of like transfers by family B to the children of family A.

Gifts to minors

10.14   Outright transfers

No difficulty has been encountered with respect to outright gifts to minors, though it is difficult to understand how an infant of three can possess and enjoy a $1,000 bill, for example. But Rev. Ruling 54–400 states: "An unqualified and unrestricted gift to a minor, with or without the appointment of a guardian, is a gift of a present interest." There are, however, practical objections to outright gifts to minors. U.S. savings bonds may be purchased for and redeemed by minors. Cash may be kept in a dry trust in a savings account in the name of the parent for the minor. But difficulties arise when other property is given to minors. Brokers are reluctant to deal in securities owned by minors. They are properly fearful of a minor's disaffirming a sale of stock that subsequently rises in value. Titles in minors are, to a large extent, frozen. The minor's signature to a deed of real estate gives the buyer no assurance of permanent title. Of course, the appointment of a legal guardian will avoid these objections. But guardianship laws are more rigid than those regarding the powers that may be conferred upon a trustee. The guardian must generally post bond; he must account periodically to the Court; and in addition the sureties on his bond will exercise a supervisory control. Generally donors will be well advised to use a trust to obtain any reasonable degree of flexibility.

10.15   Gifts in trust

Gifts of substantial amounts in trust for infants have not caused any difficulty in those cases where the income was required to be distributed annually. But, if such gifts were limited to $3,000, exclusions could be obtained only in part. To avoid this reduction in the amount of the allowable exclusion, prior to the 1954 Code, the draftsman would provide that in addition to the right to income, an infant beneficiary had the immediate and absolute power to withdraw the corpus in whole or in part at any time. This privilege technically gave the infant the immediate right to the possession of the corpus. Some courts allowed the full exclusion in these cases, recognizing that the power gave the infant the equivalent of the powers he would have if he were the outright owner. Other courts took the view that as a practical matter an infant of tender years could not make a demand and if he did the trustee would undoubtedly refuse to honor it. Of course, a guardian could make the demand for him. But suppose no guardian had been appointed at the date of the creation of the trust? Was it a future interest because it would take time after the creation of the trust to have a guardian appointed? It seems absurd to make the result turn upon the existence of a guardian, since in all such cases there was little likelihood that the power would ever, in fact, be exercised during the minority. But the case law was and is still uncertain; and for that reason, if one desires to make a $3,000 gift in trust for an infant and to obtain the $3,000 exclusion, he should follow the 1954 Code provisions precisely.

10.16   The 1954 Code provisions

The 1954 Code makes it possible for a donor to obtain the exclusion by a gift in trust to an infant, if he is willing to meet the requirements of the statute. Section 2503(c) provides that a gift to a minor shall not be considered a gift of future interest if:

1. The income and principal may be expended by or on behalf of the beneficiary; and

2. To the extent not so expended will pass to him at 21, or if he dies prior to that time to his estate or to his appointees under a general power of appointment.

Under this statute, the trustee must accumulate the income in his discretion, but the entire fund (capital and accumulated income) must be distributed to the infant at 21. It is unfortunate to require that the capital be forced upon the infant at majority. This may be the very worst thing that could happen to him. Normally, donors do not direct termination of trusts at 21, particularly when the beneficiaries are so young at the time of the gift that no one can possibly foresee the kind of persons they will be at 21. It is regrettable that Congress didn't make the age 30.

The donor should not be the trustee or one of the trustees. If he is, the corpus will be taxed as part of his estate because of the power to "alter, amend, revoke or terminate." In the *Lober* case, the grantor-trustee had created an irrevocable trust for his children. The income was to be paid to the children until they reached a certain age at which time they were to receive the principal. The only retained power was one to advance principal to them from time to time in the discretion of the trustees. Since the grantor, as trustee, could accelerate the termination date, he was held to have retained a forbidden power. Similarly the trustee of a minor's trust must have the same power to terminate to qualify the trust. Hence the adverse estate tax consequences if the grantor is the trustee or one of the trustees.

10.17   The Stock Exchange Act

While the 1954 statute removed the tax uncertainty of gifts in trust, donors objected to the expense involved in setting up small trusts. They sought a substitute that would avoid the trust expense but achieve the benefits of the management and investment characteristics of a trust. The New York Stock Exchange attempted to furnish the answer to this problem by a proposed model law concerning gifts of securities to infants.[3]

This law or a comparable one has been adopted in all 50 states. It provides for registration of a stock certificate by a donor in his own name or in the name of any adult member of the minor's family "as custodian for . . . . , a minor" with delivery of the certificate to the custodian.

---

[3] Many states include insurance policies among the assets that may be held by a custodian.

To qualify the gift for the exclusion the Act provides in Section (a):

> The custodian shall hold, manage, invest and reinvest the property held by him as custodian, including any unexpended income therefrom, as hereinafter provided. He shall collect the income therefrom and apply so much or the whole thereof and so much or the whole of the other property held by him as custodian as he may deem advisable for the support, maintenance, education and general use and benefit of the minor, in such manner, at such time or times, and to such extent as the custodian in his absolute discretion may deem suitable and proper, without court order, without regard to the duty of any other person to support the minor and without regard to any other funds which may be applicable or available for the purpose. To the extent that property held by the custodian and the income thereof is not so expended, it shall be delivered or paid over to the minor upon the minor's attaining the age of twenty-one (21) years, and in the event that the minor dies before attaining the age of twenty-one (21) years it shall thereupon be delivered or paid over to the estate of the minor.

Many donors, adopting programs of small annual gifts, are using this device. The Service has ruled, by letter ruling, that gifts under the act qualify for the exclusion.

Marital privileges

10.18   Gift splitting

The introduction of the marital deduction in the estate tax and the income-splitting technique in the income tax called for corresponding revisions in the gift tax. Again these gift tax changes may best be understood by comparing the situation of the resident of a community property state with the resident of a common law jurisdiction. For example, assume that a successful real estate operator in Texas earned a $66,000 commission and made a gift of it to his son, he paid no gift tax since half the asset belonged to his wife by operation of law. He parted with $33,000; she parted with $33,000. Since each had an exemption and an exclusion, no gift tax liability arose. If, instead of giving it to his son, he had given it to his wife, his total gift would amount to only $33,000, since she already owned the balance. And, of course, she would still continue to have her lifetime exemption. Thus the revision in the gift tax field was directed towards two concepts, gift splitting and a gift tax marital deduction.

Gift splitting applies to gifts to third persons. Any gift made by either spouse may be treated as if he gave only half and his spouse gave the other half, if the nondonor spouse consents. There are no restrictions on the type or form of gift—i.e., nothing corresponding to the terminable interest rule. However, splitting will be denied if the other spouse is given a general power of appointment over the property. Further, if any gift is split all gifts during the quarter period must be split. Assume Husband gives Son $46,000. He had made no previous gifts. Wife had, however, used $20,000 of her exemption in a previous year. They may not use his $30,000 and his $3,000 plus her $10,000 and her $3,000. They must split the gross gift, treating each as having given $23,000. The result is that the return for Husband will show no taxable amount, the return for Wife will show a net taxable gift of $10,000. This result may be avoided, however, if, for example, Husband gives $26,000 in December and the balance in January, since the option to split arises anew for each reporting period. Presumably the option would not be exercised the second period but charged against the exclusion and the remaining portion of his exemption.

Splitting is available only as to gifts during marriage. Hence gifts made in the quarter-year of the marriage but prior to the wedding may not be split nor may gifts made after the death of one spouse, but within the quarter-year of death, be split. But gifts made prior to death may be split if the executor of the deceased spouse consents.

It should be noted that it may sometimes be more costly to split that to report the full gift separately. Suppose Wife has already made $100,000 of net gifts in prior years or period and Husband makes a $50,000 gift in the current quarter. Here splitting would throw $22,000 (after deducting her exclusion) into Wife's much higher bracket because of the cumulative method of computation.

Where it is advantageous to split, the payment of the tax by one spouse is not treated as itself a gift.

10.19   Gift tax marital deduction

One half of any gift to a spouse is deductible, provided the transfer is not classifiable as a terminable interest or can be brought within one of the exceptions to that rule. The rules regarding the gift tax marital deduction parallel the estate tax marital deduction requirements except that there is an additional gift tax exception to the terminable interest rule which permits joint tenancies to qualify.

A transfer to a spouse will qualify for the deduction if it is:

1. A fee,
2. An indefeasibly vested remainder,
3. A life estate with unrestricted power to appoint the corpus,
4. A life estate with remainder to the estate of the spouse,
5. A power of appointment trust,
6. An estate trust,
7. A joint tenancy. (An interest as tenant in common would qualify under 1 above.)

A detailed discussion of the various types of transfers noted above will be found in sections 4.13 through 4.18, where they are treated in connection with the estate tax marital deduction.

The following will illustrate the operation of the marital deduction. Assume Husband gives Wife property worth $80,000. He deducts $40,000, marital deduction, $30,000 lifetime exemption, $3,000 annual exclusion and the net taxable gift amounts to $7,000.

A further example will illustrate how the exemptions, exclusions, gift splitting, and gift tax marital deduction operates, in transfers to both a spouse and a third person.

Assume a gift of $100,000 in trust by Husband for Son for life, remainder to Wife, her heirs and assigns forever. Assume further that the actuarial value of Son's life estate is $60,000. Husband and Wife may split the $60,000 gift to Son and, since it is a present interest, each is entitled to an exclusion. Husband

may take the gift tax marital deduction for the gift to Wife
since it is not a terminable one but will be denied the exclusion
because the remainder is a future interest.

The husband's return would show:

Gift to son	$30,000	
Less exclusion	3,000	
Net gift to son		$27,000
Gift to wife	$40,000	
Less marital deduction	20,000	
Net gift to wife		$20,000
Total gifts		$47,000
Less lifetime exemption		$30,000
Taxable gift		$17,000

The wife's return would show:

Gift to son	$30,000	
Less exclusion	3,000	
Net gift to son		$27,000
Less lifetime exemption		$30,000
Taxable Gift		0

Halstead v. *Commissioner* represents an extremely strict interpretation of the requirement that, in the case of a trust,
the wife be entitled to all the income for life, if the trust is
to qualify for the gift tax marital deduction. In that case the
trust consisted largely of life insurance policies on the life of
the grantor. Income was to be used to pay premiums. As the
income was insufficient the grantor made contributions to the
trust. The questions were whether, as to these contributions,
the grantor was entitled to both the annual exclusion and the
marital deduction. The Court held the gifts were present interests since the wife had an absolute right to demand the trust
principal at any time. This holding is in line with the gifts to
minor cases (see section 10.15). However, the gift tax marital
deduction was denied becuse the trust was not designed to be
income producing. This seems wrong since in view of her unlimited withdrawal privilege the wife had the power to make
herself outright owner at any time. The trust could hold unproductive property only with her consent in the sense that she
could have terminated it at will. Realistically looked at the
power to terminate includes the lesser power of controlling
the investments. For all practical purposes she, and she alone,

could determine the extent to which the trust assets might continue to be unproductive. The decision is unfortunate as it may make it impossible to qualify an unfunded irrevocable insurance trust for the gift tax marital deduction.

Valuation

10.20 In general

Valuation problems are as numerous as there are properties to be valued. The Regulations use the "willing-buyer-willing-seller" standard but unfortunately this does not eliminate all valuation problems since aside from the cases in which there is no market for the item transferred, there are many situations where there are several markets each with differing prices. Is it the market to which the donor must go in order to buy, or the one to which he must resort if he wants to sell? He may have to pay $2,000 for a piece of jewelry because he can buy only in the retail market. But, as a seller, he will be lucky to realize $500. He must resort to a market of middlemen, who may offer only $500, since they can't get more than $1,000 from the retailer, who in turn will mark it up to $2,000.

Securities traded on a recognized market present no difficulty. Appraisals may be obtained for real estate, mortgages, notes, bonds, etc. The problem of the closely held business presents the most uncertainty. See chapter 16. With respect to personal property where there may be more than one market, the courts have insisted on replacement value where the article is purchased new for the purpose of giving. Thus in *Ryerson and Guggenheim* gifts were made of fully paid up life insurance policies. Assume, for example, a $300,000 face amount single premium life insurance policy which cost $250,000. Immediately after purchase it has a cash surrender value of $200,000. On the day after purchase, it is transferred by gift. All the donee can realize on the surrender is $200,000, but the Supreme Court has held that the replacement cost, $250,000, is the value of the gift for tax purposes. The same result has been reached where a husband purchased a valuable piece of jewelry for his wife. These results seem sound since the purchase and gift may be viewed as part of the same transaction.

On the other hand, a gift of a diamond ring purchased 12 years before ought to be measured by what the donor or donee could have sold it for, not by what either would have been willing to pay for it. This measure is, in fact, used if the donee promptly sells and the result ought not be different if he keeps, but there is little discussion of this problem in the cases.

10.21   Pledged property

It is well settled that a gift of property subject to an encumbrance, is to be measured by the value of the equity. Thus, in one case, the taxpayer owned securities having a market value of $129,270 which were pledged as collateral for a note in the amount of $120,000. He transferred the securities to his wife subject to the debt. The Treasury contended the value of the gift was the full value of the securities, less $24,000. This represented the Commissioner's determination of a reasonable discount "based on the donor's ability to pay, considering all the circumstances." The Court, however, held that the gift was $9,270. Any reduction thereafter made by the husband would, of course, constitute a further gift to the wife. Thus if he desired to make her annual gifts of $6,000 a year, he could do so by reducing the loan by that amount each year.

10.22   Property burdened with gift tax liability

Frequently a donor will insist the donee must pay the gift tax. This is sometimes accomplished by borrowing on the security of the property, the amount of the tax and then transferring the property either subject to the burden or with an assumption of the burden. Query, if this is desirable? It has the effect of reducing the amount of the gift and hence of the tax but there are other pitfalls. If the donee takes subject to the obligation and the donor dies before it is fully liquidated, has the donor in effect reserved the income from the property for a period which in fact did not end before his death? If so, does he not have a reserved life estate for estate tax purposes? And might not the income used to pay the tax be taxable to the donor as income used to discharge his obligation? The *Morgan* case so held.[4] On the whole it is undesirable to give property burdened with gift tax liability, though unfortunately, there is a surface appeal to the rugged individualist who somehow believes that shifting the burden of the tax represents a real accomplishment, when, in fact, nothing is actually achieved and a number of unnecessary risks are assumed.

10.23 Gifts of contingent interests

A gift tax may be imposed on an interest even though there is some considerable likelihood that the donee may never in fact enjoy the property. Thus to A for life and then to B, if he survives A, otherwise the property to return to the donor. If B should die before A he will never have the benefit of the gift. However the Supreme Court in a gift of this type held that the full value of the property was to be taxed less the value of the interest retained by the grantor. The burden of showing how much was to be subtracted from the full value of the property is put upon the donor and in cases where he cannot show the value of the reserved right no reduction is permitted.

10.24 Restrictive agreements

Suppose stock is given subject to the right of the donor to repurchase it at any time within the next five years for $30

---

[4] However, in *Schaeffer* the trustee borrowed the money to pay the tax and then repaid the loan from income. It was held the income used to repay the loan was not taxable to the grantor.

a share. Does this fix the value for gift tax purposes? It may well fix it for estate tax purposes on the death of the donee since his estate must sell at $30. See chapter 16. Further it is clear that no buyer during the donee's life, and while the restriction is operative, would pay more than $30. But the stock has use values as well as sale values. Assume it pays dividends of $10 a year. Obviously it is worth more than $30; how much more depends on the probabilities that the option will not be exercised. In some fact situations this may give it a value very substantially in excess of $30 and close to the value of similar unrestricted shares. In every case, however, there should be some discount because the option limits the sale value, one of the privileges of ownership. Because of what has been said above this device does not represent a worthwhile technique in gift transactions.

It has been suggested by some agents on behalf of charitable donees that a gift of stock subject to a repurchase option may prove attractive to prospective charitable donors. Thus it has been said that if X contributes General Motors to a charity, at a time when it is selling for $45 with an option to repurchase at $50, he will get a charitable income tax deduction of $45, without any realization of gain even if the stock cost him considerably less than $45 and he can repurchase the stock if and when it increases in value above $50. A little reflection will indicate, however, that the value of what is given to charity is very much less than $45. If the reader will assume that he now has 100 shares of General Motors and consider how much he would charge for the privilege of giving X an option to purchase it at any time within the next five years at 5 points over the present market price, he will realize how valuable is the retained privilege. In view of the history of the General Motors stock, the writer would want something like $20 or $25, assuming General Motors is now selling at $45, for the call privilege. This would indicate that the value of what the charity would get in the above proposal is worth something like $20 or $25 and the income tax deduction will be accordingly so limited.

Selection of gift property

10.25   Cost basis of donee

The value for gift tax purposes is always fair market value at date of the gift. But for income tax gain purposes the donee takes the donor's cost, plus, in most cases, the amount of the gift tax paid. Thus, if the stock which cost the donor $10, is given away at $20, and subsequently sold by the donee for $30, the donee has a $20 capital gain. For loss purposes, the donee's cost is either the cost to the donor or the fair market value at the date of the gift, which ever is lower. This makes it impossible to transfer "losses." Assume the donor paid $30, gave it away at $20, and the donee later sold it for $10, his loss would be limited to $10. Where the property which cost the donor $30, is given away at a time when it is worth $10 and is later sold by the donee for $20, there is neither gain nor loss. There is no gain, because the cost basis to determine gain is $30; there is no loss because the cost basis for determining loss is $10. Thus neither gain nor loss is recognized on the assumed sale at $20.

These capital gain rules makes the selection of the property to be given important. It is foolish to give low cost stock, if other assets are readily available, since such stock is burdened with a potential tax liability. If such stock is retained until death, it will get a new basis, the market value at the date of death, and the increase in value during life will wholly escape income tax. On the other hand, it is equally foolish to give high cost basis stock, since thereby a potential income tax deduction is lost. Here it is preferable to sell the asset, realize the loss, and give away the proceeds. Generally speaking the ideal gift property is property with a cost basis that approximates its current value.

It should not be assumed that it will always be undesirable to give away low basis stock. While the donor will generally be subject on sale to the 25 percent alternative capital gains rate, his donee, assuming he has little other income, may by including one half of the gain in ordinary income have the actual gain taxed at considerably less than 25 percent. While the Act now provides that the standard deduction is not available for use against unearned income in the case of a taxpayer who is claimed as the dependent of another, the exemption ($750 for 1972) will still be available. Thus, if the actual capital gain is $1,500 or less and the donee has no other income, no tax at will be incurred on a sale by him.

10.26 *Income assets*

A gift of property will shift the income taxes on the future dividends or interest to the donee. But the property given must constitute a capital asset. One may not shift the income tax liability on his earnings by an assignment of part of his salary, whether such salary is already earned or is to be earned in the future. Similarly one may not avoid the tax on dividends or interest coupons by assigning such rights to his donee, retaining the stock or bond. Gifts of next year's income from a trust will not be recognized for income tax purposes. For a more detailed discussion of this subject, see section 11.28.

10.27 *Income-producing property*

Where the objective is to reduce family income taxes as well as to eliminate estate taxes, high income-producing assets should be selected for the gift. A 6 percent mortgage is preferable to a 2 percent bond if the donee is in a lower income tax bracket than the donor. This consideration is no longer significant where the gift is to a spouse, since the income tax splitting provision of the Internal Revenue Code has, generally speaking, eliminated the income tax advantages formerly resulting from inter vivos gifts between spouses. Gifts of income-producing assets to other members of the family may still be used effectively to reduce the overall family income tax burden.

10.28   *Property likely to increase in value*

Another consideration which should not be ignored is that, to the extent possible, the property selected should consist of assets which are likely to increase in value rather than decrease. If the assets in fact increase in value while in the hands of the donee, the estate tax saving will be proportionally increased, whereas any substantial decrease in value correspondingly reduces the anticipated saving. Gifts of leasehold interests, patent rights, and other property which necessarily decrease in value with the mere passage of time should be especially avoided.

10.29   *Jointly owned assets*

See Chapter 8.

10.30   *Life insurance*

See Chapter 15.

I I

Taxable transfers

11.1   Introduction

There is no correlation between the income, gift, and estate tax concepts. Transfers complete for gift tax purposes may be incomplete for either income or estate tax purposes. For this reason the fact that a gift tax has been paid is no assurance that the income from property has been shifted to the donee or that the estate tax, on the death of the transferor, has been avoided. A gift tax is payable on a transfer in contemplation of death in spite of the fact that the property transferred will be subjected to estate tax on the death of the donor. Suppose an attorney transfers by way of gift fees due him for services rendered. The assignment will attract gift tax but the amount of the fees, when collected, must be included in the income tax return of the assignor. Generally the Courts have construed the gift tax sections as requiring the imposition of the tax if the transfer is such that it shifts either income or estate tax. This carries out the Congressional policy which was to compensate for the loss in either or both income and estate tax revenues that gifts achieve. Thus, in the contemplation of death transfer assumed above, the income tax on the income from the transferred property is taxable to the donee. The gift is complete for income tax purposes but not for estate tax purposes. In the fee assignment example the gift may be complete for estate tax purposes, though incomplete for income tax purposes. There is at least one situation where a gift tax will be incurred even though the gift is incomplete for both income and estate tax. Suppose A transfers Blackacre to B, reserving a life estate in the property. A will be taxed on the rental income and Blackacre will be part of his estate at death. A gift tax will, nevertheless, be imposed. But here the gift tax may be justified since any later capital gains tax on a sale of the property is shifted from the donor.

Gifts distinguished from other transfers

11.2 Services gratuitously rendered

One may freely give his services without incurring gift taxes. In *Hogle* the taxpayer had created Clifford-type trusts for his children. Because of his control he was taxable on the income but the court refused to assess a gift tax based on the contention that Hogle had given his expert services in managing the trust operations. His services, however valuable, did not constitute a transfer of property rights, which the gift tax contemplates.

In *Alexander* v. *Commissioner* a rancher gave cattle and grazing land to his daughter. He continued to manage the cattle. While this was an income tax case (the profits being all taxed to the daughter) it seems clear that he did not make a taxable gift because he failed to charge for his services. This rule is also recognized in the charity cases.

The rule that services may be freely given was abused to a very considerable extent in the family partnership cases, and has led to a limitation on the rule in those cases. See section 11.27.

Suppose Father permits Son to occupy real estate as a residence, rent free. Has he made a taxable gift measured by the fair rental value of the property? Apparently not. The Code is aimed at transfers rather than permitted use. In I.T. 3918 it was ruled that the owner of property who permitted a charitable corporation to occupy it was not entitled to a charitable income tax deduction, the ruling being predicated on the theory that "such an arrangement does not constitute a gift of property." Thus, while parents have no legal obligation to support adult children, furnishing them with the use of property, real or personal, should not involve gift tax consequences.

11.3   Gift or compensation

Not every gratuitous transfer constitutes a gift. In *Fisher* v. *Commissioner* the issue was whether an amount of $6,000 received by the taxpayer from his employer was a tax-free gift to the employee or additional compensation for services rendered. After 24 years of service the taxpayer had resigned, effective the following December. He has risen from office boy to general traffic manager of the Holmes Electric Protective Company. He had been told at the time of submitting his resignation that the company "would do something for him." On December 23rd he was given a check for $6,000. He had never before received a bonus, there was no agreement to pay him anything in addition to the regular monthly compensation he had always received. He had performed no services outside the scope of his normal duties. The taxpayer contended it must be a gift because there was (1) no contractual obligation, (2) no extra services, (3) no payment for loss of employment, since the resignation was voluntary. But the court held the payment taxable as compensation since the prime motivation was to further recognize past services. Gifts spring primarily from motives of love and affection; and not from the desire to more liberally compensate. For this reason gifts outside the family are rare. Tips constitute taxable income. They have been held not to be gifts within the meaning of the income tax exclusion "for gifts, bequests, devises, and inheritances." On the other hand, a pension provided for a minister upon retirement "motivated solely and sincerely by the congregation's love and affection for Dr. Mutch" was held within the income tax gift exclusion. A "gift" to an officer of the company "as an expression of good will, esteem and kind feeling," however, was held income taxable. In each case it is a question of fact, the vital consideration being the donor's motives in making the transfer. Since gifts flow from love and affection the interfamily transfer is most likely to be held a gift, even though the recipient has rendered past services. Transfers to persons outside the immediate family will rarely be found to have the requisite gift motive. The minister cases are not an exception but a recognition that the religious leader occupies a position more akin to a family member than an employed individual.

11.4   Gift or dividend

Generally speaking any distribution from a corporation to a stockholder constitutes a dividend to the extent of the corporation's earnings and profits. The fact that the distribution is not pro rata does not prevent its being taxed as a dividend. To the extent that the distribution exceeds earnings and profits, it is treated as a return of capital, reducing the stockholder's cost basis, if in excess thereof, it gives rise to capital gain.

It is possible, however, that a corporate distribution may constitute a gift. If Father and Mother own all the stock of X Corporation and a distribution of $10,000 is voted to Son, Father and Mother are each treated as having made gifts in proportion to their stock ownership. See section 10.7. Suppose Son is also a stockholder, each owning one-third of the issued stock. Here two thirds of the distribution may be treated as gifts by Father and Mother, one third as a dividend to Son. In each of the cases suggested Father and Mother will be treated as having constructively received their proportionate shares and then having given them to Son, so that the transaction will have both income and gift tax consequences for them.

Whether a distribution to a stockholder is a dividend in whole or only in part, will depend upon whether it is made to him because of his stock ownership or because of the love and affection of the other stockholders. Like the compensation cases, section 11.2, unequal distributions to a stockholder, unrelated by blood or marriage, to his fellow stockholders, will almost always be found to be a dividend in full. But in family corporations the unequal distribution is most likely the result of love and affection or a feeling of family responsibility, i.e., typical gift motives, and so will generally result in a finding that the excess over the recipient's proportionate interest, constitutes (1) constructive dividends to the other stockholders and (2) gifts by them to the actual distributee.

11.5 Gift or sale

The Code makes it clear that any transfer for less than a full and adequate consideration in money or money's worth constitutes a gift in part. Thus, if Father sells Blackacre worth $40,000 to Daughter for $10,000, he has made her a gift of $30,000. It is not possible, therefore, to avoid the gift tax by sales for inadequate considerations. The same gift result would follow if Father employed Daughter at $10,000 a year requiring in exchange services having a fair market value of $2,000.

11.6 Sham gifts

Gifts will result in income and estate tax savings but they must be genuine transfers, not pretenses designed to have no real economic significance other than the hoped for tax consequences. There is a fundamental principle that a transaction will be recognized for tax purposes only if it makes some sense, apart from its tax sense. This is generally referred to as the business purpose doctrine but, in the opinion of the writer, it is of broader application in that it is not limited to business transactions.

A taxpayer wanted to deduct from his income taxes the allowances he was making to his adult children. He, therefore, went to the X Bank and borrowed $100,000. He immediately transferred the $100,000 to the same X Bank, as trustee, with instructions to invest the capital and pay the income to his children. The trust instrument contained a provision authorizing the trustee to loan money to the grantor. The taxpayer-grantor next borrowed $100,000 from the trustee, giving his 6 percent promissory note. He used this sum to discharge his debt to the Bank. Mirabli dictu, he thought he had a $6,000 yearly deduction for the interest paid at the end of the year!

What meaning, apart from the tax meaning, did these separate steps have? Did the combination of steps, viewed as a single transaction, represent rational conduct, aside from taxes?

Bobby Jones, the golfer, had a contract with Warner Brothers to make a series of pictures depicting his form and style in playing golf. He was to receive $120,000 plus a royalty of 50 percent on the earnings of the pictures. Before making any pictures he sold his services to his father for $1,000 a year and transferred his rights under the contract to his father. His father then transferred the rights under the contract to himself as trustee for Jones' three children. The court held the plan was without legal effect and the income was all taxable to Jones.

All letter perfect plans should be submitted to the test: Does this make sense, apart from its tax sense? If not, the proposal should not be adopted. Tax consequences depend on something more than the words used. Like all other transactions they will be legally recognized if they have a rational basis, but the courts will always look through the form to the substance.

It is not enough to go through the form of giving, if there is, in fact, no intention to make a present transfer. Parents will frequently execute and record deeds of their real estate to their children with the secret understanding that the parent is to have the continued possession and use of the property and the right to sell and dispose of it at any time. If, in any particular case, such an agreement is found to exist, the parent will be held to be the owner, and the property will be included in his estate at least for purposes of satisfying his debts and determining the amount of his death taxes. The children hold the title merely as his nominees; see Section 3.7. Nor is proof of such secret arrangements difficult to obtain. Investigation of the uses to which such property is put following the conveyance will generally furnish telling evidence of the presence or absence of such an agreement. For example, if the parent continues to collect the rent, pay the taxes, order repairs, make annual leases, discuss offers of sale, obtain and use the proceeds of mortgages placed on the land and otherwise deal with it as owner, securing the submissive signatures of his nominees when necessary, a strong case of a sham transfer will be made. The same evidence will be available where other income-producing property such as stocks and bonds is used. The endorsement over of the dividend checks and the delivery of the coupons to the donor, and the use by him of the securities as collateral for loans, the decisions by him as to reinvestments, will point strongly to him as the real owner.

Requirements for gifts

11.7   Formalities

Two elements are required for a gift to obtain legal recognition: (1) an intention to give, (2) certain objective manifestations of that intention. There must be a delivery of the physical property or a formal writing, duly delivered. In *Richardson* two brothers owned shares of stock which they kept in safety deposit boxes in a different city than the one in which they resided. On May 18, 1932, they told a clerk that they were making gifts of the stock to their wives. The clerk made notations of the gifts on cards. They told their wives what they had done and the wives said they accepted. On May 27 they asked a business associate, after telling him what they had done, to prepare the necessary papers. He made out blank stock assignments which they executed and returned to him. The gift tax law was enacted June 6th. On June 9th the stock was removed from the safety deposit boxes and mailed to the business associate. On June 29th the shares were transferred on the books of the corporation to the wives.

The brothers argued, unsuccessfully, that the gifts were made before the gift tax became law. However, there was no physical delivery to the donees prior to June 6th. Nor was there any formal instrument of transfer delivered to the donees. The business associate was acting as agent for the donors, not the donees.

It is possible to make gifts without delivery to the donees. What is required is a question of state law. The brothers might have formally declared themselves trustees of the stock for their wives. The formal declaration is generally sufficient under trust law to vest indefeasible interests in the beneficiaries, even though they do not yet know of the gifts. Delivery might have been made to the business associate as agent for the wives. If he purported to so act, the gift by state property law would, in most, if not all, jurisdictions, be valid and complete. Thus the first requirement of a gift, for tax purposes, is that it be a valid transfer under the state law governing the transaction. It does not have to be classified as a gift under state law but an effective transfer of title must have occurred.

11.8   Contracts to make gifts in the future

Suppose a prospective husband agrees, in consideration of marriage, that he will give his wife $50,000 a year for ten years. Such a transfer will not avoid gift tax simply because the consideration is sufficient to make the transaction a binding contract under state law. See section 11.19. The problem here is whether the taxable event is the execution of the binding contract or the actual transfer of the property interests pursuant to the contract.

In *Estate of Copley,* Ira C. Copley and his intended wife entered into an agreement in 1931 in contemplation of and in consideration of marriage whereby he agreed to pay her the sum of $1,000,000, immediately after the solemnization of the marriage. The parties were married but no immediate payment was made. In 1936 Copley transferred $500,000 of corporation notes to her. In 1944 he transferred $500,000 of preferred stock to her. These transfers were in performance of the prenuptial agreement. The Commissioner determined that taxable gifts were made in 1936 and in 1944 but the Court held these transfers were not gifts but were in discharge of his 1931 obligation. Apparently the Court assumed the gift occurred in 1931 through this issue was not before it since there was no tax on gifts at that time.

This type of arrangement can raise difficult problems and

there are some cases contra. Suppose the wife releases her husband from the contractual obligation? Has she made a gift? Suppose the statute of limitations bars the assertion of the claim. Is there any gift tax due from the wife? If the claim is barred or released, does the husband have income under the cancellation of indebtedness cases? If the husband fulfills his obligation with low cost basis stock, does he have capital gain income.

The opposite view seems preferable since a gift requires the transfer of property, not a promise to make a transfer in the future. But note an assignment of future rents may constitute a present transfer. Thus in *Galt* v. *Commissioner,* the taxpayer leased real estate to a trotting association for 20 years. The rentals were measured in part by a percentage of the wagering done at the track. Taxpayer made a gratuitous assignment of 20 percent of the percentage rental for the full term of the lease to each of his three sons. Later the lessee made payments to the sons. The assignment was held to constitute gifts, measured by the present value of all the anticipated payments over the 20-year period. The gifts were made on the date of the assignment of the rentals rather than when the payments were actually made each year. The property rights were acquired by the sons on the earlier date. It should not be assumed, however, that because a gift tax was paid the income was, therefore, shifted for income tax purposes from the father to the sons. See section 11.23.

11.9   *Completeness required for gifts*

A transfer remains incomplete for gift tax purposes so long as the donor retains the power to revoke. No taxable gift occurs when Father deposits funds in the joint checking account of Father and Son, since he may freely withdraw the deposit. The taxable event will occur when and if Son withdraws. This will be the first time he will acquire indefeasible rights and, what is really decisive, Father will have irrevocably parted with the asset. *Totten* trusts, where the donor makes a deposit in a savings account entitled "Donor in Trust for Donee" and retains the possession of the book, are regarded as revocable transfers. Hence no gift tax liability arises. The same is true of government bonds, registered in joint names, if the donor retains the power to redeem the bonds for his individual benefit. In *Commissioner* v. *Allen* the question was whether a transfer, without consideration by an infant, was effective on the date of the transfer so as to incur gift tax or whether the taxable event occurred in the year in which he attained his majority and failed to disaffirm. The Court held it immaterial that the power arose by operation of law rather than by the terms of the gift. "The difference in the inception of the powers is merely one of immaterial form and not of substance. The thing that renders the giving in the first instance less than a gift is the power of the donor to nullify the grant . . . with the extinguishment or termination of the power, however created, comes the change of legal rights and shifting of economic benefits" which Congress intended to tax.

The gift of the donor's check is not complete until the check is paid or negotiated to a third person for value. The same is true as to the donor's note. Until payment or transfer to a bona fide holder the maker does not, because of the absence of consideration, come under any legal obligation to honor the instrument. Thus, where checks were given on December 25, 1925, but cashed on January 2, 1926, the tax was incurred in 1926.

11.10   Renunciations

A husband, having inherited all his property from his first wife, desired to leave it to the sons of that marriage, rather than to his second wife and their child. He had a will prepared to carry this intention into effect but died prior to executing it. Under the intestacy laws of the state of his domicile, his present wife, his son, and his daughter by the second marriage each became entitled to one-third of his estate. However, because his wife and daughter felt a moral obligation to carry out his wishes, each renounced her intestate share and the entire estate was distributed to the son. On substantially the above facts the Court held the wife and daughter had made taxable gifts to the son. The theory was that under local law (Minnesota) the heirs had no power to prevent the vesting of title in themselves. The law gave them the title and that they could not refuse it. The only method by which they could avoid ownership was by an assignment. From this it logically followed that each had made a gratuitous transfer. The same result was reached in a California case.

It is generally believed, and the regulations so state, that a legatee may renounce without the imposition of a gift tax, provided he acts with the requisite promptness. The reason is that a legatee may refuse a gift and it is regarded as never having vested in him. Query, if the tax law ought to turn on such nice common law distinctions. A relinquishment of an interest ought to have the same tax effect whether the gift was by will or intestate succession. Presumably if the state law permits an heir to renounce, as it does by statute in many states, no gift tax will result.

The renunciation must be promptly made. Most renunciations will be subject to the contention that the legatee failed to act within a reasonable time. This will always be a question of fact, but because state law places this restriction upon his power to refuse, the uncertainty is one that cannot ever be completely and absolutely avoided.

Powers, life insurance, joint ownership

11.11 Special powers

Neither the exercise nor the release of a special power of appointment results in a taxable transfer. See section 5.9, 5.10. However, the exercise or release of a special power may have additional consequences not immediately recognized. If X has a special power to appoint by deed and a general power by will, the exercise of the special power will also have the effect of releasing his general power and the release of the general power will attract gift tax. Shortly after the marital deduction provisions became law it was suggested that the estate tax marital deduction might be obtained by giving the wife the requisite general power by will only and that she could then be enabled to pass the property so bequeathed free from gift tax during her life if she were given a special power by deed. In view of what has been said above such a happy result is obviously not obtainable.

A more common situation where the exercise of a special power may attract some gift tax occurs when the donee of the power and the life tenant are the same person. Suppose A is entitled to the income from a trust for his life with a special power to appoint the corpus by deed. He appoints it to B. A has not only exercised his power but arguably he has given B his life estate in the property. See section 5.14.

11.12 General powers

The Code makes it clear that the exercise, release, or lapse of a general power constitutes a gift. The prompt renunciation of such a power, however, will not incur gift tax. For a detailed treatment of the gift taxation of general powers, see section 5.11.

11.13 Reserved powers

See chapter 14.

11.14 Life insurance

See chapter 15.

11.15 Joint ownership

See chapter 8.

Donative intent

11.16 Indirect gifts

Many gifts are made without the donor's fully realizing the effect of his conduct and without appreciating the tax consequences. It is clear from the cases that no donative intent is required. Thus if Father, to preserve the family name, pays off a judgment entered against Son, particularly if Son is solvent, he has made a gift to Son. In the *Berger* case a husband created an irrevocable trust of 15 life insurance policies. Under the terms of the trust, upon his death, $3,000 a year was to be paid to his mother for life, his wife was to receive the balance of the income, and upon the mother's death, the entire income was to go to her for life. After the deaths of his mother, his wife, and a sister (a contingent income beneficiary), the corpus was to be paid to his five brothers and sisters. His wife paid the annual premiums. She objected to the assessment of a gift tax thereon, on the ground that she was merely protecting her interest. But the absence of any donative intent was held immaterial. The court said: "We think it clear that the amount of the premiums in excess of the value to the taxpayer of her interest in the trust was a gift. The equivalent could have been obtained by her by making substantially lesser payment, for example, through the purchase of policies on her husband's life in a lesser amount to be used to purchase an annuity upon his death."

It is clear that the payments were partly for her benefit, partly for the benefit of others, i.e., the mother and the remainderman. The benefits purchased by her for others constituted gifts, whether she so intended or not.

Where a life tenant discharges the mortgage on the fee, he has under state law a right of reimbursement from the property interests owned by the remainderman. If the transaction is designed to and does destroy this right over, a gift has occurred. Difficult problems of interpreting the legal consequences of such a payment may be present. How and when is the right against the remainderman's interest barred? What is necessary to destroy this right? These are questions of local law.

11.17   Commercial transactions

The Regulations make it clear that no genuine business transaction comes within the purport of the gift tax by excluding "a sale, exchange, or the transfer of property made in the ordinary course of business, a transaction which is bona fide, at arm's length and free from any donative intent." A bad bargain will not result in gift tax, even though the disparity in consideration may be substantial. It is the interfamily transfers that cause trouble, but even here it is possible to have a genuine arm's length transaction. In one case a daughter transferred realty to her father in 1934. They became completely estranged following her marriage, and in 1942 she demanded the property back, alleging duress. After considerable negotiation the father paid her $120,000 for a general release. The Court refused to hold that a gift had occurred as the "petitioner was not actuated by love and affection or other motives which normally prompt the making of a gift . . . the settlement to which she agreed on her attorneys' advice was that which they and she regarded as advantageous economically under the circumstances."

11.18   Payments in excess of one's obligations

No gift occurs from the discharge of one's legal obligations. Thus payments made for the support of wife and minor children will not incur gift tax. But one may go beyond his obligation. Thus in *Hooker* two trusts were created by the taxpayer for the support of his minor children, pursuant to an agreement incorporated in a divorce decree. These trusts were held taxable gifts in so far as they exceeded the father's legal obligation, i.e., to support his children during minority. He may not avoid a gift tax by creating a support trust, with corpus going to the children after they reach specified ages. Only the value of that part of the transfer necessary to support the children until each reaches 21 may be deducted in computing the value of the gift. Assume a transfer in trust of $50,000, income to be used for the support of the grantor's child, now aged 16, with corpus to the child at 21. Assume further than $2,000 represents the annual support obligation. Here the taxable gift would be in excess of $40,000—the actual amount would be the present worth of the right to receive $50,000 five years from date.

Medical and hospital bills were paid by a father for his adult son, also certain living expenses, including payments on his mortgage. These were held gifts in Rev. Ruling 54–343. Parents generally have no obligation to support adult children. While there may be a tendency to question the validity of the ruling, on balance the result seems sound and desirable from the tax-payers' standpoint. A contrary ruling would have income and estate tax disadvantages. If a trust for the support of an adult child escaped gift tax because the income was being used to discharge the obligation of the grantor parent, the income would be taxable to the parent and the corpus would be part of his estate on the theory of a retained life estate. In *Greene* it was argued that since a California statute, under certain circumstances, required citizens to support needy relatives, that a legal obligation rested upon estate owners to support dependent adults. The courts held the transfers to such relatives were, nevertheless, taxable as gifts.

The extent of the parent's obligation is vague and uncertain. While family harmony exists the father determines his obligation within the widest limits. But he may go beyond recognized bounds. Thus a $25,000 piece of jewelry may not be brought within his obligation to property dress and adorn Mother or debutante Daughter. To what extent are payments for the maintenance of adult members of the household gifts? Here the law is uncertain. Furnishing them with clothing, food, shelter, use of family cars, and other personal property would seem to represent permitted use rather than transfers of property, see section 11.2. Ownership of these assets probably remains in the parent purchaser rather than the adult son or daughter to whose use they are allocated. On the other hand, actual money transfers such as monthly allowances, would clearly constitute taxable gifts.

11.19 Premarital settlements

A resident of Florida, about to marry a second time, entered into an agreement with his prospective bride under which he transferred $300,000 to her in exchange for a release of all rights she might acquire in his property as wife or widow, except the right to maintenance and support. He was worth at the time about $5,000,000. He was advanced in years and under the law of his domicile his wife was given a forced share in his estate of which she could not be deprived by will. All things considered, what she gave up most likely had a value well in excess of what she received. The Supreme Court, nevertheless, held the transfer taxable as a gift. The result carries out the policy of the gift tax. His estate was depleted by $300,000 and, had the transfer been delayed until death, no deduction for the obligation would have been allowable.[1] Hence the appropriateness of an imposition of the gift tax on the transfer.

In this type of settlement, as well as in the divorce settlements, next discussed, it should be remembered that what is a gift for gift tax purposes is not necessarily a gift for income tax purposes. If the husband had transferred securities worth $300,000 that had a cost basis to him of $100,000, it is likely he would have incurred a $200,000 capital gain, and the wife would have acquired a cost basis of $300,000 for the assets received by her.

In *Wemyss*, the taxpayer proposed marriage to a Mrs. More, a widow. Her deceased husband had set up a trust for her benefit during widowhood. She was unwilling to sacrifice this income and for that reason hesitated to accept the proposal. To induce her to marry him, the taxpayer transferred certain properties to her. The transfer was held taxable as a gift. While the promise to marry represents a valid consideration

---

[1] Other than the estate tax marital deduction.

to support a contract, it is not a consideration reducible to money value. To carry out the policy of the act, i.e., to impose a gift tax on transfers that avoid estate tax, "considerations not reducible to money value, such as love and affection, promises to marry, etc., are to be wholly disregarded."

11.20 Transfers on divorce

Suppose Husband agrees to give Wife $200,000 as a lump sum settlement on divorce in exchange for a release of all marital rights she may have in his estate. For years the taxability of such a transfer was uncertain. There is something to be said for treating it as a taxable gift since Husband reduces his estate by $200,000, whereas his obligation in most states is simply to support his spouse from month to month. On the other hand, the lump sum may have achieved a lesser payment than if spread over the period of his common law obligation which is limited to the period during which both are alive and she does not remarry. The issue finally came before the Supreme Court in the *Harris* case. The Court held the transfer in that case not a gift since the obligation was imposed by court decree, not by agreement.

The Code now makes it clear that where Husband and Wife enter into a written agreement relative to their marital and property rights and divorce occurs within two years thereafter any transfer pursuant to such agreement shall be deemed to be a transfer for full and adequate consideration in money or money's worth. Unfortunately the Code fails to include transfers based on separations or annulments. Further there is the two-year limitation which may raise occasional problems that will have to be settled under the rationale of the *Harris* case.

11.21 Gratuitous transfers pursuant to court order

Transfers made by a guardian or committee of an incompetent pursuant to court order have been held subject to gift tax. Under the laws of most, if not all, jurisdictions, the court may order distribution to relatives and dependents of an incompetent if the incompetent's estate is more than adequate for his needs and the recipients are persons who will share in his estate or to whom he would have made donations were he competent. Taxing such transfers seems clearly within the policy of the gift tax, since if the transfers were not made, the funds would incur estate tax upon the deaths of the incompetents.

Gifts of income items

11.22   Gifts of past or future earnings

The Supreme Court early held that an assignment of future earnings would not be effective to shift the income tax liability to the donee. In the famous case of *Lucas* v. *Earl,* the taxpayer had agreed in 1901, on his marriage, that his wife should own half of whatever he earned. But the Court held he was taxable on the entire income, Mr. Justice Holmes saying, "There is no doubt the statute could tax salaries to those who earn them and provide that the tax could not be escaped by anticipatory arrangements, however skillfully devised to prevent the salary when paid from vesting even for a second in the man who earned it. That seems to use the import of the statute before us and we think that no distinction can be taken according to the motives leading to the arrangement by which the fruits are attributed to the different tree than that on which they grew."

In *Eubank* the taxpayer had been a general agent for a life insurance company. After the termination of his agency he assigned renewal commissions, which would thereafter become payable to him, to his wife. The Court held the commissions, when paid, taxable to him.

A physician transferred to a trust for the benefit of his child certain accounts receivable arising out of his professional practice. The transfers were irrevocable. He was nevertheless held taxable on the amounts as collected by the trustee.

In all cases like the above gift taxes will be incurred, measured by the present worth of the rights transferred. It is immaterial that no income tax shifting occurs, since an estate tax advantage may be secured by such transfers. But gifts of earnings, future or past, are not desirable since they incur gift tax without any corresponding income tax savings.

11.23   Gifts of income from property

An assignment of next year's dividends from a certain stock or next year's rent from a certain building will not shift income tax to the donee but will incur gift tax. Thus, in *Horst,* the donor removed an unmatured interest coupon from a bond and gave the coupon to his son. The interest was held taxable to the donor. In these cases the fruit-tree doctrine of Mr. Justice Holmes was applied. In *Galt* v. *Commissioner* a father assigned 20 percent of certain rentals to each of his three sons. It will be remembered, see section 11.8, that the assignment incurred immediate gift tax. He was, nevertheless, subject to income tax on the rentals as paid to the sons.

11.24   Gifts of property

On the other hand, it is clear that if the tree is given, all future fruit will be taxed to the donee. Thus if General Motors, costing $1,000 is transferred to Son when it has a value of $3,000 and Son later sells it for $3,500, the entire gain is shifted to Son's tax return. This result is to be compared with *Austin* v. *Commissioner* in which a wife gave the children certain notes which she had received from her husband in exchange for loans made to him. At the time of the transfer, accumulated unpaid interest amounted to $43,320. The husband was killed shortly thereafter. His executor paid the interest. The wife was held taxable on the interest paid to the children covering the period when she owned the note, the children were held taxable on the interest that accrued from the time they acquired the note. This represents a logical development of the *Horst* case. The fruit that accrued while the wife owned the tree was taxable to her. It had ripened; only the act of plucking remained to be done. On the other hand, in the sale of General Motors stock something further, i.e., the sale, was required to mature the fruit.

But the fruit must have matured to have the *Austin* case apply. Thus in *Bishop* preferred stock in a closely held corporation was given by Father to Son. Shortly thereafter back dividends were paid. Held these were taxable to Son, the Court stressing the facts that no right to the dividends existed at the time of the gift.

11.25 Income or capital

From the discussion above it is clear that if a lawyer draws a will and assigns the right to receive the fee, the fee will nevertheless, be taxable to him. Suppose an artist paints a beautiful picture and gives this to his daughter. She later sells it. The cases indicate that the proceeds are taxable to the daughter, even though the receipt is essentially an income item. It is, nevertheless, property that has yet to mature. In *Campbell* v. *Protho* calves were given to the Young Men's Christian Association and sold by them.[2] The Commissioner attempted to tax the proceeds to the donor. The taxpayer prevailed in the District Court and the collector appealed.

Sustaining the lower court, the Circuit Court said:

The collector insists that, because the calves were kept for sale in the ordinary business of the partnership of which Protho was a member, the expense of raising them had been allowed as deductions, and the proceeds of the calves if sold by taxpayers would have been ordinary income, the case is ruled by *Helvering* v. *Horst,* in which it is in effect held that when the right of one to collect income is given to another and that other receives it, the giver is taxable on the income in the same way and to the same extent as he would have been if he had collected the income and then given it to the donee.

The taxpayer, analyzing and discussing the cases cited by the collector, including the *Horst* case, asserts that the transaction in question here

---

[2] Under the Tax Reform Act of 1969 the charitable deduction would be limited in this case to the donor's cost basis, if any.

is not a *Horst* case transaction, nor is it similar to the transactions dealt with in the other cases the collector cites. Expanding his views, the taxpayer says:

The fundamental defect in the Government's position in the case at bar is that the animals here in question did not per se represent "income." The plan or scheme of the income-taxing acts is that from the realized and recognized gross income of the taxpayers, there is subtracted or withdrawn all deductions allowed by law, and the remaining balance or net taxable income subjected to tax.

. . . Compensation for personal services and periodical returns from capital investments become "gross income" when earned, although the time when the taxpayer is required to recognize them, that is report them for taxation, depends on taxpayer's method of accounting. Gains from the sale or exchange of property, on the other hand, do not arise, and therefore do not constitute "gross income" until a sale or exchange for value has been consummated, regardless of taxpayer's method of accounting.

. . . Raised livestock does not constitute income per se. This is because raised livestock are not claims or demands representing income fully earned but are instead chattels created by the livestock raiser through the instrumentality of his breeding herd and having an independent basis for gain or loss in his hands. . . . Gains from raised animals can only be realized if and when they are sold or disposed of by their owner for value in a taxable transaction.

11.26   Gifts of life estates

In *Blair* v. *Commissioner* the life income beneficiary of a trust assigned all his right, title and interest therein to his children. The Supreme Court held the income taxable to the donees, on the theory that something more than the right to future income was given. "The will creating the trust entitled the petitioner during his life to the net income from the trust. He thus became the owner of an equitable interest in the corpus of the property." The Court thought of the life estate as the tree rather than the fruit. Query, if this is the place to draw the line. The decision has been criticized but never overruled. Thus in *Bell's Estate,* the Circuit Court said "There can be no question that the Supreme Court ruled that the assignments of life interests . . . are transfers of interests in trust assets and not merely assignments of income. . . . The

Supreme Court has not, expressly or by implication, overruled or modified its decision and it is not for this Court to unmake it."

The Treasury has recently ruled, in conformity with the codification of the Clifford Regulations, see chapter 14, that where an assignment of trust income is for a period of ten years or more "the life income beneficiary will be considered to have made a disposition of a substantial interest in the trust property" and the income will be taxable to the assignee. Further it is now settled by the Code that a trust to last for at least ten years will shift the income tax to the donee, even though the donor retains an indefeasibly vested reversion in the corpus.

On the other hand the assignment of rentals under a 20-year lease was held ineffective to shift the tax to the donee in *Galt* v. *Commissioner* and it is at least doubtful that a gift of 11 years of unmatured coupons would have changed the result in the *Horst* case.

Why the trust should have received favored treatment is difficult to understand other than as a matter of historical accident. Under present law trusts are not to be taxed under Section 61, the catch-all section of the Code defining gross income. While this was not true prior to 1954 the Courts were reluctant to disregard the special trust sections and the Supreme Court did it only for what were called short-term trusts. It also seems illogical to recognize for tax purposes the assignment of a life interest (where the expectancy may be 10 or less years) but to refuse to recognize the assignment of 20 years of income from a lease.

11.27 Family partnerships

With high corporate taxes during the war there was a tremendous shift to the partnership form of doing business. This was followed by gifts of partnership interests to wives and children in order to keep the earnings in lower tax brackets. In one case it was said that the instruments had been fully drafted with a blank left for the insertion of the name of the momentarily expected offspring as soon as word of the sex was received from the hospital. The pressure for additional partners was such that one wife, in response to questioning on cross examination concerning her participation in management of the business, stated she was too busy producing partners to be otherwise productive in the business.

Most of the partnerships were obviously sham. Father would come home one evening with a batch of papers to be signed. They had something to do with business and taxes. That was enough for the family to know. When Mother discovered her status as partner, a mild request that the blond secretary be discharged would be met by Father's curt statement, that if Mother would run the home, he would run the business.

The first Supreme Court case placed heavy emphasis on the rendition of services or the contribution of capital as vital elements in determining whether the partnership was genuine. The later *Culbertson* case indicated that what was important was that "the partners really and truly intended to join together for the purpose of carrying on the business," . . . "Whether the parties in good faith and acting with a business purpose intended to join together in the present conduct of the enterprise." These statements appear again and again in the opinion. The Court pointed out "that things may not be what they seem," that later conduct may belie the words of the written agreement. The test is and was whether the partnership was real or a sham. What partner, with 20 percent interest in the capital, would work 12 or 14 hours a day without compensation, while his 4 fellow partners and equal sharers in the profits, lolled on the sands of Florida? Such an arrangement would make no business sense. Yet this was typical of the family partnership. Father who had previously earned $100,000 a year, with always a large portion, and frequently the lion's share, being due to his untiring personal service, would suddenly wind up with $20,000 a year, though he still did all the work and assumed all the responsibility, Mother and three children dividing the other $80,000.

These partnerships may be classified into two groups, (1) where capital is the substantial income-producing factor, and

(2) where services are the substantial income-producing factor. Both will be factors in practically all businesses but in many one or the other will predominate in varying degrees. In the pure personal service business the family partnership arrangement is obviously an assignment of future earnings. As capital becomes more important in the production of the income, the partnership may be more readily justified. But even here, if the contract is to be accepted as having a business purpose, the working partner's services require some monetary recognition. This is the result which Congress finally evolved.

Section 704 (e) of the Internal Revenue Code now provides:

1. *Recognition of interest created by purchase or gift*   A person shall be recognized as a partner for purposes of this subtitle if he owns a capital interest in a partnership in which capital is a material income-producing factor, whether or not such interest was derived by purchase or gift from any other person.

2. *Distributive share of donee includible in gross income*   In the case of any partnership interest created by gift, the distributive share of the donee under the partnership agreement shall be includible in his gross income, except to the extent that such share is determined without allowance of reasonable compensation for services rendered to the partnership by the donor, and except to the extent that the portion of such share of the donor attributable to the donor's capital. The distributive share of a partner in the earnings of the partnership shall not be diminished because of absence due to military service.

3. *Purchase of interest by member of family*   For the purposes of this section, an interest purchased by one member of a family from another shall be considered to be created by gift from the seller, and the fair market value of the purchased interest shall be considered to be donated capital. The "family" of any individual shall include only his spouse, ancestors, and lineal descendants, and any trusts for the primary benefit of such persons.

The Senate Finance Committee Report in explaining the Section, states:

Section 339 of your committee's bill (Sec. 191, '39 Code; Sec. 704(e), '54 Code) is intended to harmonize the rules governing interests in the so-called family partnership with those generally applicable to other forms of property or business. Two principles governing attribution of income have long been accepted as basic: (1) income from property is attributable to the owner of the property; (2) income from personal services is attributable to the person rendering the services. There is no reason for applying different principles to partnership income. If an individual makes a bona fide gift of real estate, or of a share of corporate stock, the rent or dividend income is taxable to the donee. Your committee's amendment makes it clear that however the owner of a partnership interest may have acquired such interest, the income is taxable to the owner, if he is the real owner. If the ownership is real, it does not matter what motivated the transfer to him or whether the business benefited from the entrance of the new partner.

Although there is no basis under existing statutes for any different treatment of partnership interests, some decisions in this field have ignored the principle that income from property is to be taxed to the owner of the property. Many court decisions since the decision of the Supreme Court in *Commissioner* v. *Culbertson* have held invalid for tax purposes family partnerships which arose by virtue of a gift of a partnership interest from one member of a family to another, where the donee performed no vital services for the partnership. Some of these cases apparently proceed upon the theory that a partnership cannot be valid for tax purposes unless the intrafamily gift of capital is motivated by a desire to benefit the partnership business. Others seem to assume that a gift of a partnership interest is not complete because the donor contemplates the continued participation in the business of the donated capital. However, the frequency with which the Tax Court, since the *Culbertson* decision, has held invalid family partnerships based upon donations of capital, would seem to indicate that, although the opinions often refer to "intention," "business purpose," "reality," and "control" they have in practical effect reached results which suggest that an intrafamily gift of a partnership interest, where the donee performs no substantial services, will not usually be the basis of a valid partnership for tax purposes. We are informed that the settlement of many cases in the field is being held up by the reliance of the field officer of the Bureau of Internal Revenue upon some such theory. Whether or not the opinion of the Supreme Court in *Commissioner* v. *Tower* and the opinion of the Supreme Court in *Commissioner* v. *Culbertson,* which attempted to explain the *Tower* decision, afford any justification for the confusion is not material—the confusion exists.

The amendment leaves the Commissioner and the courts free to inquire in any case whether the donee or purchaser actually owns the interest in the partnership, which the transferor purports to have given or sold him. Cases will arise where the gift or sale is a mere sham. Other cases will arise where the transferor retains so many of the incidents of ownership that he will continue to be recognized as a substantial owner of the interest which he purports to have given away, as was held by the Supreme Court in an analogous trust situation involved in the case of *Helvering* v. *Clifford.* The same standards apply in determining the bona fides of alleged family partnerships as in determining the bona fides of other transactions between family members. Transactions between persons in a close family group, whether or not involving partnership interests, afford much opportunity for the deception and should be subject to close scrutiny. All the facts and circumstances at the time of the purported gift and during the periods preceding and following it may be taken into consideration in determining the bona fides or lack of bona fides of a purported gift or sale.

Not every restriction upon the complete and unfettered control by the donee of the property donated will be indicative of sham in the transaction. Contractual restriction may be of the character incident to the normal relationships among partners. Substantial powers may be retained by the transferor as a managing partner or in any other fiduciary capacity which, when considered in the light of all circumstances, will not indicate any lack of true ownership in the transferee. In weighing the effect of a retention of any power upon the bona fides of a purported gift or sale, a power exercisable for the benefit of others must be distinguished from a power vested in the transferor for his own benefit.

Since legislation is now necessary to make clear the fundamental principle that, where there is a real transfer of ownership, a gift of a family partnership interest is to be respected for tax purposes without regard to the motives which actuated the transfer, it is considered appropriate at the same time to provide specific safeguards—whether or not such safeguards may be inherent in the general rule—against the use of partnership device to accomplish the deflection of income from the real owner.

Therefore, the bill provides that in the case of any partnership interest created by gift the allocation of income, according to the terms of the partnership agreement, shall be controlling for income tax purposes except when the shares are allocated without proper allowance of reasonable compensation for services rendered to the partnership by the donor, and except to the extent that the allocation to the donated capital is proportionately greater than that attributable to the donor's capital. In such cases a reasonable allowance will be made for the services rendered by the partners, and the balance of the income will be allocated according to the amount of capital which the several partners have invested. However, the distributive share of a partner in the earnings of the partnership will not be diminished because of absence due to military service.

11.28 Family corporations

Gifts of stock in closely held family corporations have been held to shift the income tax on the earnings to the new owners, even though they rendered no service and had contributed no capital of their own to the venture. The obvious reason is that the working stockholder (except in Subchapter S cases) always drew a salary commensurate with the value of his services. The corporate income tax deduction for compensation paid was enough to assure that this would be true in practically all cases. Thus the profits going to the donee-nonworkers was most likely to bear a reasonable relation to the value of the capital owned by them. Since this made business sense the transfers escaped being classified as sham. But like the family partnership, the allocation of interests in the family corporation must have rational basis. In *Overton,* X and Y owned all the stock of a corporation. They caused the corporation to issue a new class B stock, entitled to dividends only after the old stock had been paid $10 a share. The B stock was to receive $1 on dissolution, all other assets going to the old stock. The old stock retained all voting rights. The B stock was given to the wives of X and Y. The wives then received large dividends. Held: These were taxable to the husbands on the theory they were assignments of future dividends, not gifts of capital. The court said:

The Tax Court was of opinion that the 1936 arrangement, though made in the form of a gift of stock, was in reality an assignment of part of the taxpayers' future dividends. Unless form is to be exalted above substance this conclusion is inescapable. Since the total issue of B stock represented only $1,000 of the corporate assets, it is plain that the property which earned the large dividends received by the B shareholder was the property represented by the A stock held by the husbands. In transferring the B shares to their wives they parted with no substantial part of their interest in the corporate property. Had they been content to transfer some of the original common stock, they could have accomplished their purpose of lessening taxes on the family group, but they would then have made substantial gifts of capital. The arrangement they put into effect gave the wives nothing, or substantially nothing, but the right to future earnings flowing from property retained by the husbands. That anticipatory assignments of income, whatever their formal cloak, are ineffective taxwise is a principle too firmly established to be subject to question."

I 2

Gifts in contemplation of death

12.1   Introduction

From the standpoint of the estate planner the problems raised by the possibility that gifts may be held to be in contemplation of death represent a major consideration in most planning. The obvious reason is that estate owners generally are hesitant about making substantial transfers until they reach relatively mature ages, or are visited with illnesses that may prove fatal. At 50 or 55 the average man prefers to retain control over his wealth. He wants to avoid estate taxes but understandably believes that this is an objective he can achieve at 70, as easily as now. He remembers the depression and appreciates the ease with which inflated values can disappear into thin air with any substantial business recession. While there are exceptions, the person willing to make gifts is generally between 70 and 80 and frequently older before he is willing to part with any material portion of his property. His health will almost always leave something to be desired. This is not to suggest that all such gifts are motivated primarily by thoughts of death. With age comes a lessening of the acquisitive instinct. The need for substantial reserves diminishes. The burdens and problems of property management become more annoying. The capacity of grown children, now in the middle of life, to manage is more clearly recognized. The heavy impact of income taxes on income used for the family, rather than the owner, furnishes a potent argument for gifts. Frequently the children upon whose advice and guidance the aged parent has come to rely, will be the ones who in fact contemplate the death as they urge that gifts be made.

Motives will generally be mixed. There will be recognition on the part of the donor that gifts will remove property from his taxable estate but there will also be other motives and the issue will therefore always be a factual one.

12.2   The Statute

Section 2035 requires the inclusion in the gross estate of all transfers, for less than a full and adequate consideration, made by the decedent within three years of the date of his death, in contemplation thereof. All such transfers are presumptively so made but the Commissioner may not include any gifts completed more than three years before death, no matter how clear the evidence that death was the primary motivation.

12.3 The requirement of a transfer

The term transfer includes any exercise or release of a power of appointment. Thus if X, having a general power of appointment under the will of his father, exercises or releases it within three years of death, the property over which the power existed may, nevertheless, be included as part of his taxable estate, unless it is affirmatively demonstrated that the exercise or release was prompted by thoughts associated with continued life, rather than death. Further with respect to retained powers (as contrasted with donated powers, chapter 14) the exercise or release of any power which would have caused the inclusion of the property in the gross estate of the grantor may be attacked as a transfer in contemplation of death, if death occurs within the three-year period.

On the other hand, renunciations of donated powers may be freely made, since, while the exercise or release of a power is treated as a transfer, a renunciation is not. Suppose Grandfather leaves his estate to Son, with a further provision that, if the bequest lapses, it shall pass to Grandson. Son, being in poor health and anticipating an early death, declines to accept the bequest. His prompt refusal does not constitute a transfer within the statute. But note that if Grandfather had died intestate the result might be different since, under the laws of some jurisdictions, an heir has no power to renounce. The law vests the property in him and he can get rid of it only by an assignment. See section 11.10.

The requirement of a "transfer" has important tax consequences in other situations. Suppose Husband and Wife own Blackacre as joint tenants with right of survivorship. Husband paid the full purchase price and therefore on his death the full value of Blackacre will be included in his taxable estate. In contemplation of his death they convey the property to Son. Most cases have held that only one-half the value of Blackacre may be included in Husband's estate since he transferred only one-half.

12.4   *Valuation*

The value of the property to be included in the estate is its fair market value at the date of death rather than at the date of gift, less the value of any improvements or additions made by the donee. This can present difficult problems if the asset given is converted into other property by the donee prior to the donor's death. Assume a gift of 1000 shares of X Motors worth $50,000 on the date of gift, $100,000 on the date of the donor's death. Further assume the donee sold the X Motors for $45,000 shortly after the gift and purchased Y Motors, which on the date of death had declined in value to $25,000. There are three possible solutions, any one of which might be adopted: (1) The specific property transferred might be valued as of the date of death in spite of the prior sale; (2) the property might be valued as of the date of sale; or (3) the proceeds might be traced and the substituted property acquired by the donee be valued at the date of death. In the case suggested, the application of the first alternative might create a tremendous hardship; there seems no legal basis for the second; the third would appear to operate most fairly except for the often insoluble problem of tracing the gift through a series of reinvestments in which the proceeds of individual transactions have been temporarily mingled with the donee's general funds.

There are no published rulings by the Internal Revenue Service on this question. The practice, however, is generally to make a distinction between outright gifts and gifts in trust. In the case of transfers in trust the property is regarded as a single unit, the trust fund; no attention is paid to the specific items making up the fund. Thus the property comprising the trust fund at death is valued, whenever this becomes necessary, regardless of any reinvestments which may have been made. But in the case of the outright gift it is understood to be the

Treasury practice to value the specific property transferred as of the date of death, even though it is no longer owned by the donee. This would, of course, operate to favor the estate if X Motors had gone down and Y Motors, up. But in planning for the unpredictable future, conservatism would suggest the use of a trust. If the new investment has increased in value while the old decreases, an added tax will be incurred, but there will be funds with which to pay the heavier tax. If, however, the reverse happens and the gift has been outright, taxes will be imposed on nonexistent values.

Motives

12.5 Definition

The ultimate fact to be found in determining whether the gift was in contemplation of death is whether the transfer was motivated by thoughts of living or by thoughts of dying. The leading case in the Supreme Court is *United States* v. *Wells*. There the Court said:

. . . It is recognized that the reference is not to the general expectation of death which all entertain. It must be a particular concern, giving rise to a definite motive. The provision is not confined to gifts causa mortis, which are made in anticipation of impending death, are revocable, and are defeated if the donor survives the apprehended peril. The statutory description embraces gifts inter vivos, despite the fact that they are fully executed, are irrevocable and indefeasible. The quality which brings the transfer within the statute is indicated by the context and manifest purpose. Transfers in contemplation of death are included within the same category, for the purpose of taxation, with transfers intended to take effect at or after the death of the transferor. The dominant purpose is to reach substitutes for testamentary dispositions and thus to prevent the evasion of the estate tax.

As the test, despite varying circumstances, is always to be found in motive, it cannot be said that the determinative motive is lacking merely because of the absence of a consciousness that death is imminent. It is contemplation of death, not necessarily contemplation of imminent death to which the statute refers. It is conceivable that the idea of death may possess the mind so as to furnish a controlling motive for the disposition of property, although death is not thought to be close at hand. Old age may give premonitions and promptings independent of mortal disease. Yet age in itself cannot be regarded as furnishing a decisive test, for sound health and purposes associated with life, rather than with death, may motivate the transfer. The words, "in contemplation of death" mean that the thought of death is the impelling cause of the transfer, and while the belief in the imminence of death may afford convincing evidence, the statute is not to be limited, and its purpose thwarted, by a rule of construction which in place of contemplation of death makes the final criterion to be an apprehension that death is "near at hand."

It is apparent that there can be no precise delimitation of the transactions embraced within the conception of transfers in "contemplation of death," as there can be none in relation to fraud, undue influence, due process of law, or other familiar legal concepts which are applicable to many varying circumstances. There is no escape from the necessity of carefully scrutinizing the circumstances of each case to detect the dominant motive of the donor in the light of his bodily and mental condition, and thus give effect to the manifest purpose of the statute.

We think that the Government is right in its criticism of the narrowness of the rule laid down by the Court of Claims, in requiring that there be a condition "creating a reasonable fear that death is near at hand" and that "such reasonable fear or apprehension" must be "the only cause of the transfer." It is sufficient if contemplation of death be the inducing cause of the transfer whether or not death is believed to be near.

12.6 *Mixed motives*

There will practically always be several motives. The *Wells* case is generally accepted as requiring that death be found to be the primary reason, before the transfer may be included as one in contemplation of death within the meaning of the statute. This interpretation has not, however, gone unchallenged. In *Farmers Loan and Trust Co.* v. *Bowers* it appeared that William Waldorf Astor had given away about $46,000,000 worth of New York City real estate. Evidence of three substantial motivating influences were introduced: (1) the desire to save income taxes, (2) the fear of a capital levy, and (3) avoidance of death taxes. The trial judged instructed the jury that if they "concluded from all the evidence in the case that there were several motives for the transfers—one being to avoid the estate tax, another being to avoid or reduce income tax, and still another being to escape a possible capital levy by the British Government, and if you are of the belief that the motive of avoiding the estate tax played a substantial part in causing Astor to make the transfers, the transfers must be held to have been made in contemplation of death, and your verdict should be for the defendant."

The problem of determining the donor's motivation, frequently years after the transfer, at best calls for a wild guess. Frequently the donor himself may not have been very clear as to his motivation. Many persons, having decided on a course of action, begin to marshall reasons to justify contemplated acts. Further, in the case of gifts, the real or the supposed real reasons may be carefully concealed by the donor for any one of a dozen family reasons. The concept, while necessary to protect the estate tax, is extremely vague and unsatisfactory. It seems unfortunate to add to it the complexities of the "substantial producing cause" doctrine, rather than the simple and more accurate test of "the primary" or "the compelling clause," particularly in view of the frequency with which this issue is litigated to a jury. Further this latter test would appear to be required by the clear language of the *Wells* case.

12.7   *Motives associated with thoughts of continued life*

Where thoughts of continued life motivate the transfer, the gift is not one in contemplation of death. Among the motives associated with life rather than death a few may be listed as illustrative of the concept.

1. The desire to avoid income taxes.
2. The desire to be relieved of the burdens of property management.
3. The desire to fulfill moral obligations.
4. The desire to be relieved of harassment from constant money demands of children and other near relatives.
5. The desire to see children independently settled in life.
6. The desire to see how the children manage property in

order to determine the form that later testamentary gifts should take.

The list could be continued endlessly. Transfers may be made to avoid marital difficulties in the family, to induce a son to remain in the family business, to encourage children to go into business of their own, to develop financial responsibility, to equalize the children's wealths where one inherits from a relative to the exclusion of the others, etc. Professor Griswold has said, "It is the rare case that does not leave the lawyer an opening to show that some motive other than the thought of death was the inducement for the gift."

If the desire is to reduce income taxes, the donor is obviously thinking about living. Only if he lives will the savings be realized through spreading the income among several tax entities, including himself. Again, if he wants to observe how the children manage property, he contemplates the opportunity of watching the results. If he thinks he is going to die, there is little point in planning to be relieved of the burdens of property management or of the harrassment that comes from constant money demands of the children, etc. Thus the attainment of many objectives are conditioned upon continued life. Others may be thought of as neutral in character, as the fulfillment of moral obligations or the equalization of children's shares, but are definitely not suggestive of thoughts of death.

12.8   Motives associated with thoughts of death

There are some motives and some transfers that are clearly testamentary in character.

1. The desire to avoid death taxes.
2. Advancements in lieu of bequests.
3. Transfers with enjoyment postponed until death.

Where a child is given a substantial portion of the estate, prior to his parent's death, with the intention that the gift shall be charged against his intestate share, or be in lieu of a bequest by will, the gift is a testamentary substitute. Antenuptial agreements are vulnerable to this argument. In *Kroger* the decedent, just before his second marriage, transferred property to his intended wife, the dominant motive being the desire to bar her from any statutory rights of dower in his estate. The transfer was held to be in contemplation of death. In *Burns,* a decedent created a trust for his incompetent son, consisting of one fourth of his estate. By will he divided the balance among his other three children. The incompetent was and had always been taken care of by the decedent. Thus there was no immediate need for the gift. The transfer was held to be in contemplation of death since only with death would the gift begin to serve any real purpose. Further it was clearly a part of the overall testamentary plan. A few cases seem to go contra to *Burns* on the theory that such a transfer may be made to obtain *present* "peace of mind" and "freedom from worry" and hence may be life motivated.

Similarly a gift, in trust, with income to be accumulated during the life of the grantor, is strongly suggestive of a primary death motive. Since the gift will take on real meaning only at the grantor's death, it is hard to think of a clearer substitute for a testamentary disposition.

12.9   *Evidential value of expressions of intent*

The donor is in a unique position with respect to the creation of evidence as to his motivation. He and his advisers set the stage, write the dialogue and direct the players in the little drama that is being prepared for the grand opening that is expected to follow if the donor dies before obtaining the shelter of the three-year statutory limitation. Too often the script, because of its very perfection, belies the words used. Whether thoughts of death or of continued life motivate the transfer, the estate owners' advisers are bound to recognize the risk that, right or wrong, the issue of contemplation of death may be raised. Hence the instrument of transfer will often recite life reasons and studiously avoid any possible recitations of motives that might be suggestive of thoughts of death. Query if zealous counsel do not too often overemphasize this motivation to the detriment of the estate. In any event, objective evidence will frequently rebut the recitations in the instrument. For this reason it is believed that, if life motives predominate, more care should be taken in the selection of the type and amount of property, the form and terms of the gift, and the evidence concerning the health of the donor, than in studying the decided cases to determine what verbal expressions of intent may help to avoid a finding of contemplation of death.

Significant evidentiary factors

12.10 Age

Age will always be an extremely vital factor but advanced age is never conclusive. Transfers by decedents in their 80s have been held not to have been in contemplation of death. Much depends on the health, vigor, future plans of the donor and the validity of the lifetime motives that may have prompted the gift. In any event there is nothing the estate planner can do but accept the fact of his client's age, with the realization that clients who are 85 sometimes live until 88. And, as appears later, nothing is to be lost even if the contemplated transfer is determined to have been made in contemplation of death.

12.11 Health

Health is one of the most important evidentiary factors. Where a donor is demonstrably in poor health at the date of the gift and dies shortly thereafter, it is extremely difficult to avoid the inference that failing health prompted the transfer. But as the test is subjective, i.e., what was actually in the mind of the donor, if it can be shown that he had no knowledge of the disease or malady, the inference from his poor health loses its validity.

12.12   Percentage of property given

It is frequently stated that where a large percentage of the estate owner's assets, in relation to his overall wealth, is given, this points to contemplation of death. It is true that only in advanced age is one likely to strip himself of the major part of his property but it is equally true that this may occur without any thought of approaching death. With age, needs and desires decrease. Pleasures come from seeing others comfortably settled in life. Management problems become irksome. The decided cases do not bear out the conclusion that the percentage given has more than very slight evidentiary value. Of course, there will be cases when a comparison with what was given and what was retained is strongly suggestive of the fact that both gift and estate tax tables were carefully studied to arrive at the maximum amount that could be transferred cheaper by gift than at death. Generally, however, other factors will account for the size of the transfer, i.e., the nature of the properties, the objectives the transfer was intended to achieve, etc.

12.13   The nature of the property given

Perhaps the most important factor is the type of property given. A life insurance policy is particularly vulnerable to attack, as insurance is intimately connected with death. As a practical matter, enjoyment is delayed until the death of the insured. Unproductive property is subject to the same criticism. Unless the donee really gets something he can immediately enjoy, the validity of the lifetime reasons becomes doubtful. These transfers are similar to those trusts in which the trustee is directed to accumulate the income until the death of the grantor.

Learned Hand has put the argument most strongly in *Vanderlip* v. *Commissioner* when he said:

All gifts necessarily differ from bequests in that they deprive the donor of future control over the property, and for that reason they can never be perfect substitutes; but if the effect of the gift is substantially the same as the gift of a remainder; that is, if the donor reserves the income to himself during his life, it is as nearly a substitute for a bequest as it can be and still remain a gift at all. . . . When the property produces no income, living the donor, . . . it may be open to question whether any motive can exclude it from his estate. . . . Situations may be put in which it might be plausibly argued that motive would be relevant: for example, the donor may wish to protect the property against the hazards of his business, or against a possible change in his feelings towards the donee, or he may contemplate getting married and losing power of disposal over all his property. Whether these would affect the result, we leave open because here the donor only desired to avoid estate taxes, and we cannot see how that can be classed among those motives which will on any theory take a gift out of the Section. A gift differs from a bequest,—apart from the inevitable loss of control over the property— only in so far as it secures enjoyment to the donee during the donor's life; and the donor's motives are relevant to exclude the property only so far as they touch upon his enjoyment in that period. The motive to avoid taxes does not touch that at all; a donor, interested in saving taxes, is not concerned with the donee's enjoyment while he himself lives; he is interested in relieving his legatees from taxes after he dies, and, not only may his legatees not be the donees, but when they are, their relief will not concern their enjoyment of the property while he lives. Such a motive is necessarily testamentary, and not donative.

12.14 Concurrent making of will

If the estate owner executes a new will at the same time the deeds of gift are executed and delivered, it may be difficult to escape the conclusion that he was thinking about death in connection with the overall transaction. At least, this has been said to be true. The inference, however, is most unfortunate and its correctness may be questioned. Wholly aside from the motivation for the lifetime transfer, the fact that the client is in his lawyer's office, makes the occasion appropriate for the execution of a new will. Wills ought to be reviewed periodically. Rarely does a client take the initiative of suggesting a review. Lawyers are heistant to urge such action lest they be thought of as seeking business. In the course of a conference on unrelated matters the question is likely to arise. Thus the revision of a will may occur at a time when contracts or deeds of sale are being drafted as well as when gift transactions are under consideration.

**Reasons for making gifts that may be vulnerable
to the contemplation of death section**

12.15   The three-year limitation

One should never hesitate to make gifts in contemplation of death, provided the amount given is not so large that the cost by gift is in excess of the cost of giving by death. It is surprising how many people who are 80 live to be 83. If the client is in reasonably good health there will generally be a fair chance that he may outlive the three-year statutory period. If he does, the Commissioner may not include the transfer as one in contemplation of death, no matter how clear the evidence that the gift was so motivated.

12.16   Litigation possibilities

The government has not been particularly successful in the contemplation of death cases, having lost considerably more than they have won. While estimates vary, it is generally said that the taxpayer is successful in about 70 percent of the cases tried. The reason is that executors usually pay the tax and sue for a refund in the District Court in order to have the issue determined by a jury. Juries have generally been sympathetic to the taxpayers.

12.17   Possibility of settlement by compromise

Because of the Government's lack of success in litigation the Service is generally eager to settle these cases by compromise. In *Horlick* $8,000,000 of stock was given to the children. The Commissioner included it as a gift in contemplation of death. After some negotiation the taxpayer consented to a proposed deficiency of $4,000,000 on account of the gift. This was a pure compromise. It is not clear whether it was arrived at by valuing the total stock at half its value or by treating half of the property as given in contemplation and half not. On its face either proposition would seem absurd. The property was worth twice $4,000,000 and since it was all given the same day, it is a little difficult to see how he could have been motivated by thoughts of dying as to half the shares and not as to the other half. However, the Commissioner has authority to settle cases whenever there is substantial doubt as to the law or the facts. Whenever there are risks that the case may be decided either way, he can settle on a fair appraisal of those risks.

Every estate tax return will have in it a number of questionable items. There may be gifts in each of the three years immediately preceding death. Here, depending on the strength of the arguments, the taxpayer may yield on the last or last two gifts in exchange for an agreement not to include the first.

In every estate there will be valuation problems. Reasonable minds may differ considerably as to the value of closely held stock or unimproved real estate. Assume the Commissioner is arguing for a $200,000 valuation of the stock in the family business, the taxpayer for a figure around $125,000. This can be settled only by each side giving a little. In this type situation it is extremely comforting to have a contemplation-of-death issue. Even if a weak case it will furnish a powerful bargaining weapon in settling the other issues. The taxpayer may concede the gift as in contemplation of death in exchange for a low value. Or he may concede a high value if the gift is omitted.

12.18 Cases that cannot be settled

There may be gifts so clearly promoted by thoughts of death that no compromise is possible and the taxpayer either concedes the issue or loses after litigation. Even in these extreme cases the gift in contemplation of death will prove profitable because of the peculiar wording of the statutory provisions. There is a kind of double deduction that can best be illustrated by an example (which sacrifices technical accuracy for simplicity).

1. Net taxable estate..........................		$400,000	
Estate tax................................		94,500	
Passes to heir............................			$305,500
2. Net estate..............................		$400,000	
Gifts to heir.............	$200,000		
Gift tax...............	31,000		
Total......................................		231,000	
		$169,000	
Net estate at death......	169,000		
Inclusion of gift in contemplation of death.....	200,000		
Net taxable estate................		$369,000	
Estate tax..............	84,900		
Less gift tax credit.......	31,000		
Total tax payable.................		53,900	
Net estate at death..........................		$169,000	
Tax after credit..............................		53,900	
		$115,100	
Passes to heir on death......................................			$115,100
Passes by inter vivos gift...................................			200,000
			$315,100

SUMMARY

Property passing to heir, partly by gift in contemplation of death, partly by will...	$315,100
Property passing to heir by will.............................	305,500
Difference...	$ 9,600

A gift in contemplation of death always saves an amount equal to the top estate tax bracket on the amount of gift tax incurred, except where a larger gift tax is incurred than the estate tax avoided. Thus an estate owner with a building worth $60,000 and $10,000 of other assets conveyed the building to his daughter two months before his death. It had a cost basis to him of $20,000. She sold it for $60,000 shortly thereafter. Confronted with a long-term capital gain of $40,000, she for the first time sought advice. Could she avoid the capital gains tax if the transfer was in contemplation of death? Quite possibly yes, but her father's estate owed a gift tax of more than the estate tax he hoped to avoid, since he had made a gift of $60,000 minus his $30,000 exemption and $3,000 exclusion.

13

Sales within the family

13.1   *Introduction*

The capital gains provisions of the Code offer certain opportunities for tax savings within the family such as bargain sales, sales to offset losses, sales to obtain a stepped-up basis, sales in exchange for private annuities, etc. But there are pitfalls and uncertainties. The statutory language frequently fails to furnish a complete answer. Indeed, too strict a reliance upon the words of the statute may prove disastrous. In this area, much of the law is judge made and the existing body of authority may not be regarded as the final words to be uttered. Thus, in many situations, the lawyer must approach the problems with caution and the realization that judicial trends may be more important than the holdings of specific cases.

It seems appropriate, at the outset, to discuss capital gains in general in order to lay a foundation for the discussion of particular estate-planning objectives that planners have attempted to solve through use of the sale rather than the gift technique.

Capital gains taxation in brief

13.2 How capital gains are taxed

A short-term capital gain is a capital gain resulting from the sale or exchange of a capital asset held for not more than six months. A loss resulting from such a sale is a short-term loss. If capital assets, held for more than six months, are sold at a profit, the gain is a long-term gain; any loss is a long-term loss.

All short-term transactions are first lumped together. Thus, if there is a short-term gain of $10,000 and a short-term loss of $6,000, there would be a net short-term gain of $4,000. This initial calculation will result in either a net short-term gain or a net short-term loss. The same computation is then made with respect to all long-term transactions. Again, there may be either a net long-term gain or a net long-term loss.

Next, short-term and long-term transactions are lumped unless there are both short-term and long-term gains.

1. *Overall loss*   If there is an overall loss, either long- or short-term or both, $1,000 is deductible from ordinary income.[1] Beginning with 1970 a $2,000 net long-term loss is needed to offset $1,000 of ordinary income. In other words,

---

[1] The deduction of $1,000 is not available to corporations.

a long-term loss must be reduced by 50 percent when it is taken as a deduction against ordinary income. Any excess loss is carried forward as a capital loss (long or short) indefinitely. It may be used in later years to offset capital gains, and, if not thus exhausted, any excess, to the extent of $1,000 yearly, may be deducted from ordinary income. Where there are both long- and short-term excess losses the short-term losses must first be used for the deduction against ordinary income.

Example: Jones has ordinary income of $15,000 and a $10,000 long-term loss. He may deduct $1,000, thereby reducing his ordinary income to $14,000. He carries $8,000 forward as a long-term loss. In the following year he again has $15,000 of ordinary income and a $4,000 capital gain, either long- or short-term. He uses $4,000 of his carry-over to offset his gain, deducts $1,000 from his ordinary income and carries $2,000 forward. This carry-over must first be used to offset gains, so that if he had had a $10,000 gain instead of a $4,000 gain the second year, he would report $2,000 gain (long or short) and would have no deduction from ordinary income.

2. *Net short-term gain*   If there is a net gain, which is short-term, the gain is taxable in full at ordinary rates.

Example: Jones has net short-term gains of $6,000, net long-term losses of $3,000, and $15,000 ordinary income. His net short-term gain is $3,000. This is added to his ordinary income, making it $18,000, which is taxable at the regular graduated rates.

3. *Net long-term gain*   If there is a net gain, which is long-term, the taxpayer may, at his option, either deduct 50 percent of the gain and carry the remaining 50 percent into his ordinary income or he may have the full amount of the gain taxed at the alternative rate which is 25 percent of the first $50,000 of long-term gain. One half of the excess over $50,000 must be included in his ordinary income and taxed at progressive rates. The maximum tax on the excess is thus 35 percent (29.5 percent in 1970, 32.5 percent in 1971), since the present highest tax bracket is 70 percent. The effect of this option is that long-term gains up to $50,000 bear a maximum tax of 25 percent.

Example: Jones, a married man, has net short-term losses of $5,000, net long-term gains of $8,000. His ordinary income is $15,000. Here he would elect to deduct $1,500 of the long-term gain and add the remaining $1,500 to his ordinary income. Only if adding 50 percent of the actual gains puts him in a tax bracket higher than 50 percent is it advantageous to use the alternative rate. Thus it is erroneous to think of long-term capital gains as bearing at least a 25 percent tax, since in many instances the tax will be very much less, sometimes as little as one half of the beginning rates.

4. *Both net short- and net long-term gains*   If there are both short-term and long-term gains, the net short-term gain is taxed in full at ordinary rates, the net long-term gain either at 25 percent of the first $50,000 or by treating 50 percent of the actual gain as ordinary income.

While capital gains are given preferred treatment, not every profit derived from a capital asset will qualify for this special tax treatment, as will appear from the sections that follow.

13.3   *What is a capital asset*

The Code defines a capital asset as all property except:

1. Stock in trade, inventory, or property held primarily for resale to customers in the ordinary course of business.

2. Property used in the trade or business of a character which is subject to an allowance for depreciation or real property used in the trade or business.

3. Certain literary, musical, or artistic productions created by the taxpayer and under the Tax Reform of 1969 letters and memoranda held by a person by whom or for whom (Donee) they were prepared.

4. Certain accounts receivable.

5. Certain obligations issued at a discount.

The last three came into the Section to plug loopholes. The second exception is designed to give the business taxpayer ordinary loss treatment on sales of property used in his business, if sold at less than cost, but capital gain treatment if sold at a profit. This technically is accomplished by eliminating all such property from the capital asset definition and then, in a subsequent section (1231) granting capital gain treatment to any profits. Section 1231 affords similar treatment to certain sales of coal and timber, livestock and unharvested crops. But the Code requires that all 1231 transactions be first netted. Thus if two pieces of real property (1231 assets) held for more than six months are sold during the year, one at a gain of $40,000 the other at a loss of $30,000, the taxpayer has a net 1231 gain of $10,000, taxable as a long-term capital gain. The timing of 1231 transactions can have important tax consequences. If he had sold the first parcel in 1969 and the second in 1970 he would have had a long-term gain of $40,000, in 1969 but an ordinary loss of $30,000 in 1970.

Speaking generally, the Code attempts to distinguish between property held for sale and property held for investment. When a merchant buys property for resale to customers, the gain is ordinary income since in large part the profit is due to the personal services of the taxpayer. When an investor purchases property the gain is usually the result of economic factors beyond his control and not due to his personal efforts. Here the gain is capital. While all gains are taxable, not all losses are deductible because of the Code requirement that only business losses, losses from transactions entered into for profit, and a very limited number of specifically designated personal losses, are recognized.

It may be helpful to keep in mind five major classifications and the tax consequences of each.

1. Property held for sale to customers in the ordinary course of trade or business. Ordinary income, ordinary loss.

2. Property used in the trade or business, held for more than six months. Capital gain, ordinary loss.

3. Property held for investment. Capital gain, capital loss.

4. Property held for personal use, such as the family residence. Capital gain, loss disallowed.

5. Property essentially "ordinary income" in character. This last group includes sales of future income items such as dividends, rents, unrealized receivables, etc. Here the case law

is confusing and unsatisfactory. Sometimes capital gain treatment is achieved, sometimes not.

Difficult questions of fact, as to the proper classification of property as investment or held for resale are constantly arising. It should be noted however, that it is not the type of property that determines its classification but the use to which a particular owner puts it. Thus an automobile may be held for sale to customers, may be used in the trade or business, or may be held for personal use.

It is clear that if a wealthy widow purchases an apartment house, her sole real estate holding, derives rental income from it for several years and then sells it, she has capital gain on any profit. Suppose, however, a doctor or lawyer acquires a number of rental properties and over the years becomes active in the buying and selling of real estate. Eventually his trading activities will become sufficiently numerous so that he will be regarded as being in the real estate business and his profit therefrom will be taxable as ordinary income. At what point of time his activities cease to be those of an investor and become those of a dealer will be difficult to determine. His classification will depend on the time and the amount of activity in seeking buyers for his properties, the number of sales, etc. A trader in securities, on the other hand, no matter how much time he devotes to "playing" the market, will never be classified as a dealer since he does not sell to customers but over recognized exchanges. The basic distinction is between one who buys seeking a profit through increase in value due to economic conditions in general and one who buys seeking a profit through a markup in price which he hopes to obtain because he has established a market for the properties purchased.

13.4   What is a sale or exchange

The requirement that there be a sale or exchange has caused and still causes unfortunate results, though many of the unhappy consequences have been eliminated by specific statutory provisions requiring certain events to be treated as though they were sales or exchanges. Thus stock and bond retirements, corporate liquidations, securities becoming worthless, losses by fire, government seizures, and other involuntary conversions are treated in the Code as though they arose as a result of a sale or exchange. But arbitrary results continue to be reached. Thus amounts received in excess of cost by one who purchases the right to legacy will not receive capital gain treatment. The purchaser of a judgment, later satisfied, will have the gain, if any, taxed as ordinary income.

Assume X purchases a defaulted $20,000 mortgage as an investment for $10,000. He subsequently, due to changes in economic conditions, collects in full several years later. He has $10,000 of ordinary income. If he is in a 60 percent tax bracket, his net profit is $4,000. Suppose, instead, he had sold the mortgage prior to collection but when it had a value equal to its face of $20,000, for $19,000. The Buyer is assured a clear profit of $1,000. X is better off by $2,750 because he sold rather than collected the debt. On a sale he would realize a long-term capital gain of $9,000, with a maximum tax of $2,250. His gross profit by sale is $9,000, but his net profit is $6,750. However, had he allowed the mortgage to mature and collected $20,000 his gross profit would be $10,000 but his net profit only $4,000. This absurdity results because payment does not constitute a sale or exchange.

While it ought to be clear that a transfer of property in cancellation of an obligation results in a sale or exchange of the property, this result is frequently overlooked. An executor who transfers stock, having a cost basis to him of $8,000 but a present market value of $12,000, in payment of a $12,000 legacy, realizes $4,000 of capital gain income. Similarly on divorce, where a husband transfers the family residence held in his name, cost $15,000, and securities, cost $50,000, to his wife in partial settlement of his marital obligations, he may be held to have capital gain measured by the difference between his cost and current value. Assume the home is worth $30,000 and the securities $70,000 on the date of the transfer, he may be charged with a $35,000 capital gain. In a case involving this question it was argued that there was no way to value the consideration received by the husband. To this the Court replied, "In the case at bar the amount of the taxpayer's obligation to his wife was fixed in part in terms of stock by the parties themselves who really dealt at arm's length with one another . . . . We think that we may make the practical assumption that a man who . . . . gives property of a fixed value for an unliquidated claim is getting his money's worth." In other words the parties themselves fixed the value of the obligation by the market value of the assets transferred. The Supreme Court in the recent *Davis* case agreed with this reasoning.

Exchanges of property, except where they can be brought within the nonrecognition provisions of the Code, will result in the realization of gain. Thus if General Motors, cost $10,000 current value $25,000, is transferred for Blackacre, cost $15,000 current value $25,000, the buyer of Blackacre has $15,000 capital gain on the transfer of his General Motors, the seller of Blackacre realizes $10,000 capital gain on the transfer of Blackacre. Each has a cost basis for the new asset of $25,000.

Occasionally no gain will be immediately realized upon a sale if the amount received has no fair market value. In *Burnet* v. *Logan* property was sold for some cash plus an agreement to pay 60¢ a ton, no gain was immediately recognized as the cash received was less than the seller's cost basis. While this rule can occasionally be useful in postponing the recognition of gain it should be noted that the Regulations provide that only in rare and extraordinary cases will property be regarded as not having a market value.

13.5 Disposition by gift or at death

It has long been the established rule that transfers by gift or at death do not result in the realization of income.

Thus property cost $10 may be given away at a time when it is worth $20 without any recognition of gain. Since the donee takes the donor's cost as his basis, plus the gift tax paid, the gain will be taxed if, but only if, he later sells. Further, where the disposition is by will, the gain will never be taxed because the legatee receives a new cost basis, i.e. market value at date of death. This aspect of the doctrine of realization offers avoidance opportunities, some of which are treated at section 11.24.

Gift property continues, for purposes of gain, to take the donor's cost and holding period. However, to avoid too easy a transfer of losses to family members who can profitably use losses on their returns, the cost basis, for loss, is fair market value at the date of the gift or the donor's cost, whichever is lower. If stock costing the donor $20, is given away at a time when it is worth $10, and it is later sold for $5, the donee's loss is limited to $5. See section 10.25, where these rules are stated somewhat more fully. Inherited property receives a new basis, market value at date of death or six months from the date of death, in the event the executor elects the estate tax valuation option. See section 3.24. Prior to 1954 this step-up in basis was limited to property acquired by devise, bequest, or inheritance, with unhappy tax consequences. Jointly owned assets, gifts in contemplation of death, transfers with reserved life estates, or with possibilities of reverter, etc., were all included in the taxable estate of the donor as substantially testamentary in character, yet because the donee's title had been technically acquired in an inter vivos transfer, he was treated as a donee, rather than a legatee and saddled with his donor's cost rather than the market value at the donor's death. This inequity has been corrected by the 1954 Code. All property included in the taxable estate now receives the new basis, other than "income-in-respect-of-a-decedent" items.

13.6 Identification of assets sold

Suppose X owns 3 shares of General Motors, one acquired in 1960 at a cost of $10, one acquired in 1964 at cost of $20 and the third purchased in April, 1970, for $50. In May, 1970, when the price is $45 he decides to sell one share. He may select the particular certificate to be sold. Thus he may sell the 1960 share and incur long-term gain of $35, or the 1964 share and have long-term gain of $25, or the 1970 share and sustain a short-term loss of $5. Which one he should select will depend on his other transactions during the year. The cases in this area have been quite strict. Thus in *Davidson* v. *Commissioner* the taxpayer instructed his broker to sell shares purchased on a certain date and directed his bank to send the shares to the broker. By mistake the bank sent the wrong certificate purchased at a different time and for a different amount. The Court held the gain was to be computed on the certificate actually sold. In the absence of identification, the Regulations provide that the first-in, first-out rule shall apply. This problem of identification can become extremely complex where securities are held in companies that make a practice of paying stock dividends or where a number of stock splits occur. Only through the exercise of considerable care is it possible to have the certificates issued in such a way as to make identification practical. Where a number of securities are merged into a single security, as may occur in connection with a reorganization, gain or loss may be determined on an average basis. Estate owners, giving or selling assets to family members will find it extremely profitable to keep these rules in mind in selecting the particular properties or certificates for transfer to the objects of their bounty.

13.7   Allocation of cost to units purchased

Suppose X purchases 100 shares of General Motors for $5,000. He subsequently sells 50 shares for $3,000. He might well take the position that the entire amount represented return of cost and that no gain was to be recognized unless and until he had received his full $5,000 investment from sales. But the rule has always been otherwise. His cost must be allocated among the maximum units into which the property is divisible. This obviously presents no difficulty in the case of stocks. But suppose the property consists of 200 acres of undeveloped land. Here a normal division or apportionment will generally suggest itself on inspection. It may be into acres, with some parcels having a value considerably in excess of the others or it may be a division into lots. Much will depend on the contemplated use. But only in the rarest cases will an apportionment of the price not be required. One such case is *Inaja Land Company, Ltd.* v. *Commissioner* in which it was held that the amount received on the sale of an easement over land was not immediately taxable but was to be used to reduce the basis of the land and treated as return of capital.

Allocation problems become extremely complex, when the securities sold represent an original purchase plus a series of stock dividends and stock acquired as the result of stock rights. Assume X purchased one share of common stock of ABC, Inc., for $100. Later he received in a nontaxable transaction a new common and a new preferred in exchange for the old common. On the date of exchange the new common had a market value of $50 and the preferred of $100. Here he must allocate $33.33 of his original cost to the common, $66.67 to the preferred. Further assume that subsequently he was given a right to purchase an additional share of common for $25, at a time when the common was still selling at $50. He exercised the privilege. A portion (½) of the new stock is attributable to the original purchase. The cost of this half is $11.11, the total cost of the new share $36.11. The cost of the original share of common must now be reduced to $22.22. Fortunately, lawyers and others preparing tax returns may avoid the necessity for extremely complicated mathematics by referring to the capital adjustment manuals published by both Commerce Clearing House and Prentice-Hall, which show in detail the proper percentage allocation for all capital changes of most of the securities that will be found in the usual investment portfolio.

13.8 Apportionment of the cost to different items purchased

In *Williams* v. *McGowen* the court held, on the sale of a sole proprietorship for a lump sum, that the price must be apportioned to the various items sold, some of which consisted of capital assets, some 1231 assets, some ordinary assets. Assume the sale of a drugstore as a going business for $50,000. What is actually sold is (1) medicines, drugs, and other inventory, all classifiable as property held for sale to customers in the ordinary course of business; (2) counters, tables, equipment, etc. (1231 assets); (3) receivables, profit on which is ordinary income; and (4) goodwill. The last is a capital asset. In order to determine ordinary income or ordinary loss on the inventory items, a portion of the price must be allotted to this group. To determine capital gain or ordinary loss on the equipment, the price to be attributed to it must be fixed, the same is true of the receivables and the goodwill. The buyer is faced with identical problems since he must compute his ordinary income on the sale of merchandise, his depreciation on the items used in the business, etc. If the parties fail to make the allocation, the Commissioner will do it and frequently not in a way completely satisfactory to the taxpayers involved. Generally speaking the Commissioner will not upset, indeed the Courts will not permit him to upset, any reasonable apportionment made by the parties in an arm's length transaction; for here each is obviously bargaining in his own economic interest and their interests are adverse. The seller desires the minimum apportionment to the property held for resale, since this will result in ordinary income to him. The buyer, however, would prefer the maximum allocation to these items, in order to reduce the amount of his later profits.

However, where the allocation is for any reason obviously unreasonable the Commissioner may disregard it. In one case, the taxpayer owned a winery. X wanted to buy a large quantity of wine but, because of OPA Regulations, the taxpayer was restricted as to the sale price. He therefore offered to sell both the wine and the winery for $350,000, $77,000 for the wine, $273,000 for the winery. The Commissioner in assessing a tax deficiency on the sale as reported, allocated $302,000 to the wine. This allocation was sustained by the Court.

Since family sales will rarely be at arm's length, particular care should be exercised to apportion the price in a manner that the fact situation justifies. Any obvious effort to gain an unfair tax advantage will generally have unhappy tax consequences, as the Commissioner, in the exercise of his discretion, may allocate maximum values to the most immediately vulnerable tax assets and minimum values to others.

13.9   Ordinary income or capital gain

Because of the tremendous differential in rates or (at the option of the taxpayer) the 50 percent deduction for capital gains profits, much thought goes into the devising of plans to turn ordinary income into capital gain. Since the concept of a capital asset is arbitrary, the results have sometimes been arbitrary. Assume X owns stock which cost him $10,000 and has a present worth of $50,000. This resulted from the fact that the corporation had plowed earnings back in the business until it had a surplus attributable to his shares of $40,000. $20,000 of this surplus was in liquid assets, accumulated for the purpose of an expansion project, which at the last moment, became undesirable. The corporation is thinking, therefore, of declaring a large cash dividend since it no longer needs its liquid surplus. If X sells his shares before the dividend is declared for $50,000, he will have a long term gain of $40,000, with a maximum tax of $10,000. If he waits until the dividend is declared (assume to be $20,000) his stock will decrease in value to $30,000 and if he is a 60 percent taxpayer he will net $8,000 from the dividend. Thus he will be worth $38,000, instead of $40,000 had he sold. What of buyer? He would have to pay, if he is also a 60 percent taxpayer, $12,000 in income taxes on what to him was return of capital. He would be worth $38,000 instead of the $50,000 he paid for the stock. If X, after the supposed sale, goes back into the market and repurchases an equivalent number of shares with his $30,000, he will have a $30,000 cost basis for his stock instead of $10,000. Thus a sale and a later repurchase is worth much more than the mere $2,000 saved in immediate tax, since his new stock is no longer burdened with the potential capital gain liability that it had before the sale and repurchase, when the cost basis was $10,000.

Other examples are noted in section 13.4 where a sale of assets that will ripen into ordinary income will convert the profit into capital gain.

But taxpayers have not always been successful in their efforts. Thus the sale of a dividend after the record date will result in ordinary income. The proceeds from the sale of accounts receivable that have not been taken into ordinary income will be treated as taxable in full at ordinary rates. Both Truman and Eisenhower received capital gain treatment on the sale of the copyrights to their books, whereas royalties received would have constituted ordinary income, but specific legislation now makes this impossible for other amateur authors. Some other loopholes have been closed by Congress. In other cases the Courts have and will continue to struggle with the problem. Thus in *Hort* v. *Commissioner,* the taxpayer inherited improved real estate from his father which was under lease to the Irving Trust Co. at an annual rental of $25,000 for a 15-year term. In 1933 when the lease had nine years to run, the tenant, finding it unprofitable to continue banking operations at the location, offered the taxpayer, and he accepted, $140,000 for the cancellation of the lease. The taxpayer reported a loss of $21,000 on the transaction, on the theory that the amount he received was $21,000 less than the difference between the present value of the unmatured rentals and the fair rental value of the premises for the unexpired term. The government contended the entire $140,000 was taxable as ordinary income. The Supreme Court sustained the government's position, on the theory that the landlord had merely anticipated income that otherwise would have been received over the years. He had not transferred any capital. He still owned the capital asset, the real estate, and while it had decreased very substantially in value as a result of the cancellation of the lease, no gain or loss is recognized on mere fluctuations in market value. The result seems sound, though unfortunate. The landlord who collects ten years rent in advance has immediate income whether he is a cash or accrual basis taxpayer. Here Hort had collected nine years fruit in advance. His position is not different from that of the discharged executive who settles his claim for breach of a nine-year contract of employment for a lump sum. Hort had no cost basis for his lease, apart from the land, since every dollar of rent collected over the years would be taxable in full as ordinary income.

The result is unhappy in the particular case but stems directly from the arbitrary distinction between income and capital gain. A few assumptions will illustrate this. At the date of the father's death in 1928, assume the land had a value of $300,000. In 1933 it was worth $200,000 due to the depression and the absence of available tenants to occupy the balance of the building. The value, we may assume, would have been about $60,000, if it were not for the one substantial tenant who was committed for nine years. On these assumptions, with the cancellation of the lease the value of the retained fee would be worth $60,000; of the $140,000 he received, the Government collected about $100,000, leaving him $40,000 cash. He might have sold the building to the tenant for $140,000 and been richer by $40,000 even though his capital loss would have been wasted, or he might have spread the payments over the years and thus kept them in very much lower brackets.[2] Thus there were other methods of handling the transaction that would have eliminated the confiscatory tax.

Suppose a tenant has a valuable long-term lease executed during the 30s. The monthly rental is $1,000, current fair market rental is $3,000. The term has ten years to run. If he subleases for $3,000 a month, he will realize $24,000 of ordinary income each year. Suppose, instead, he sells the lease for $100,000, or accepts $100,000 from the landlord for cancellation of the lease and surrender of the premises, does he have ordinary income, as did the landlord in Hort, or does he have capital gain? What he has done in substance is to anticipate income just as Mr. Hort did. But there are technical differ-

---

[2] Some relief is provided by the averaging provisions of the 1964 Code.

ences. He sold his entire interest. The tenant's lease is property and technically within the definition of a capital asset whereas the lease in the hands of the landlord is not recognized as having any independent existence. In any event the Court gave the tenant capital gain treatment and this rule was specifically written into the 1954 Code, the Committee Report noting that the statute was not intended to change the result of the *Hort* case.

Other distinctions present pitfalls or windfall opportunities. Suppose an accountant sells his practice for $50,000. Physical assets may not be worth more than $5,000. What is really being paid for is goodwill. If the accountant continued in business every dollar that the goodwill produced would be taxable as ordinary income. Yet he obtains capital gain treatment when he anticipates these profits by sale. The Courts also sanctioned this where a partner sold his interest in a law firm, even though much of the purchase price was attributable to the unrealized receivables, work in progress, and going concern value of the firm. As to partnerships the rule has been modified by the 1954 Code, making the portion of the price allocable to unrealized receivables ordinary income, but still making it optional with the parties, upon the liquidation of a partnership interest, whether the amount paid for goodwill shall be taxed as capital gain or ordinary income. This is achieved by providing that capital gain shall apply only to the amount paid for the partner's capital interest in the business and that this shall not include unrealized receivables or goodwill, except to the extent a payment for goodwill is specifically provided for in the agreement. Thus if a partnership interest is liquidated for $50,000, and the physical assets are worth $5,000, there will be $45,000 of ordinary income. But if the agreement provides for $5,000 for the physical assets, $25,000 for goodwill, $20,000 for work in progress, then only $20,000 will be taxable as ordinary income, assuming the allocation of $25,000 to goodwill is not unreasonable. Here, however, the remaining partners will be less well off, since they will forfeit any deduction for the amount paid for goodwill. It will enter into their costs basis

253

but, being nondepreciable, will be of no tax value to any of them unless and until one of them sells or liquidates his interest in the partnership during his life.

A further illustration of the vagaries of the distinction between capital gain and ordinary income may be appropriate. Suppose on the sale of a business the Buyer insists on a noncompetition clause. In *Hamlin Trust* the negotiations culminated in an offer of $1,000,000 ($200 per share) for the stock of the corporation plus an agreement on the part of the selling stockholders not to compete for ten years. Just prior to putting the contract in final form, the Buyers inquired whether the Sellers would object to valuing the stock at $150 a share and the restraining order at $50. They stated they desired this to make the provision enforceable and to help them tax-wise. The Sellers readily agreed, apparently thinking it would make no difference to them. But the tax difference was tremendous. The Sellers were in receipt of $250,000 of ordinary income, rather than capital gain. The Buyers had a deduction to be spread over the ten-year period for compensation paid of $250,000.

Would the result have been different if the contract had not separated the price? It very well might be for the cases have held that where the covenant "constitutes a nonseverable element of a transaction in which the owner of a going business sells the property and transfers the goodwill, the covenant is a contributing element to the assets transferred and the entire revenue received is subject to tax as a capital gain."

13.10   Losses disallowed

1. Losses sustained on the sale of stock or securities will be disallowed, if, within a period beginning 30 days before the sale and ending 30 days after the sale, the taxpayer acquired or has entered into a contract or option to acquire substantially identical stock or securities. This is known as the "wash sale" provision and is obviously designed to prevent the realization of tax losses without any real change in the economic position

of the taxpayer. Absent this section, taxpayers could sell stock exchange securities in the morning and buy back the identical stock interests in the afternoon solely to gain the tax advantage of a loss to offset gains. The provision, however, largely fails to accomplish its purpose since a seller can almost always protect himself against the risk of a substantial rise during the 30-day waiting period by acquiring stock in comparable companies whose price changes are influenced by the same business factors. Thus on selling General Motors, he can immediately buy and hold Chrysler for 30 days before switching back to General Motors. Sears Roebuck and Montgomery Ward, Standard Oil of California and Standard Oil of New Jersey, Consolidated Edison and Brooklyn Union Gas are examples of other comparable securities. Most stock exchange houses publish lists of substitute companies where the economic risks are the same and hence reduce to a minimum any chance that the market will get away from the seller within the 30-day period.

The provision relates only to losses and only to securities. Frequently it will be desirable to sell at a gain in the morning and repurchase in the afternoon. Thus, assume X has $20,000 of losses, and a security which cost him $15,000 and is now selling at $35,000. The sale will create a gain to offset his loss, and the afternoon purchase will give him a $20,000 increase in cost basis that will be valuable on any later sale.

2. Losses on sales to related taxpayers are disallowed under Code Section 267. See discussion in section 13.19.

3. Losses on sales of property held for personal use are not deductible because of the Code requirement that only business losses and losses arising out of transactions entered into for profit shall be recognized. No one who had purchased an overcoat for $100 would expect a $90 deduction on its sale for $10 four years later, after he had worn it threadbare. But objection is frequently raised to the disallowance on the sale of a residence though the same reasoning applies.

Problems arise when property held for personal use is shifted to property held for the production of income. Suppose X purchased a residence in 1940 for $30,000. He occupied it until

1942, when it was worth $25,000. He then rented it until 1945, at which time he sold it for $20,000. During the rental period he took depreciation of $1,000 per year. His cost for loss is the market value at the date of conversion, $25,000, reduced by the allowed depreciation of $3,000. Thus, the amount of loss recognized on the sale was $2,000. Assume the sale price was $26,000. Here he would have neither gain nor loss. There is no gain since his basis is $27,000 (original cost less allowable depreciation); no loss since what he recovered exceeded his basis for loss. If the sale price had been $32,000, he would have incurred a $5,000 capital gain.[3]

The courts have been strict in the evidence required to show that a conversion has taken place. Apparently nothing short of actual rental will suffice. Thus, in *Horrmann* v. *Commissioner* the taxpayer ceased to occupy the property and attempted for three years to sell or rent it. It was finally sold. The court held these efforts did not convert the holding "into a transaction entered into for profit"; but that it did result in causing the property to be "held for the production of income" so that depreciation was allowable under Code Section 167(a)(2) and maintenance expenses under Code Section 212. It is unfortunate that these sections should receive different interpretations since, while the phraseology is different, the policy considerations are the same.

Where a residence is inherited, its character depends on the use the new owner puts it to. Thus in *Campbell* v. *Commissioner* the devisee son immediately attempted to sell or rent. He was finally successful in selling the property seven years later, not having occupied it in the meantime. The loss was held deductible.

13.11   Nonrecognition of gains or losses

There are a considerable number of situations where neither gain nor loss is recognized. Others where the recognition of

---

[3] This example assumes no depreciation recapture.

gain may be postponed at the option of the taxpayer. Many of these refer to corporate reorganizations and are extremely complex. The estate planner is more likely to be concerned with the nonreorganization sections.

1. No gain or loss is recognized upon the transfer of assets to a corporation in exchange for stock or securities if the transferors are in control of the corporation immediately after the transfer. X owning Blackacre, which cost him $20,000, present value $50,000, may transfer it to Blackacre, Inc., in exchange for all its stock. The cost basis of Blackacre to the Corporation will be $20,000. X's cost basis for his stock will be $20,000. Gain will, however, be recognized on liquidation. Assume X decides that forming the corporation was a mistake. He causes it to be dissolved, in receiving Blackacre back he may incur a $30,000 capital gain, since the value of Blackacre exceeds the cost basis of his stock by $30,000, unless he can bring himself within the elective provisions at Code Section 333.[4] It will be long term, however, as his stock takes the holding period as well as the cost basis of Blackacre, the asset transferred to the corporation. Taxpayers should proceed slowly and only after full consideration of all the facts to incorporate their properties. No tax consequences need attach to the organization of a corporation but large taxes may be incurred when and if it is desired to retrace steps and dissolve.

2. No gain or loss is recognized on exchanges of property held for productive use in trade or business or for investment for property of like kind to be held for a like use. There is a specific exception for stocks, bonds, notes, or other securities. Thus, X, who owns Blackacre, cost $10,000, may exchange it for Whiteacre worth $25,000 without recognition of gain, if Blackacre was and Whiteacre will be held for investment.

---

[4] Section 333 provides that a corporation may at the shareholders' election be liquidated without recognition of gain to the individual shareholders, except that any gain shall be taxed as ordinary income to the extent of accumulated earnings and profits and except that capital gains shall be recognized with respect to liquid assets if acquired shortly before liquidation. It is thus favorable to liquidation of closely held corporations owning assets that have substantially appreciated in value and without a large earned surplus. The assets take the shareholders' basis.

His cost basis for Whiteacre will be $10,000. If money or non-qualifying property is also received, gain will be recognized to the extent of such cash or other property with a corresponding basis adjustment. On the other hand, because of the exception, one may not exchange General Motors for Chrysler without immediate tax consequences.

3. Further no gain will be recognized on the involuntary conversion of property (as a result of its destruction in whole or in part, theft, seizure, or condemnation) if the proceeds are reinvested in property similar or related in service or use.[5] Normally the reinvestment must occur within two years after the close of the taxable year in which the loss or transfer occurs but an extension of time may be secured. Note that these involuntary conversions relate to any property, even if held for personal use. Thus if jewelry with a cost basis of $1,000, is stolen at a time when it is worth $2,000 and there is a $2,000 recovery from the taxpayer's insurer, he may delay the recognition of any gain by investing the $2,000 in another item of jewelry. The cost basis of the new piece will be $1,000.

4. There are elaborate provisions for the nonrecognition of gain on the sale of a residence if the seller acquires a new residence within a year before or a year after the date of sale.

There is an exclusion of the portion of the gain allocable to the first $20,000 of the sale's price on the sale of his residence by a taxpayer over 65.

13.12 Summary

No effort has been made to completely treat all aspects of the taxation of capital gains. The objective rather has been to touch on those rules that are most likely to have application in the more usual family transactions and to suggest some of the unsettled problems that these rules may pose for the planner when he uses the sale rather than the gift technique to achieve family estate-planning objectives.

---

[5] In case of condemnation "like property."

Family sales

13.13   Bargain sales

Many donors, motivated by the desire to avoid estate taxes through lifetime gifts, nevertheless, insist that their donees pay something for the property given. It is believed by them that what is paid for, even at a bargain price, is more appreciated and better taken care of by the recipient. There may be much to be said for this approach. In any event it exists and its tax consequences must therefore be considered when the client desires to use this method of transfer.

In a number of other cases donors will desire to spread a gift over several years in order to obtain the full benefit of several years of exclusions. Thus Blackacre, with a value of $24,000 may be sold by Father to Son for $18,000, the entire purchase price being represented by a purchase money mortgage, with a series of six promissory notes each in the sum of $3,000. The plan is to cancel two of the notes each year and charge them against the annual exclusions of Father and Mother.

First, the bargain sale will result in a gift transaction to the extent the value of the property transferred exceeds the consideration received. Thus if Whiteacre, worth $40,000, is sold by Father to Daughter for $20,000, Father has made a taxable gift of $20,000. This gift tax consequence is generally recognized. But donors are more likely to overlook the income tax problems in such a sale. To what extent does such a transfer give rise to gain or loss? What is the transferee's cost basis for the property? These are troublesome questions and are not wholly answered by present case law. In Fincke property was transferred to a trust at a price considerably less than its value but equal to the transferor's cost. The court held the seller realized no gain on the part-sale part-gift transaction.

From this the following rules may be inferred.

1. *Sales price exceeds cost*   Blackacre, cost $10,000 is sold for $20,000 at a time when it is worth $40,000. The Seller

realizes a capital gain of $10,000. The Buyer's cost basis is $20,000.

2. *Sales price less than cost*   Blackacre, cost $20,000, is sold for $10,000 at a time when it is worth $40,000. Here the loss will not be recognized because of Code Section 267, disallowing losses on sales between members of the family. Even without this Section the loss would undoubtedly be disallowed because of the gift element. The Buyer's basis, however, should be $20,000, since if the transfer had been all gift it would be $20,000 and it ought not be less when he actually paid something for it.

3. *Market value less than cost*   Blackacre, costing $40,000 is sold for $10,000 at a time when it is worth $20,000. No loss will be allowed. B's basis should be $20,000, fair market value, for the purpose of any later loss. Arguably it should be $40,000 for the purpose of computing any gain. But these rules are yet to be worked out by the courts.

Donors who insist on selling rather than giving, would be well advised to fix the price in terms of cost to them and thus avoid any gain problem. They should also avoid using property which has a market value substantially less than its cost basis to them.

Under the Tax Reform Act of 1969 bargain sales to charities have lost much of their attractiveness. If property is sold to a charity for less than its fair market value, the cost basis of the property must be allocated between the portion sold and the portion given. Thus, a donor-seller will realize some gain even if the selling price does not exceed the cost basis of the entire property.

13.14   Sales of life estates

These offered attractive tax-saving possibilities prior to 1969. Assume Mother was income beneficiary of a $200,000 trust producing $8,000 a year, Son was remainderman. Son would purchase Mother's life estate for $100,000, its fair value based upon Mother's expectancy. The courts had held that Mother had a shifting basis that would normally approximate $100,000, and hence she had no income. Son, on the other hand, was allowed to amortize his cost as he received the $8,000 income each year. If Mother's expectancy was 20 years, Son amortized his cost $5,000 a year and paid tax on $3,000. Thus, $60,000 of what would have been taxable income wholly escaped any tax.

To eliminate this loophole the Tax Reform Act of 1969 provided that on the sale of a life estate no cost basis is to be attributed to the life tenant, where the estate was acquired by gift. This means that the entire $100,000 would, in the example above, be taxable to Mother in the year it was received. Presumably it would be treated as capital gain income.

13.15   Who is the real seller

In an earlier chapter (section 10.25) it was suggested that if Father was about to sell stock (cost $10,000) for $30,000, considerable taxes might be saved if the stock were transferred to the children who then made the sale. But the children must be the real sellers, not the agent of Father for the completion of a transaction which he, in substance, brought to fruition.

In *Court Holding Co.,* Husband and Wife owned all the stock of Blackacre, Inc. The corporation's sole asset was a building which it had agreed to sell at a price which would net a large profit. For purposes of illustration, assume the cost basis of the property to have been $50,000, the sale price $200,000. When Husband and Wife consulted tax counsel they were advised that the sale would incur capital gains tax by the corporation and that there would be a second capital gains tax on the liquidation of the company and the distribution of the portion of the purchase price left after payment of the tax, to the extent that that amount ($167,500) exceeded the cost basis of the stock held by Husband and Wife. If their combined cost basis were also $50,000, the taxable profit on the liquidation would amount to $112,500. One of these taxes, counsel pointed out, might be avoided, if the corporation first liquidated and the stockholders then sold. The reasoning was that on liquidation and receipt of Blackacre, the stockholders would incur a capital gains tax on their profit, $150,000. But they would get a new cost basis, $200,000 for Blackacre. Hence, on the later sale for $200,000 there would be no further gain.

The deal was momentarily called off. The dissolution and liquidation took place and this was followed by a sale by the stockholders to the same purchaser for the same amount and on the same terms. In fact a $1,000 down payment made to the corporation was retained and later credited on the stockholder's sale. The Supreme Court held that the sale was really made by the corporation which had negotiated all the terms of the contract and that it had merely taken a circuitous route in making the transfer. On the other hand, in *Cumberland Public Service Co.,* buyers approached a corporation, offering to buy its assets. The corporation declined to consider a sale because of the large capital gains tax involved. Stockholders of the corporation then approached the buyers and negotiated a contract of sale, on their assurance that they could acquire the assets by liquidating the corporation. This was done and the sale made. The Supreme Court held that the corporation was not taxable in this case since it had not acted as seller. Negotiations had originated, been carried on, and concluded with the stockholders who were the real sellers. Congress has changed the rule of the *Court Holding Co.* case by providing that any sale by a corporation of its assets shall not result in taxable gain if the corporation liquidates within 12 months after the sale.

But the lesson the *Court Holding Co.* case teaches is still important in the family gift cases followed by sales. Assume Father owns Blackacre which has a low cost basis to him. If he negotiates a contract and, to reduce the taxes on the prospective profit, transfers the property by gift to the children, who then complete the transfer, the gain may be taxed back to him. To be safe all negotiations for any sale should be commenced after the transfer, not before.

13.16   Sales to obtain a stepped-up basis

Suppose Father has a $30,000 capital loss with no offsetting gains. He owns X stock which he wants to keep within the family. Assume it cost him $10,000 and is worth $40,000. He may sell it to Mother for $40,000, thereby realizing a gain. The gain, however, will incur no tax since, on our assumption, the loss will eliminate the gain on his tax return. While losses within the family are disallowed (see section 13.17) there is no restriction on the recognition of gains.

In another area this principle may sometimes be advantageously used. Suppose Father owns a large undeveloped tract of land suitable for a subdivision. His cost is $50,000. On the sale of the lots it is hoped to realize $300,000. But, unless he can bring himself within the new Code Provision granting capital gain treatment, under certain highly restricted conditions, on the sale of subdivided real property, he will hesitate to develop the land as the profit may be subjected to tax as ordinary income. On these facts he may sell the property to a member of the family and, always assuming a bona fide sale, he will incur capital gains tax, with the family member having ordinary income on the profit he makes. However, this latter profit will be relatively small because of the high cost basis acquired on the purchase. Thus, if Father sells the land in bulk for $250,000, he will have more net profit because of the maximum capital gains tax, than if he sells the individual lots for a gross amount of $300,000. The family member will, if he grosses $300,000, have $50,000 of income subject to ordinary rates. Within the family $200,000 of the $250,000 profit would have been converted from ordinary income into capital gain.

This principle led to some abuses which Congress has attempted to correct by Code Section 1239. Husband, after depreciating an office building to zero, sold it to Wife for

$100,000, its fair market value.[6] He immediately incurred a capital gains tax but this was more than compensated for by the fact that Wife now had a depreciation basis of $100,000 (less the cost attributable to the land). Over the years, to 70 percent taxpayers, allowable depreciation, worth 70 cents on the $1.00, could thus be acquired at a cost of 25 cents on the $1.00.

Congress has plugged this loophole by providing that in the case of a sale between husband and wife or between an individual and a corporation, more than 80 percent of the value of which is owned by him, his spouse, his minor children, and grandchildren, any gain on such sale shall result in ordinary income, not capital gain. The section, however, applies only to a sale of property which is depreciable by the transferees. Thus, the opportunity for family sales to obtain higher basis is still available except for the highly restricted coverage of Code Section 1239.

13.17   Losses on sales within the family

All losses on sales within the family are disallowed. Even if the sale is bona fide, no deduction is allowed if it is made, directly or indirectly between (1) husband and wife, (2) brothers and sisters, (3) ancestors and lineal descendants. The statute extends far beyond family members. Thus sales to controlled corporations, partnerships, and exempt organizations may result in the nonrecognition of losses. The same is true with respect to sales to trusts created by the seller, or between two trusts with a common grantor or to a trust of which the seller is beneficiary, etc. In short the statute includes all entites that might conceivably be regarded as "second pocketbooks." There is the further rule of constructive ownership under which an individual is regarded as owning stock owned by other family members, etc. Nor will a loss on a sale by a wife, for example, on the New York Stock Exchange, followed by

---

[6] This practice was common prior to the depreciation recapture provision of the Code.

the purchase of identical securities by her husband, be recognized. Such transactions have been held to be indirect sales between husband and wife.

Further the section has been strictly construed. Suppose A has 100 shares of X stock which cost him $1,000, and 100 shares which cost him $3,000. He sells the 200 shares to his brother, at a time when the fair market value of the shares is $4,000, for $4,000. He will be treated as having a $1,000 gain on the first 100 shares and a loss, which will be disallowed, of $1,000 on the second 100 shares.

Because of the wide range of the inclusions no sale should ever be undertaken where the parties are not completely strangers without a careful study of the Code Section. Perhaps no other section contains more pitfalls for the unwary.

13.18   Private annuities

The interfamily annuity has at first glance an attractiveness that unfortunately, in most cases, begins to fade on more mature consideration. On rare occasions, however, it may be found to be a useful estate planning device.

The plan contemplates that Father, for example, will sell appreciated property to Son in return for Son's promise to pay Father an annuity as long as Father lives. It has the following advantages.

1. The property is removed from Father's estate.

2. No gift tax need be paid, if the present value of the promised annuity payments equals the value of the property.

3. Any capital gains tax that may be incurred will be spread over the life of the Father, rather than having the total gain recognized immediately.

4. Father will enjoy a fixed income for life. This is frequently thought of as comparable to a retained life estate but without the estate and income tax consequences of such an estate.

But the picture is not quite that rosy.

1. Father may not require that the income from the prop-

erty be applied to satisfy the annual payments. If he does, he may be held to have a retained life estate. Father may not take a mortgage on the property to secure the payments without incurring an immediate capital gains tax. He must rely solely on the unsecured promise of Son. This obviously has its drawbacks.

2. To avoid any gift tax the value of the annuity must equal the value of the property and it frequently will be difficult to fix, with any degree of certainty, either the value of the property, such as closely held stock, or the value of the annuity, where Father's health leaves something to be desired. But this risk may be worth running. Any disparity in the values as ultimately determined will result in some gift but always much less than the full value of the property. If Father dies within three years, a portion of the value of the property may be included in his taxable estate as a transfer in contemplation of death for less than a full and adequate consideration in money or money's worth. If, however, Father survives the transfer for more than three years this risk will automatically be eliminated.

3. Father will be taxed on a portion of each payment as ordinary income and on a portion of each payment as capital gain. Assume his cost basis in the property is $20,000, its present value is $80,000, and the expected payments amount to $120,000 ($10,000 a year for 12 years). Assume also that the present value of the promised annuity payments equals $80,000, hence no gift is involved. Father's ratio exclusion is 16.66 percent ($20,000 investment in contract, $120,000 expected return). Thus, from each $10,000 payment he excludes $1,666.66. Of the remaining $8,333.33, each year he must report $5,000 as capital gain and $3,333.33 as ordinary income. See Revenue Ruling 69-74.

4. Son will not obtain any deduction for the annual payments since each payment represents part of the cost of the property. In most cases, if the values are fairly fixed, the income from the property, after taxes, will fall short of the annual payments, a substantial hardship to Son.

5. If Father dies within a few years after the transfer Son

will find himself with an extremely low cost basis for the property.

6. If Father outlives his expectancy, the unanticipated profit will have the effect of increasing rather than decreasing his estate.

Occasionally the transfer of property, which has appreciated in value, to a family member in return for a promised annuity (which promise must be unsecured) may prove a happy solution but generally the uncertainties will suggest the wisdom of some other plan, the results of which are more definitely predictable.

14

Trusts

14.1 Introduction

From a tax standpoint, substantial gifts should generally be made to trusts for the benefit of the intended donees.

The outright gift will be subjected to estate tax on the death of the primary donee. This may be avoided by a transfer to the donee for life, remainder (for example) to his children. But legal life estates are generally unsatisfactory. See section 5.4. The gift in trust may avoid the inclusion of the property in the taxable estate of the donee, without depriving him of all access to the capital and without the objectionable features of legal life estates. The same techniques may be used in life time trusts as were suggested for residuary testamentary trusts in chapter 5. Thus, a life tenant may be given:

1. The income from the property.

2. A noncumulative annual power to withdraw at pleasure $5,000 or 5 percent of the capital, whichever is larger.

3. A power to demand capital in excess of the 5 percent or $5,000 limitation, to whatever extent needed to enable him to maintain his accustomed standard of living.

4. The trustee may be authorized to distribute capital to the life tenant in any amount, at any time, and for any reason that the trustee may determine in his absolute discretion.

5. The life tenant may be given a special power of appointment by deed which will enable him to direct distributions of capital to objects of his bounty at any time and in any amount that he may desire during his life.

6. The life tenant may be given a special power of appointment by will which will enable him to dispose of the capital at his death as though he owned it, provided he is deprived of the doubtful privilege of being allowed to give it to the creditors of his estate.

The trust plan also lends itself to arrangements that will reduce overall family income taxes. The techniques suggested in chapter 6 for residuary income bequests may be adopted equally well for living trusts. Thus a trust instrument may provide for:

1. Separate trusts,
2. Discretionary accumulation powers,
3. Sprinkle powers,
4. Authority to purchase life insurance,
5. Authority to allocate receipts and disbursements between income and principal.

There are, however, pitfalls in lifetime trusts that are not encountered in testamentary trusts because of the understandable desires of most donors to retain some interest in or control over the donated properties. Too many donors would both eat their cake and have it. To prevent too easy avoidance, the law has become extremely complex in this area. Further there is a distressing lack of any relationship between the income, gift, and estate tax concepts as to what constitutes a completed gift. A transfer may be complete for one tax, incomplete for another. The fact that a gift tax has been paid on a transfer is no assurance that the tax on the income from the property will be shifted to the donee or that the estate tax will be avoided by the donor.

Estate and income tax savings can be achieved through lifetime gifts if the donor is willing to completely divorce himself from all interest in and control over the property, select an independent trustee and eliminate any possibility of his, at any time, obtaining any benefits, direct or indirect, from the trust. Less absolute transfers may sometimes obtain the same results but the permissible bypaths are full of traps for the unwary. The topic will be divided into (1) transfers with possession and enjoyment delayed until the death of the donor, (2) transfers with reserved possibilities of reverter, (3) transfers with reserved life estates, (4) transfers with reserved reversions—short term trusts, (5) transfers that may possibly benefit the donor, including retained administrative powers, (6) transfers with powers to invade corpus, and (7) transfers with retained powers to alter, amend, revoke or terminate.

Transfers with delayed possession and enjoyment until the death of the donor

14.2   Delayed enjoyment

Many a donor is perfectly willing to give, provided his donee does not actually receive the properties until the donor's death. He wants to avoid the estate tax but to retain the satisfactions that belong to the holder of the family purse strings. In one of the first estate tax cases to reach the Supreme Court, a man, when he was 56 years old and had a life expectancy of 16 years, created a trust for his sons under the terms of which the income was to be accumulated for 30 years. Shortly thereafter he died and the government attempted to include the trust corpus in his estate on the theory that he had made a transfer intended to take effect in possession and enjoyment at or after his death. The Court held for the executors, stating that the decedent had parted with his entire interest during his life and that the enjoyment of his beneficiares was no way contingent on his death. Had the donor lived to be 86 his sons would have come into the enjoyment of the property even though he were still alive.

In the later *Reinecke* case the donor has created a number of trusts which were to end five years after his death or upon the earlier death of a designated beneficiary, if he survived the donor and died within the five-year period. The Court recognized that this case, unlike the earlier case, fell within the literal description of a "transfer to take effect in possession or enjoyment at or after death." Only after the donor's death would the beneficiaries come into the enjoyment of the capital.

271

But the court held the transfer not taxable because the donor had retained no interest in the property during his life and nothing passed from him at his death. With this case, the law became settled that Father could transfer property in trust, income to be accumulated until his death, such disposition of the accumulated income and capital thereafter as he desired, without having the property included in his tax estate at death.

This remained the law until 1949 at which time, probably because of the implications in the *Spiegel* case Congress decided to tax all transfers where the donee's rights to enjoyment commenced at the donor's death even though the donor had parted long before his death with his entire interest in the property. However present Code Section 2037, passed in 1954, indicates a Congressional change of heart. The Ways and Means Committee Report of that year states:

Under present law property previously transferred by a decedent is includible in his gross estate if possession or enjoyment of the property can be obtained only by surviving him. This rule applies even though the decedent has retained no interest in the property. Where the decedent has disposed of all, or substantially all, of his rights to property long before his death, it appears unduly harsh to subject the property to estate tax merely because the ultimate taker of the property is determined at the time of the decedent's death. This rule has been discarded by your committee's bill. In the future property previously transferred by a decedent will be includible in his estate only if he still had (either expressly or by operation of law) immediately before his death a reversionary interest in the property exceeding five percent of its value, that is, if he, prior to his death, had one chance in twenty that the property would be returned to him.

Thus, under current law it is again possible to give away the property for estate tax purposes and at the same time to withhold it from the donee until the donor's death. Such a gift comes about as close to a testamentary disposition as one can imagine. For this reason transfers of this type are peculiarly vulnerable to the contemplation of death section of the Code. They will be found useful, however, to the estate planner in a number of situations. The income from an accumulation trust will be initially taxable to the trust. While the children will ultimately be subject to the throwback rule, see section 6.12, this will not necessary result in additional taxes. Thus, considerable income tax savings may be realized, with the possibility of increasing the spendable income of an estate owner. Assume X has $500,000 of investment capital, $20,000 of investment income, and $30,000 of compensation income. He is a widower and presently disinclined to make his children financially independent of him. Suppose he creates a trust of $150,000 with securities which produce $6,000 of annual income. If the transfer is complete and the income is to be accumulated, he will have removed $150,000 from a 32 percent estate tax bracket by paying a gift tax of $20,000.[1] The estate tax reduction will amount to $48,000 a net saving of $28,000. While he lives the $6,000 will bear a tax of $890 instead of $3,568. Since he is accumulating funds for his children in the trust pocketbook, he should feel free to invade his retained capital to the extent of the reduction, or $2,678 each year.

Transfers with reserved possibilities of reverter

14.3 Possibilities of reverter

The possibility of reverter is to be distinguished from the indefeasibly vested reversion. Suppose A creates a trust, income to his wife for life, then to his daughter for her life, capital to be returned to him, if living at the death of the survivor of his wife or daughter, otherwise to his estate. Here A has an indefeasibly vested reversion. The tax consequences of such reversions will be discussed in the second next subdivision, in connection with ten-year trusts. The possibility of reverter differs from the indefeasibly vested reversion in that the estate may or may not return to the grantor, depending on future contingencies. Suppose A creates a trust to pay the income

---

[1] Because of the power to accumulate, the $3,000 annual exclusion is not available.

to his wife for life, remainder to his daughter, but if his wife predeceases him the corpus is to be returned to him instead of going to his daughter. Here A has a possibility of reverter, not a certain reversion. His wife has a life estate, his daughter has the fee subject to the possibility that it may be divested and return to the grantor, A, on the happening of the stated contingency, his surviving his wife.

Reverters and reversions exist because the grantor has given less than his entire interest absolutely and unconditionally. For this reason the regulations recognize that the possibility that the property may return to the grantor by inheritance is not a possibility of reverter.

When Husband gives Wife 100 shares of General Motors, it is quite possible that on her death the stock may return to him under her will or under the law of intestacy, but such a chance does not constitute a possibility of reverter. It does not stem from his earlier transfer but rather he acquires a new unrelated title through an act of hers or by operation of law upon her property.

Possibilities of reverter are extremely common in trust transfers. The prospective donor wants to give the property to his wife and then to his children. But what if they all predecease him? There being no one else in whom he is interested at the moment, the logical provision to add to the instrument of transfer is to have the property revert to him, should such an extremely remote contingency occur. In other cases, the donor will be willing to part with his property so long as his wife remains owner, but if she should happen to predecease him, he would prefer it to return to him rather than pass to the children, while he is still alive. But the retention of these possible interests, some extremely valuable and some practically valueless, has caused unhappy estate tax consequences.

In the leading case of *Helvering* v. *Hallock* a donor gave property to his wife but if she died before he did the title was to return to him. He died while his wife was still alive. The Court included the full value of the property, less the value of the wife's outstanding life estate, in his taxable estate. In *Spiegel,* the donor had created a trust, income to his three children for the life of the grantor. If any child predeceased the donor, the income was to be paid to his issue, etc. On the donor's death the corpus was to be distributed to the three children, and if any were then dead, to that child's issue, etc. Spiegel, however, failed to provide for any takers in the unlikely event that all the children and all grandchildren might predecease him. Since he had given away less than all in every conceivable contingency, he had, by the operation of law, a possibility of reverter. As a matter of fact, all three children survived him and the actuarial chance, computed as of immediately before his death, that the property might come back to him was absurdly remote. The trust consisted of assets worth $1,000,000. His chance was valued at $70. That is the amount a gambler, based on the mathematics of the case would have paid for the chance of his ever again becoming owner of the property. But because of this possibility, the entire $1,000,000 was taxed as part of Spiegel's estate.

It will be remembered that in the earlier case a deduction was allowed for the value of the outstanding life estate. No deduction was allowed here because the donees had to survive the grantor to take. In *Hallock,* the wife's life estate was in no way dependent on surviving the grantor; hence that estate had no relationship to his death.

Spiegel varied from *Hallock* in another respect. In *Hallock* the reverter existed because it was expressly retained by the words of the instruments of transfer. In *Spiegel* the possibility arose by operation of law because the grantor had failed to provide for every possible contingency. In *Hallock* the grantor had consciously retained the reverter by expressly providing for it. In *Spiegel* it may have been inadvertently retained. The then statutory section required the inclusion of transfers "intended to take effect in possession and enjoyment at 'death." This might mean that the state of mind of the grantor was decisive. The Supreme Court, however, refused to give the words such a restrictive interpretation, and properly so. To make the result turn on whether the reverter arose because of words in the deed or because of the absence of words would be a triumph of form over substance.

14.4   Current law

Transfers prior to October 8, 1949, the date of the *Spiegel* decision, are treated differently from those made on or after that date.

With respect to pre-October 8th, 1949, transfers:

1. The decedent must have retained a reversionary interest by the express terms of the instrument of transfer.

2. The reversionary interest must have had a value immediately before the death of the decedent in excess of 5 percent of the full value of the property.

3. Possession and enjoyment of the property by the donees must have been conditioned upon their survivorship.

With respect to transfers made on or after October 8th, 1949, the rules are the same except that the interest need not be expressly retained. It may arise by operation of law.

In either case nothing is to be included in the estate of a grantor, if prior to his death, the beneficiary could have obtained possession and enjoyment through the exercise of a general power of appointment which was exercisable immediately before the decedent's death. Assume A created a trust, income to be accumulated until his death at which time the corpus and accumulated income were to be distributed to his then surviving children, if any. He gave Wife a general power of appointment by deed. Further assume Wife survived A. Nothing is to be included in A's estate since possession and enjoyment of the property could have been obtained by Wife during A's life.

A few examples will illustrate the survivorship requirement.

Suppose A transferred property in trust, income to his wife, remainder to his then surviving children, if none, back to A or if he be dead to his estate. Since both the wife and the children can possess and enjoy the property without surviving A, nothing will be included in his estate under the possibility of reverter section of the code. However, the value of the contingent remainder interest, assuming it is not too speculative to be valued, will be included under the general section.

Suppose A transfers property in trust, income to his wife for life, remainder to his son, but if son is not living at the date of wife's death, to A or if he be dead, to his brother B. Assume A was survived by his wife, his son and B. Only B need survive A in order to obtain possession and enjoyment. If the possibility that A might survive his wife and son and thereby recover the property was a better than a 20 to 1 chance, the value of B's remainder interest, and only that amount, is includible.

The value of the reversionary interest is to be determined as of a time immediately before the death of the donor by recognized valuation principles for determining the value for estate tax purposes of future or conditional interests in property.

Suppose A created a trust, income to his wife for life, corpus to be returned to him if he survives, otherwise to his daughter. Assume he is survived by both his wife, age 60, and his daughter. Further assume that the value of the wife's life estate is approximately 40 percent of the whole. This is to be included in determining whether his interest is worth in excess of 5 percent of the property. As he had a better than 20 to 1 chance of outliving his wife, the transfer is taxable as part of his estate. However, the interest of his wife is not included in the estate tax valuation. Thus if the property were worth $100,000, and the wife's life estate worth $40,000 only $60,000, i.e., the excess over the value of the outstanding life estate, will be included in his gross taxable estate.

14.5   *Eliminating possibilities of reverter*

In most cases it will be desirable for the draftsman to eliminate any possibility of reverter. The lawyer will do this by providing for final distribution to the estate of the last surviving named beneficiary, in the event all the beneficiaries predecease the termination date of the trust. Generally the possibility will be too remote to bother retaining. The suggested solution may well have the effect of returning the property to the grantor, in whole or in part, through the laws of inheritance, should the unlikely contingency occur. There will always be a danger in retaining unimportant possibilities of reverter because the valuation date is the uncertain future date of the grantor's death. Assume a transfer to A for life, then to A's wife for the life of the grantor, remainder to A's children living at the time of the grantor's death, if none, to the grantor. As of the date of the conveyance grantor and A are 50, A's wife is 45, A's children are 20 and 18. Here the risk that the property may ever return to the grantor may well be considerably less than 1 in 20. But suppose A and one child die two weeks before the grantor. Under the changed circumstances the likelihood of the property coming back to the grantor is greatly increased. Since people have a habit of dying out of order, computations made at the date of the gift are completely unreliable. Frequently the motivation is not the desire to have the property return but rather that the children shall not come into possession and enjoyment before the donor's death. If the transfer is to wife for life, remainder to the children but if wife predeceases the grantor, the property to return to him, the possibility retained will most likely cause the inclusion of the property in the grantor's estate, less the value of the outstanding life estate, assuming the wife survives. To avoid this result and achieve the objective the transfer may be to the wife for life, and upon her death, income to be accumulated during the life of the grantor, with distribution to the children upon the death of the survivor of the grantor and his wife. See section 14.2.

There will be cases where it will be important to the donor to retain the possibility. Where the stock of a family company is involved he may not want it to get out of the bloodstream. Father may be willing to give it to Mother or Son or Grandson but he is fearful that if all predecease him it may wind up in the hands of Daughter-in-Law through inheritance from either Son or Grandson. Here he will prefer to run the risk of inclusion in his estate, since, if Son and Grandson predecease him and thus increase the value of his possibility he will be less concerned with the amount of the estate taxes that may be incurred on his death.

14.6   Gift taxes

A transfer with a retained possibility of reverter will incur gift tax even though the property may be later taxed as part of his estate.

As we saw in section 10.23, if Husband transfers property to Wife for life, and upon her death, to him if he survives, otherwise to his children, a gift tax measured by the full value of the property, less the value of his possibility of reverter, must be paid. The fact that the interests of the children are contingent does not prevent the imposition of a gift tax.

14.7   Income taxes

The justification for the imposition of a gift tax in these cases would seem to be that such transfers, even if incomplete for estate tax purposes, may be complete for income tax purposes. If the income is paid to the life tenant, it will be taxable to him, not to the grantor. Thus a gift, even with a substantial possibility of reverter may be used to reduce family income taxes, by shifting the tax on the income to lower income bracket members of the family. Only in those trusts where the trustee is to accumulate the income, is there a risk that the transfer may be treated as incomplete for income tax purposes. Code Section 677 makes the grantor taxable on income which may be "held or accumulated for future distribution" to him or his spouse. Suppose the transfer is in trust to accumulate the income during the life of the grantor and then to make distribution to X, if living. This creates a possibility of reverter by operation of law; if X should die, the property together with the accumulations would return to the grantor. Does this amount to an accumulation for later possible distribution to the grantor? The case law has not taxed the income, so accumulated, to the grantor under Section 677 where the possibility of reverter was extremely remote, though the Regulations appear to be to the contrary.

Transfers with reserved life estates

14.8   Introduction

The 1954 Code provides that the full value of any property transferred during life by gift is includible in the estate of the transferor if he has reserved the possession or use of the property or the right to the income.

1. For his life,
2. For a period not ascertainable without reference to his death,
3. For a period which does not in fact end before his death.

Transfers made before March 1, 1931, are exempted from the statute since prior to that date the statute had not included such transfers in the taxable estate.

14.9   Indirect reservations of income

The courts have been astute to look through disguised transactions and find reserved enjoyment of income wherever the facts warranted such a conclusion. In *Estate of Cornelia B. Schwartz* the decedent had transferred property to the children in exchange for a promise to pay her an annuity for life. The children immediately transferred the property to a trust, directing the trustee to make the payments to the mother. The court held the property includible in the mother's estate on the theory that she had retained the possession and enjoyment of the property. The result seems sound. There was obviously a family understanding of what was to be done. The same result will be reached if the income from gift property, after being received by the donee, is in fact handed over regularly to the donor.

Suppose X, about to sell Blackacre, for $50,000, requires the purchaser, instead of paying him the purchase price, to create a trust, income to X for life, remainder to X's children. Here the purchaser is the nominal grantor, X is the real grantor.

The courts look at substance rather than form. Assume Father, owning all the stock of X Corporation, transfers the stock to the children, after having arranged with his corporation to pay him a salary for life equal to the anticipated earnings. Here he has in substance retained the income from the property.

14.10 Trusts to satisfy legal obligations

If the income is to be used to discharge the grantor's legal obligations he will be held to have reserved the income from the property. Thus, there is no advantage to the creation of a trust with, for example, Wife as beneficiary but with the income to be used to pay household expenses. The same is true of trusts, the income of which is in fact used for the support of the grantor's minor children. However, trusts may be advantageously created for the support and education of adult children since the parent has no legal obligation to maintain them once they attain 21. A more difficult question will arise if Father, owning Blackacre, borrows $50,000 on the security of the land, and then transfers it in trust, subject to the mortgage, income to be accumulated or paid to the children as the trustee may determine. Assume the trustee in fact used the income to discharge the mortgage and that before it is fully discharged Father died. Did he reserve the income from the property for a period which did not in fact end before his death? In a sense he has received the benefit of the payments since they repaid his debt. On the other hand, it is arguable that, under local law, he was not the primary debtor after the transfer. The debt is to be satisfied from the land in the first instance, Father's obligation is only secondary. In this sense it is like the cases where Grandfather or Mother sets up a trust for the education of minor children, or grandchildren. Since neither of them have the primary obligation, Father having adequate funds, they are not regarded as having reserved life estates. About all that can be said is that the mortgage and similar cases, such as having the trustee pay Father's gift tax liability (see section 10.22) are risky transfers possibly causing the later inclusion of the property in the donor's estate.

Since there is no advantage to gifts with reserved life estates or reservations which do not in fact end before the death of the grantor, and since disguised transactions will not avoid the rule, donors should be careful to avoid even the appearance of such interests, where gifts are planned for the purposes of reducing estate taxes.

Transfers with reversions—short-term trusts

14.11   Clifford

Clifford declared himself trustee of certain securities owned by him for a term of five years or the earlier death of either himself or his wife. All the net income was to be paid or held for the benefit of his wife. At the end of the term the securities were to revert to him. As trustee he retained broad investment powers. The wife's interest was not assignable and the instrument contained an exculpatory clause protecting him from all liability except such as might arise from his "willful and deliberate" breach of trust duties. The Supreme Court held the income during each of the five years taxable to Clifford on the theory that he remained the substantial owner of the property throughout. The Court stated:

> So far as his dominion and control were concerned it seems clear that the trust did not effect any substantial change. In substance his control over the corpus was in all essential respects the same after the trust was created, as before. The wide powers which he retained included for all practical purposes most of the control which he as an individual would have.
>
> We have at best a temporary reallocation of income within an intimate family group. Since the income remains in the family and since the husband retains control over the investment, he has rather complete assurance that the trust will not effect any substantial change in his economic position. It is hard to imagine that respondent felt himself the poorer after this trust had been executed or, if he did, that it had any rational foundation in fact. For, as a result of the terms of the trust and the intimacy of the familial relationship, respondent retained

the substance of full enjoyment of all the rights which previously he had in the property.

14.12   Aftermath of Clifford

The Court had stressed three factors in the *Clifford* case:
1. Short duration of the trust;
2. Wife as beneficiary;
3. Retention of administrative control.

Because of the vagueness of the Supreme Court opinion the lower courts were swamped with *Clifford-type trusts,* and the resulting judicial confusion seems only to have increased litigation rather than to have clarified the rule of substantial ownership.

1. Suppose the trust was to last for 7, 10, or 15 years?

2. What if the beneficiary was the grantor's mother or a charity rather than his wife?

3. What if the grantor's wife or brother-in-law or a lawyer was trustee?

4. Suppose the grantor retained only the power to vote the stock in the trust, having appointed a corporate trustee?

5. Should there be one rule for a ten-year term if the beneficiary was outside the family group and the trustee completely independent, and a different rule if the spouse were beneficiary and the administrative control was retained?

Finally in an effort to rationalize the hundreds of confusing and contradictory decisions the Treasury issued the famous Clifford Regulations. Ten years were set as the dividing line, except that the time was extended to 15 if the beneficiary was not a tax-exempt organization and the grantor or his spouse had certain administrative powers. The duration of the trust was ruled immaterial however if the grantor or a nonadverse party had power to control the beneficial enjoyment of income or corpus. Trusts, also without regard to the period of their duration, were ruled vulnerable to the Clifford doctrine if the grantor had retained certain administrative controls which could be exercised primarily for his benefit. These are discussed later in this chapter.

The Clifford Regulations, with some modification, were incorporated in the 1954 Code.

14.13   Current law

Under the Code the income from a trust, whose duration is more than ten years, will be taxed to the beneficiary to whom it is distributable or initially to the trustee and later to the beneficiary under the throwback rule if it is in fact accumulated, rather than to the grantor, assuming no retained powers to control beneficial enjoyment, and no retained administrative powers. The tax on the trust income may be shifted even if the duration is likely to be less than ten years provided it is measured by the life of the income beneficiary. Thus, it is possible to create a short-term trust for the benefit of an aged parent and provide that it shall terminate either at the end of ten years and a day or upon the death of the parent, whichever event shall first occur.

A gift tax is payable on the creation of a ten-year trust. The value of the gift is the discounted value of the right to income for ten years. This amounts to 44.16 percent of the value of the property. Assume a gift in trust of $100,000, income to A for ten years, on termination, corpus to be returned to the grantor. The value of the retained reversion is $55,840. The availability of the annual gift tax exclusion depends on whether the interest given is present or future. Thus if the income must be paid to the beneficiary, the gift is of present interest. If the trustee is directed or authorized to accumulate the income the gift is of a future interest and the exclusion will be denied. See section 10.12.

If the grantor dies at any time during the ten-year period the value of his reversionary interest will be included as part of his taxable estate. If he died the day after the transfer (assuming it was not in contemplation of death) $55,840 would be included. This figure will constantly increase as the termination date approaches. For this reason short-term trusts achieve no substantial estate tax reduction. Their principal, if not sole, advantage is to reduce income taxes.

14.14   Tax savings through ten-year trusts

Short-term trusts offer attractive savings to limited groups who have no real interest in estate taxes or who hesitate to part irrevocably and finally with their capital. The relatively young man of wealth, the high salaried executive with limited capital, the individual whose principal source of income is a life estate in real property or a trust; none of these people are immediately troubled by death taxes. They are looking only for relief from the heavy burden of high income tax brackets.

To take a concrete example: Jones is a top executive with salary of $60,000 and capital assets of $100,000. He is married and 55 years of age. Once he retires, his capital and the income it produces will be really important to him. But at the moment the heavy tax drain ($3,127 after the dividend credit on the $6,000 his capital produces) is his big concern. He can create, under the Code provisions, three ten-year trusts of his capital, income to be accumulated for his three children or used to pay insurance premiums on policies on their lives (but not on his life or the life of his spouse), corpus to be returned to him at 65 and the accumulations or the policies delivered to his children. Such gifts have a gift tax value of about $45,000—well within his and his wife's lifetime exemptions. The trusts over the ten-year period will pay income taxes of about $9,000 whereas if he retained the assets during the period he would pay income taxes of about $30,000. What the exact tax savings may be will depend on the tax brackets of the children since as distributees they would be subject to the unlimited throwback rule. See Section 6.12 where this rule is discussed in detail.

Further Jones has not substantially changed his economic position during the ten-year period. He has, the moment after the transfer, an indefeasibly vested reversion. It has a present value of 55 percent of the value of the trust corpus. It is presently useable as collateral and, indeed, may be sold, if necessary. What he has is very similar to the present ownership of a noninterest bearing note, payable ten years from date.

14.15   Charitable trusts

It is no longer possible to provide for a two-year short-term charitable trust. Further the Tax Reform Act of 1969 has made gifts of income interests of any duration to trusts with noncharitable remainder interests most unattractive from a tax standpoint. Prior to these changes Father would transfer, for example, $25,000 in trust, income to charity for ten years, distribution of the corpus at the end of the period to Son. Father received an immediate income tax deduction for the value of the ten-year interest, $7,200. If he were in a 70 percent bracket, this resulted in a current tax saving of $5,140. Of course, he or his son lost the use of the income $1,000 a year (if we assume a 4 percent return) for the ten-year period, but if Father was in a 70 percent bracket, the net loss to him was only $300 per year or a total of $3,000. Thus, the "profit" from the gift could be more than $2,000.

There was the further risk that the trustee would either receive and retain or would invest in low-yield securities to the detriment of the charity. In *Hipp* v. *United States,* low-yield life insurance company stock was put in such a trust and while the charitable deduction was based upon an assumed 3½ percent return, the actual return was very substantially less. In many of these cases the low return, frequently less than 1 percent, resulted from the fact that earnings were being retained by the corporation and were thus reflected in growth in capital value of the stock. Thus the deduction was frequently allowed for property that in large part went not to charity but at the end of the ten-year period to the family.

To prevent these abuses no deduction is to be allowed under the Tax Reform Act of 1969 for trust income interests to be paid to charity unless: (1) The income will continue to be taxed to the grantor under the Clifford rules, and (2) the charity is given an annuity or unitrust interest. Further, if for any reason the grantor ceases to be taxable on the income, there is to be a "recapture" of the deduction by requiring the donor to report as income the amount of the proper deduction reduced by the trust income already taxed to him.

**Transfers that may benefit the grantor including
retained administrative powers and the payment
of life insurance premiums**

14.16   Administrative powers

One of the three decisive factors in *Clifford* was the retention of broad administrative powers by the grantor as trustee.
As a result of the emphasis on this factor in the Supreme Court
opinion a considerable body of case law developed taxing the
income of trusts to grantors where the terms of the instrument
or the actual operation of the trust suggested that administrative control might be exercised primarily for the benefit of the
grantor, rather than for the benefit of the named beneficiaries.
Thus, if the grantor could borrow the trust assets without interest or security, he could effectively recapture the property at
will. The same would be true if he could purchase the trust
assets for less than a fair consideration. In other situations a
retention of voting power could enable him to continue to exercise important ownership rights in the property purportedly
given away. For these reasons the Codes lists four prohibited
controls, if taxation of the income is to be shifted from the
grantor to a trust created by him. Further the Code recognizes
that control may be retained through vesting it in persons,
other than the grantor, on whom presumably he may safely
rely to do his bidding.

1. If the grantor, or a nonadverse party, i.e., any person
who does not have a beneficial interest in the trust property,
has a power which enables the grantor to acquire the trust
property for less than a full and adequate consideration, the
income of the trust will be taxable to the grantor. This prevents
the grantor from shifting the income tax and at the same time
retaining the power to recapture the property. This prohibition
also requires the income to be taxed to the grantor if the trust
property may be sold to any person for an inadequate consideration. The theory behind this restriction is that such a power
would enable the grantor to control the beneficial enjoyment.
He could deprive the named beneficiary of part of his interest

and give it to another by arranging for a bargain sale to such other person.

2. If the grantor has the power to borrow trust assets or trust income without adequate interest or security the income is taxable to him unless the consent of a person with an adverse interest is required. The trustee, as such, does not have an adverse interest. This subsection does not apply, however, if the trustee (other than the grantor) is authorized under a general loaning power to make loans to any person without regard to interest or security. The power to borrow without security and interest is obviously a power to recapture and is made fatal if the grantor is singled out as the recipient of this favorable treatment, even in the case of an independent trustee.

3. If the grantor has actually borrowed the corpus or income and has not completely repaid the loan before the beginning of the tax year he is treated as the owner of the income. This is also designed to prevent his recapturing the trust assets. The restriction, however, does not apply to a loan which provides for adequate interest and security and is made by an independent trustee, i.e., a trustee other than the grantor and other than a related or subordinate trustee subservient to the grantor. Note that the earlier prohibitions included the power in any nonadverse person. This is a broader term and includes any person who does not have a beneficial interest in the trust. A related person, on the other hand, includes only the grantor's spouse, if living with the grantor, his father, mother, issue, brother, or sister. A subordinate person includes only an employee of the grantor, a corporation or employee of a corporation in which the stock holdings of the grantor and of the trust are significant from the standpoint of voting control or a subordinate employee of a corporation in which the grantor is an executive. Related and subordinate persons are presumed subservient to the grantor unless the predominance of the evidence establishes the contrary.

4. If any person in a nonfiduciary capacity has any one of the following powers, the grantor will be treated as owner of the income.

a) A power to vote or direct the voting of stock where the holdings of the grantor and the trust are significant from the viewpoint of voting control,

b) A power to control investments to the extent the funds consist of stock in which the holdings of the grantor and the trust are significant from the viewpoint of voting control, or

c) A power to reacquire the trust corpus by substituting other property of equal value.

If the power is exercisable by a person as trustee, it is presumed exercisable in a fiduciary capacity primarily in the interests of the beneficiary. The Regulations state that clear and convincing evidence is needed to rebut this presumption. If the power is vested in a person other than the named trustee, the determination of whether it is exercisable in a fiduciary or nonfiduciary capacity will be based upon the terms of the trust and the actual way in which the trust is being operated.

This last group of prohibited powers is the one that most commonly causes concern in the setting up of trusts. Frequently the only available assets will be stock in family corporations and the donors will hesitate to surrender voting control or run the risk that a trustee might dispose of the family stock to outside interests. Hence they will insist on retaining voting power or vesting it in others whom they are confident they can control. This will often create a real stumbling block to the making of lifetime gifts. Not infrequently, however, it may be overcome by a nontaxable stock dividend wherein one share of nonvoting stock, for each share of voting stock held, will be issued to the stockholders. A donor may then transfer the nonvoting common to the trust without any dilution in his control. The use of nonvoting common may be preferable to preferred since it avoids the stigma of Section 306. See section 17.30.

It should be noted that we have been concerned only with the income tax consequences of administrative powers. The Clifford doctrine of substantial ownership has not been carried over to the estate tax field.[2] For this reason transfers with the prohibited powers may avoid inclusion of the properties in the

---

[2] The recent attempt of the Treasury to tax as part of the estate of a grantor trusts over which such grantor retained investment control has not been successful.

estates of the grantors, even though they are treated as owners for income tax purposes. It is clear that all such transfers will incur gift tax, however. Hence in the absence of very special circumstances, they should be avoided. It is foolish to pay gift tax which achieves the avoidance of only one tax when a gift tax of the same amount can avoid both taxes.

14.17   Trust income applied to the payment of insurance premiums

In earlier sections we saw that the grantor was treated as owner of trust income that could be used for his benefit as in the retained life estate trusts and those accumulation trusts where the retained possibility of reverter was not very remote. There is a third situation which does not fall within the retained life estate principle but which offers such widespread avoidance opportunities that Congress specifically included it in what is now Code Section 677(a)(3).

During the 20s thousands of grantors created funded life insurance trusts consisting of policies on their own lives plus assets which were expected to produce sufficient income to meet the annual premium payments. Assume X in a 70 percent income tax bracket created a trust which produced $2,000 a year. The trustee used the income to pay premiums on insurance policies on X's life which he had transferred to the trust. If this $2,000 were taxable to the trustee, the rate would be 14–17 percent instead of 70 percent; thus the net income available for premiums would be $1,690 instead of $600. There were difficulties in treating the grantor as owner since the income was not being applied for his benefit, he being under no legal obligation to carry insurance for the benefit of his family. On the other hand, the moral obligation for expenditures for premiums is generally recognized as being as compelling as the payment of household and other support obligations. Congress therefore provided that any income from a trust that could be applied, without the consent of a person with an adverse interest, to the payment of premiums on insurance on the life of the grantor, (or his spouse under the Tax Reform Act of 1969) should be taxable to him rather than to the trustee, on the theory that he was deriving substantial factual benefits from such payments. The Supreme Court in *Burnet* v. *Wells* sustained the constitutionality of the statute. The Court reasoned "insurance for dependents is today in the thought of many a pressing social duty. Even if not a duty, it is a common item in the family budget, kept up very often at the cost of painful sacrifice, and abandoned only under dire compulsion. It will be a vain effort at persuasion to argue to the average man that a trust created by a father to pay premiums on the life policies for the use of sons and daughters is not a benefit to the one who will have to pay the premiums if the policies are not to lapse. Only by closing our minds to common modes of thought, to everyday realities, shall we find it in our power to form another judgment."

The Code contains a special exception where the proceeds of the policies are irrevocably payable to charitable organizations. It should also be noted that while there are no income tax advantages in the creation of funded life insurance trusts where the policies are on the lives of grantors or their spouses, trusts holding policies on the lives of others offer tremendous income and estate tax saving opportunities. See section 14.36.

Again, as in the case of the prohibited administrative powers, it is only for income tax purposes that the grantor is treated as owner. The fact that the grantor paid or provided the funds for the payment of the premiums will not require the inclusion of the proceeds in his taxable estate. However, because of the income tax disadvantage, funded insurance trusts with policies on the lives of the grantors or their spouses, have lost their attractiveness.

Transfers with powers to invade

14.18 *Revocable trusts*

The purely revocable trust has no tax consequences. No gift tax is incurred on its creation. The income will continue to be taxed to the grantor, whether paid to him or another. The corpus will be part of the grantor's gross taxable estate upon his death. Early efforts were made to avoid this rule of inclusion in the estate of the grantor by providing that the power to revoke should be conditioned by the giving of a stated number of months' notice of an intention to revoke. If no such notice were given, it was argued and sometimes held that the power to revoke did not exist at the date of death. Section 2039(b) now provides that the power to revoke shall be considered to exist on the date of the decedent's death even though the exercise of the power was subject to a precedent giving of notice or could take effect only after a stated period following its exercise. Revocable trusts, as that term is broadly used in the Code to include the power to alter, amend, or terminate either by the grantor alone or in conjunction with another or by a nonadverse party are treated in the next subdivision. It seems appropriate however to consider the tax consequences of an absolute power in the grantor to recapture the trust assets with the comparable power in a third person to withdraw the trust assets, since the doctrine of constructive receipt is equally applicable in both cases.

14.19   Powers of invasions

If the grantor retains the right to recapture the property at will, he is said to have a power of revocation. If a beneficiary is given the power to withdraw the trust assets at any time, he is said to have a power of invasion. Where such a power is absolute the beneficiary is treated as the owner for tax purposes. Thus, in *Richardson,* Father transferred property to a trustee to pay the income to Son and at a stated age to distribute the corpus to him. Mother, however, was given an absolute power to withdraw any or all of the trust assets at any time she desired for her own use and benefit. The trustee paid the income to Son, Mother having failed to exercise her power. It was hers for the asking and therefore constructively received by her. It is clear that Mother made taxable gifts each year in the amount paid to the Son. On Mother's death the corpus would be part of her estate. She had the equivalent of a general power of appointment. Thus for all three taxes she is treated as owner.

Code Section 678(a), however, makes it clear that a person other than the grantor shall be treated as owner for income tax purposes only if the power is exercisable solely by him. Code Section 2041 makes it clear that the power of invasion will subject the property to estate tax only if the power is exercisable solely by the decedent or by the decedent in conjunction with a person who does not have an adverse interest. If joint action with a person in whose favor the power is also exercisable is required, then only that fractional part of the property subject to the power, determined by dividing the value of the property by the number of such persons in favor of whom it may be exercised, is includible in the estate of the decedent. Assume A, B, or C may withdraw principal but only upon the written request of all three. Here A would be treated as the owner, for estate tax purposes, of one-third of the corpus.

These rules as to third parties make possible extremely flexible trust provisions in favor of nongrantors without adverse tax consequences to them. See section 5.14. However as we shall see in a moment, the retention of the narrowest powers exercisable in favor of grantors may have serious tax consequences.

Transfers with retained powers to alter, amend, or terminate

14.20   *Difference in estate and income tax language*

The estate tax section of the Code dealing with revocable transfers requires the inclusion of property in the taxable estate of the grantor, if he, alone or in conjunction with any other person, has the power to alter, amend, revoke, or terminate.

The corresponding income tax section speaks of the power to revoke exercisable by the grantor or by a nonadverse party or both.

Suppose X creates a trust, income to his children for their lives, remainder to their issue. X retains a power to revoke, exercisable only with the consent of his children, all of whom are adults.

The trust is revocable for estate tax purposes. X has retained a power to revoke in conjunction with other persons. The fact that all the other persons have substantial adverse interests is immaterial since the statutory words are "alone or in conjunction with any other person."

The trust is not revocable for income tax purposes. The income will be taxed to beneficiaries, not to X, because his power to revoke requires the consent of persons whose interests would be adversely affected by such action. The statutory words are "by the grantor or by a nonadverse party or both."

Suppose X had created the same trust except that, instead of the power to revoke with the consent of the children, the trustee was authorized in his sole discretion to return the corpus to the grantor at any time. Here the trust is revocable for income tax purposes since the trustee is a nonadverse party. It is irrevocable for estate tax purposes since the grantor does not have the power either "alone or in conjunction with" the trustee. It is vested exclusively in a third party and the fact that his interests would not be adversely affected is immaterial.

There is an element of unreality in this whole area. How important is it that the grantor retain the power to act with another? Presumably he will select a trustee on whom he feels he can rely to follow his suggestions. It is doubtful if his position is strengthened by having to sign the consent with the trustee. Whether both must act or only the trustee, the trustee must still be persuaded. How important is it that the action must be taken with the consent of adverse parties? Suppose Father creates a trust, for Son, the corpus of which may be returned to him by the trustee only with the consent of Son. Here the gift is complete for both estate and income taxes. But if Father, whose wealth is, as it generally will be, ten times the value of the trust, suggests that he would like the corpus back, is Son likely to object? Any hesitancy on Son's part can effectively be dispelled if Father has the forethought to leave his Last Will and Testament at a prominent place on the table around which the suggestion is being discussed.

But the law has to draw lines. It is, however, unfortunate that the estate rules should differ from the income tax rules where the policy would seem to be the same. The discussion that follows should convince the reader that the only safe procedure in advising on the selection of trustees is to insist (1) that the donor retain no voice whatever in the administration of the trust and (2) that the trustee selected be a corporation or a completely independent person, unrelated to the donor and not associated with him in business.

14.21 Gift tax

In the *Sanford-type trusts*, a donor will create an irrevocable trust, expressly providing that under no circumstances shall the property ever return to him but reserving a right to change the beneficiaries or to vary their respective shares. A typical illustration would be "to T in trust, income equally to the granor's three daughters A, B, C, with power in the grantor to vary the percentage interest of any daughter at any time or to wholly exclude any daughter from thereafter sharing in the trust."

In *Porter*, the Supreme Court held that such transfers were incomplete for estate tax purposes as the grantor had retained the power to alter or amend. He could revise what he had done by taking away A's share and giving it to B. In *Sanford* such a transfer was held incomplete for gift tax purposes. In *Buck* the income, even though irrevocably payable to others, was held taxable to the grantor. Generally speaking no gift tax is incurred where the transfer is both incomplete for income and estate tax purposes, though there are exceptions to the general rule. A transfer with a reserved life estate neither shifts the income tax nor removes the property from the estate of the donor. Nevertheless, a gift tax is incurred.[3] But it is believed this is an exceptional case. If property is transferred in trust with a power to revoke by the grantor with the consent of the trustee, the gift is incomplete for both estate and income tax purposes. The property will be part of the grantor's estate because of the power to revoke "in conjunction with" another. The income will be taxed to him because the trustee does not have an adverse interest. No gift tax should result. On the other hand, if the power to revoke requires the consent of the beneficiary, a gift tax will be incurred because the transfer is complete for income tax purposes. Suppose the transfer provides "income to A for life, remainder to B, power to revoke with the consent of A." Here A's adverse interest is limited to his life estate. Hence the gift is complete to that extent only and the amount of the gift should be measured by the value of the life estate.

Where the transfer is incomplete because of a reserved power, a later release of the power constitutes the taxable event. Thus, if a donor retains a power to reallocate the income, the gift becomes complete at the time he relinquishes the power. In the case suggested where he could revoke only with the consent of A, the life tenant, a release of the power would result in a taxable gift measured by the then value of the remainder interest.

14.22 Estate tax

Code Section 2038 requires that there be included in the gross estate of a decedent the value of any transfers made during life, for less than a full and adequate consideration, where the enjoyment was subject at the date of his death to any change through the exercise of a power (in whatever capacity exercisable) by the decedent alone or by the decedent in conjunction with any other person (without regard to when or from what source the decedent acquired such power) to alter,

---

[3] It will, however, shift any later possible capital gains tax.

amend, revoke, or terminate or where any such power was relinquished in contemplation of death.

In *Helvering* v. *City Bank Farmers Trust Co.* the grantor had a power to revoke with the consent of the trust beneficiaries. It was argued that the phrase ought to be construed to mean "any person without an adverse interest." But the Supreme Court held the language was too clear to be so interpreted. Any person meant exactly that, without regard to his interest in the subject matter. On the same day the Court decided *White* v. *Poor.* In that case the donor created a trust, terminable by the joint action of the three trustees, of whom the donor was one. She subsequently resigned. A successor was appointed who thereafter himself resigned. The remaining two trustees thereupon reappointed the donor. The Court held nothing was to be included in her estate since the power to terminate resulted from her appointment by the other trustees and was therefore not reserved by her within the meaning of the statute. It was also suggested that she had the power as trustee, rather than individually. This prompted the parenthetical clauses now found in Section 2038 "(in whatever capacity exercisable) and (without regard to when or from what source the decedent acquired such power)."

In *Estate of Holmes* the sole power retained by the grantor was to distribute principal to the beneficiaries. Thus he could pay principal to the income beneficiaries or reserve it for the remainderman. The Court sustained the inclusion of the property in the grantor's estate, saying:

> It seems obvious that one who has the power to terminate contingencies upon which the right of enjoyment is staked, so as to make certain that a beneficiary will have it who may never come into it, if the power is not exercised, has power which affects not only the time of enjoyment but also the person or persons who may enjoy the donation. More therefore is involved than mere acceleration of the time of enjoyment. The very right of enjoyment is affected, the difference dependent upon the grantor's power being between present substantial benefit and the mere prospect or possibility, even the probability, that one may have it at some uncertain future time or perhaps not at all.

The *Holmes* case was followed by *Lober.* In that case the grantor declared himself trustee of certain securities for his son. He could accumulate income during the son's minority at the end of which time it was to be paid to the son. The trust was to terminate and the principal distributed to the son at 25. It was assumed that if the son died before 25 the principal would be payable to his estate. Lober retained the sensible power to pay out principal at an earlier date if he should so decide. Here the sole retained power was the right to accelerate the payment of principal. But this was sufficient to subject the property to tax at the death of the donor. The result in *Lober* would have been the same if the donor was required to obtain the consent of others before making any distribution. Thus it seems clear that if the donor is the trustee or one of several trustees, any of the usual absolute discretionary powers will prove fatal.[4]

Nor can these powers be subtly retained. Thus, it is clear that if an independent trustee is given such powers but the grantor retains the right to remove the trustee and appoint a substitute, including himself, he will be held to have the powers himself.

Suppose, however, that power to pay out or accumulate or to distribute principal may be exercised only upon the happening of future contingencies. (Other than a precedent giving of notice, see Section 14.18.) Can it then be said that the grantor has the power at the date of his death, the contingency not having yet occurred? In *Estate of Wilson* the power was to accelerate payments of interest or principal "in case of need for educational purposes or because of illness or other good reason." In *Weir* it was "for the support maintenance, education of our daughter." The parents were at all times fully able to provide for such support. While these cases also involved the effect of retained powers to remove a trustee, the opinions make it clear that because of the objective standards, and the absence of conditions warranting the exercise of the powers, the transfers were not within the statute.

In the leading case of *Jennings* v. *Smith* the trustee, of whom

---

[4] It is possible that retention of broad investment control by a grantor may prove fatal since by this device he may be able to control the flow of income by, for example, investing in unproductive property.

the donor was one, were empowered to invade corpus if the beneficiaries "should suffer prolonged illness or be overtaken by financial misfortune which the trustees deemed extraordinary." The Court held that as the trustees were not free to exercise their discretion, since the contingencies had not happened, the trust properties were not includible in the estate of the donor. On the other hand, where there was an absence of a definite standard such as a power to invade for "the best interests" or "for the comfort and happiness" of the beneficiary or "if the circumstances so require" the corpus will be taxed as part of the estate of the grantor if he had retained any voice in the decision on the theory that such vague phrases are equivalent to an absolute power.

It is possible, under the above cases, for the grantor to be one of the trustees provided all discretionary powers relating to the enjoyment of the property are limited by substantial external standards. Query, if this price is worth paying since, in so far as the estate tax is concerned, absolute discretionary power (with resultant greater flexibility) may be given to any trustee, whether he be related or subordinate in the income tax sense or not?

14.23   Income tax

One of the three bases for treating a grantor as the owner of trust income for income tax purposes is the retention of a power to control beneficial enjoyment of income or corpus. It is immaterial whether the power is retained by the grantor or is given to a nonadverse party. However, the rule is subject to a number of exceptions, some of which are noted below.

The following powers in anyone, including the grantor, will not cause the income to be taxed to the grantor.

1. A power to apply the income to the support of the grantor's dependents except to the extent actually applied.

2. A power to invade corpus for the benefit of a designated beneficiary. (Lober-type trust.)

3. A power to postpone the payment of income to the beneficiary for a reasonable time.

4. A power to postpone payment during minority or disability.

5. A power to apportion receipts and disbursements between income and principal.

Further the grantor will not be taxed on the trust income if an absolute discretionary power to apportion income and principal among a class of beneficiaries (sprinkle-type trust) is held by an independent trustee, i.e., a person who is neither a related nor subordinate trustee.

If the power to apportion among a class is limited by an external standard the power may be given to a related or subordinate trustee other than the spouse of the grantor and, of course, other than the grantor himself.

Thus some flexibility is possible with the grantor as trustee; slightly greater flexibility is possible if a related or subordinate trustee is appointed.

14.24   Selection of trustee

Too often the grantor insists on being trustee, because it appears possible. Failing this he nominates his spouse, his brother, or his chief bookkeeper. Trusts may be drawn that effect complete gifts for both estate tax and income tax purposes with the grantor or those whom he knows he can dominate as trustees. However, as appears from the above cases and statutory rules, all the usual discretionary powers that make trusts desirable must be foregone. Experience during the depression of the 30s indicated the unfortunate consequences of too rigid trusts. Income beneficiaries went hungry to preserve the rights of as yet unborn remaindermen, who could not conceivably have been the primary, or indeed other than incidental, objects of the donor's bounty. But the law of trusts grew up in England at a time when the principal objective was to maintain property in the family line for generations. Conservation of capital was as important as the production of income. Today the typical grantor is primarily interested in the life tenant. The remainderman is generally of secondary importance, often added merely to avoid an estate tax on the death of the first donee. But the old trust law prevails unless the grantor makes it clear that he is more interested in the welfare of the life tenant than in the preservation of the capital for the remainderman. For this reason trustees are understandably hesitant to act in a way that may seem to unduly favor the income beneficiary. Discretionary powers are essential if the trust is to serve the best interest of the family. To hedge them around with objective standards only further restricts the rights of those who are the main objects of the donor's bounty.

It may be argued, in answer to the objections raised above, that related or subordinate trustees are not likely to be deterred from liberally exercising discretionary powers in spite of the existence of substantial objective standards; that they probably would go along with the suggestions of grantors and beneficiaries even at the risk of assuming liabilities to the remainderman, rather confident that such risks are more theoretical than real. It is true that corporate trustees too often use the excuse of the rights of unborn future beneficiaries to justify their refusal of what to grantors and the life tenants seem reasonable requests.

But the objections to related and subordinate trustees, and indeed to all individuals, are at least fivefold.

1. A beneficiary, as trustee, must be excluded from all discretionary decisions, the exercise of which might prove beneficial to him. If he can decide how to spray the income among a class of which he is one, he will be treated as in constructive receipt of all the income, no matter how distributed. If he has this power over corpus, the trust property will be part of his estate because he has the equivalent of a general power of appointment. If he exercises either of these powers in favor of others, he will be treated as making a taxable gift.

2. Individual trustees die, resign, or become incapacitated. Trusts normally have a long duration and are created by older persons. The people they are willing to rely on are normally about their own ages. Hence in considering successor trustees the grantors, after much consideration will usually end by appointing a corporate trustee, as successor to the hand picked

individual trustees. Hence the benefits of having individual trustees are at best temporary.

3. Family discord and sometimes bitterness arises when, for what seem good reasons to the individual trustee, he refuses to accede to the desires of one or more of the beneficiaries. He frequently finds himself in the middle of family disputes that render his position unenviable.

4. Individual trustees are human, subject to temptations and pressures. Experience during the depression teaches how many honest and honorable trustees, hard pressed for the moment, "borrowed" temporarily the trust funds for their overwhelming and immediate financial needs, only to find they could not return the funds. Other individuals may become guilty of breaches of trust through arbitrary action or through ignorance of their obligations or the defalcations of agents. Too frequently there is little point in suing them to obtain worthless judgments. On the other hand, a corporate trustee while through its agents it may make mistakes or be guilty of dishonesty, will practically always be found to have the financial ability to make whatever recompense a court may order.

5. Lastly the complexities of the modern law of trusts, of taxation, and of investment and management are such that trusts have become a specialized business, rather than the incidental activity of a busy lawyer or trusted friend.

All considerations, tax and nontax, point to the selection of an independent corporate trustee.

14.25 Power to remove trustee

Many donors will insist that if a corporate trustee is to be appointed a power of removal and substitution of a new trustee shall be lodged in the beneficiaries or in other individuals in whose judgment they have confidence. Much can be said in favor of such power. Personnel in trust departments change, beneficiaries frequently develop real or imaginary grievances, and lack of harmonious relations may result. Changes in trust or local tax law may make it desirable to shift the situs of a trust from one jurisdiction to another. Most important the residence of the beneficiary may change. Frequently it is not desirable, or thought not desirable, to have a New York trustee managing the property of California beneficiaries. The lack of any personal contact will cause the trust officer handling the account to lose that personal interest that in many cases ought to be a major factor in policy decisions. For these reasons a power to remove and substitute may be valuable. Probably no tax hazard exists unless the beneficiary having the power to remove may appoint himself as successor trustee. But conservatism suggests a requirement that another corporate trustee must be designated as successor trustee. Thus the adult income beneficiaries may be given the power to remove the corporate trustee and designate its successor provided "such successor shall be another corporate trustee with capital of at least $5,000,000" or other stated amount.

Another plan is to provide that the corporate trustee may be removed and its successor designated by individuals who are neither beneficiaries nor related to the beneficiaries such as the minister, for the time being, of a certain church and/or the president, for the time being, of a particular university. This has the advantage of vesting the power in disinterested persons but the objection that, because there may be a complete lack of personal interest, such persons, who are presently unknowable, may turn out to be individuals who do not welcome the task and hence may be slow to take any action under the power. On balance the first solution generally seems more acceptable.

Reciprocal transfers

14.26   Nominal grantors

A, disappointed on learning that he could not avoid the estate tax on property transferred, subject to a reserved life estate, hit upon the happy idea of accommodating his brother B by transferring $150,000 in trust, income to B for life, remainder to B's children providing B would act in an equally brotherly fashion by creating a similar trust for A and his family. A would then enjoy the income from the trust created by B and his children would receive the principal at his death. It made no practical difference to A that the income came from B's property rather than his own.

C, another estate owner, was more interested in retaining the right to control beneficial enjoyment than in having the income himself. Learning that this could not be done without having the income taxed to him and the property taxed as part of his estate, he devised a similar reciprocal plan. He transferred property in trust for his three children, giving his wife a special power of appointment by deed or by will limited to the children. His wife, at the same time, created an identical trust except that he was given the special power. Each was in the same amount. His position and his wife's position were identical with what they would have been if each had retained the power over the trust he or she had created. But it was supposed that totally different tax results would follow.

The Courts, however, were quick to treat A as the real grantor of the trust nominally created by B. This meant that A had created a trust in which he had reserved the income for his life. Similarly C may be treated as the creator of the trust that bore his wife's name as grantor.

Assuming B and the wife of C had established the trusts because of the promises of A and C to do likewise, the holdings are obviously correct. If A gave B an apartment house in exchange for his promise to create a trust of securities for A for life, remainder to A's children, A would clearly be the grantor of the trust established by B. B is simply his nominee or agent.

In *Lehman,* the Court in discussing cross trusts between two brothers said:

The decisive point is that the decedent by transfer of his share to the brother or for the brother's use or according to the brother's direction caused the brother to make a transfer of property in trust under which the decedent had the right to withdraw $150,000 from principal. While Section 302(d) (the former version of Section 2038) speaks of a decedent having made a transfer of property with enjoyment subject to change by exercise of a power to alter, amend, or revoke in the decedent, it clearly covers a case where the decedent by paying a *quid pro quo* has caused another to make a transfer of property with enjoyment subject to change by exercise of such power by the decedent. "A person who furnishes the consideration for the creation of a trust is the settlor, even though in form the trust is created by another." (Citing *Scott* on Trusts, Section 156.3) X transfers property in trust for himself for life, with power of revocation. Y goes about it in a slightly different way; he pays cash or transfers property to another who in consideration of the cash or property sets aside or transfers securities in trust for Y for life with power in Y to terminate the trust and take the principal. Does anyone suppose that X's estate is taxable under Section 302(d) (the former version of Section 2038) but that Y's estate is not? Here the transfer by the decedent's brother, having been paid for and brought about by the decedent, was in substance a "transfer" by the decedent.

Because of the difficulties in determining whether in any particular case the transfers were in consideration for each other, the Supreme Court in 1967 in the *Grace* case held that the reciprocal doctrine applied whenever the trusts were interrelated and the arrangement left the grantors in the same economic position they would have been in if each had created the trust that bears the name of the other.

15

Life insurance*

---

* Credit for much of the material in this chapter belongs to George R. Davies, Esq., Vice President and General Counsel, retired, State Farm Life Insurance Company, Bloomington, Illinois.

15.1 Introduction

The life insurance contract creates a complex bundle of rights and mathematical privileges. The tax rules pertaining to the receipt of life insurance proceeds are peculiar to themselves because of the nature of the contract. For these reasons, it seems desirable to treat in some detail the various options available to the owner of a policy and the applicable tax rules in order to lay a background for the discussion of the uses of life insurance in estate planning.

Settlement options

15.2 In general

The owner of a policy may elect to have the cash surrender value or the proceeds payable at death paid in accordance with any one of the standard options. Usually if the owner does not avail himself of this privilege, the beneficiary of a lump sum settlement at the death of the insured may do so. Ordinarily there are five standard options available—interest option, fixed years installments, life income, fixed amount installments, and joint life income.

15.3 Interest option

Under this option, instead of receiving a lump sum payment, the sum payable may be left with the company at the guaranteed rate of interest stated in the policy. In many of the older policies, issued 25 or 30 years ago, the guaranteed minimum rate of interest may be as high as 3½ percent; currently issued contracts usually provide for 2½–3 percent. The beneficiary may also be given the privilege of withdrawing all or a part of the principal at any time.

15.4 Fixed years installments

Payment may be elected in equal monthly installments for a fixed number of years according to the Installment Table which will be found in the policy. The tables appearing immediately below are taken from the standard policy issued by the State Farm Life Insurance Company. Substantially identical tables will be found in the contracts of all other companies.

Assume a $50,000 policy, with an election to receive monthly installments for a period of 15 years. Each monthly payment would amount to $344.50 ($6.89 multiplied by 50). The annual return would amount to $4,134.00. Over the 15-year period the beneficiary would receive $62,010.00. Annual dividends, depending on the earnings of the company, may considerably increase the amount of each payment.

15.5 Life income payments

This option provides for payment in equal monthly installments during the remaining lifetime of the payee. The amount

Fixed years installments table (monthly installments that $1,000 will obtain for number of years elected)

Number of years elected	Monthly installments	Number of years elected	Monthly installments
1	$84.68	16	$6.54
2	42.96	17	6.24
3	29.06	18	5.98
4	22.12	19	5.74
5	17.95	20	5.53
6	15.18	21	5.33
7	13.20	22	5.16
8	11.71	23	5.00
9	10.56	24	4.85
10	9.64	25	4.72
11	8.88	26	4.60
12	8.26	27	4.49
13	7.73	28	4.38
14	7.28	29	4.28
15	6.89	30	4.19

Life installments table* (monthly installments for life that $1,000 will obtain)

Age last birthday Man	Woman	Life	With 5 years certain	With 10 years certain	With 15 years certain	With 20 years certain
	14	$ 3.21	$ 3.20	$3.18	$3.16	$3.13
15	19	3.28	3.27	3.25	3.23	3.19
20	24	3.37	3.36	3.34	3.31	3.28
25	29	3.47	3.47	3.44	3.41	3.38
30	34	3.61	3.60	3.58	3.54	3.50
35	39	3.79	3.77	3.75	3.70	3.65
40	44	4.01	3.99	3.96	3.90	3.84
45	49	4.30	4.28	4.23	4.16	4.06
50	54	4.68	4.65	4.58	4.47	4.33
55	59	5.18	5.14	5.03	4.86	4.63
60	64	5.88	5.81	5.61	5.31	4.94
65	69	6.84	6.71	6.34	5.81	5.22
70	74	8.21	7.93	7.20	6.28	5.41
75	79	10.22	9.56	8.11	6.63	5.50
80 and over	84 and over	13.22	11.64	8.91	6.82	5.52

* This table illustrates installments for specimen ages only. Installments for ages not shown shall be determined on the same basis as those in this table.

payable varies according to sex and age last birthday of the beneficiary on the date the option becomes effective. Payment is guaranteed for a stated number of years.

Assume a $50,000 policy, with an election by a woman 49 years of age to receive payments for her life, with 15 years certain. This means that if she dies before attaining 64, the payments will be continued to a secondary beneficiary until 15 years from the date the option became effective. If, however, she lives until 90 the payments will continue until her death. Here the monthly payments would amount to $208.00 ($4.16 multiplied by 50). The annual payments would amount to $2,496.00. Note how little would be the variance in the monthly payments if she were to select 20 years certain. Here the monthly payment would be $203.00 instead of $208.00.

15.6   Fixed amount installments

Here the principal amount is retained by the company, credited with interest annually on the then balance of the fund at a rate of not less than 3 percent or other guaranteed rate. From this fund installments of fixed amounts are paid until the fund is exhausted.

15.7   Joint life income

Payments may be elected in equal monthly installments for the lives of two beneficiaries, according to a Joint Life Installment Table, for the sex and age last birthday of each of the two payees on the date the option becomes effective. Following the first death payment is continued in either the full or a reduced amount for the life of the survivor.

Assume a $50,000 policy with an election to receive monthly payment for the lives of a man 65 and a woman 64. During their joint lives the monthly payments will amount to $260.50. As long as at least one survives, the same monthly income is payable.

Considerable flexibility may be introduced in many of the

Joint life installments table* (joint monthly installments for both lives that $1,000 will obtain with same amount to last survivor for life)

Age last birthday Man	Age last birthday Woman	Man 39 / Woman 39	Man 40 / Woman 44	Man 45 / Woman 49	Man 50 / Woman 54	Man 55 / Woman 59	Man 60 / Woman 64	Man 65 / Woman 69	Man 70 / Woman 74	Man 75 / Woman 79	Man 80 and over / Woman 84 and over
39	39	$3.52	$3.58	$3.64	$3.68	$3.72	$3.74	$3.76	$3.77	$3.78	$3.78
40	44	3.58	3.67	3.76	3.83	3.88	3.92	3.95	3.98	3.99	4.00
45	49	3.64	3.76	3.87	3.98	4.07	4.14	4.20	4.24	4.26	4.28
50	54	3.68	3.83	3.98	4.13	4.27	4.39	4.49	4.56	4.61	4.64
55	59	3.72	3.88	4.07	4.27	4.48	4.67	4.83	4.96	5.05	5.11
60	64	3.74	3.92	4.14	4.39	4.67	4.95	5.21	5.43	5.60	5.72
65	69	3.76	3.95	4.20	4.49	4.83	5.21	5.60	5.97	6.27	6.51
70	74	3.77	3.98	4.24	4.56	4.96	5.43	5.97	6.53	7.05	7.49
75	79	3.78	3.99	4.26	4.61	5.05	5.60	6.27	7.05	7.88	8.66
80 and over	84 and over	3.78	4.00	4.28	4.64	5.11	5.72	6.51	7.49	8.66	9.91

*This table illustrates joint installments for specimen age combinations only. Installments for age combinations not shown shall be determined on the same basis as those in this table.

option settlements through the use of withdrawal privileges so that the capital may be available at earlier dates if the beneficiaries desire it. Company contracts vary and, of course, each individual policy must be carefully studied.

Non-forfeiture provisions

15.8   Lifetime values

All standard policies contain provisions for cash surrender values, extended term insurance and paid-up insurance. The Table of Values appearing below is taken from the ordinary

Table of values for a policy providing $1,000 amount of insurance* (age 35; annual non-forfeiture factors: first 20 years $18.32582; thereafter $16.86452)

End of policy year	Cash surrender or maximum loan value	Extended term insurance		Paid-up insurance
		Years	*Days*	
2	$ 9.96	2	213	$ 26
3	26.26	5	297	67
4	42.88	8	83	106
5	59.80	10	23	144
6	77.02	11	171	180
7	94.52	12	209	216
8	112.30	13	161	250
9	130.37	14	47	284
10	148.70	14	241	316
11	167.30	15	27	347
12	186.15	15	139	377
13	205.22	15	221	407
14	224.50	15	276	435
15	243.98	15	308	462
16	263.62	15	320	489
17	283.43	15	314	514
18	303.40	15	292	539
19	323.49	15	257	562
20	343.72	15	212	585
Age 55	343.72	15	212	585
Age 60	437.64	14	146	677
Age 65	529.20	12	358	750

*These values do not include allowance for any paid-up dividend additions and are subject to adjustment on account of any credits or indebtedness on this policy. Values not appearing in this table will be computed on the same basis and will be furnished on request.

whole life policy, for age 35, of State Farm Life Insurance Company.

Assume a policy in the amount of $50,000 issued to a male at age 35. The annual premiums on such a policy amount of $1,097, without reference to dividends.

At the end of 15 years, the owner of the policy may:

1. Surrender the policy for its cash value, $12,199;

2. Elect to take extended term insurance for 15 years and 308 days; or

3. Take paid-up insurance in the amount of $23,100.

If he takes the cash surrender value of $12,199.00, he may take it in a lump sum or, under most policies, under one of the standard options. If he takes extended term insurance he will have protection in the face amount of the policy for 15 years and 308 days, which means that if he dies any time after age 50 (the date of election) and before age 65 plus 308 days, the policy will be payable to his named beneficiary in its face amount of $50,000. If he dies thereafter nothing will be payable. If he takes paid-up insurance the policy will be payable in the amount of $23,100 regardless of when he dies.

In planning any estate, the insurance policies should be carefully studied to determine the most advantageous method of fitting these assets into the overall plan.

Income taxation—proceeds received by reason of death

15.9 Lump sum payments

The full proceeds, if paid in a lump sum, are exempt from income tax. It is immaterial whether the beneficiary is an individual, a trust, a partnership, or a corporation (but see sections 13.11 to 13.14). Thus if A purchased a $50,000 policy, paid three premiums of $1,000 each and died, the $47,000 profit would escape income tax. Where the insured owns the policy this is in line with the general rule applicable to all assets that have increased substantially in value during life and pass at death. Thus if A had purchased General Motors stock for $25 and it had a fair market value of $50 at the date of his death, his legatee would receive the stock with a cost basis of $50 and the entire $25 profit would never be taxed. The reason probably is that since the property is subjected to estate tax it seemed unfair to subject the gain to an income tax at the same time. However, if the policy is owned by someone other than the insured, the insurance profit is still exempt from income tax even though it escapes the estate tax.[1] In this respect the insurance contract represents a favored investment.

15.10   Interest option

Where the proceeds are retained by the company under an agreement to pay interest to a primary beneficiary, the full amount of the annual interest is taxable as ordinary income. Thus if the widow is to receive the interest for life, principal payable to the children at death, each payment to the widow is taxable but the principal sum will be received tax-free by the children. Frequently the widow will be given a power to withdraw the capital. In this case the principal will form part of her taxable estate since she has the equivalent of a general power of appointment. Suppose, however, the widow may withdraw only $5,000 a year. Such a noncumulative power, limited to $5,000 or 5 percent of the corpus, is accorded special treatment which, in the case put, should result in the inclusion in the widow's tax estate of only the $5,000 subject to withdrawal in the year of death. See section 5.13.

15.11   Fixed years installments and life income payments

Under the 1939 Code the entire amount received in installments or under life annuity options was exempt, though obviously a portion of each payment included interest earned by

---

[1] Other than a transferee for value.

the companies on the retained principal amount. The 1954 Congress regarded this as unduly favorable treatment, since if the lump sum had been received and invested by the beneficiary the earnings on the property would have constituted taxable income. Hence they changed the rule with respect to persons dying after August 16, 1954, to tax the interest element in the monthly payments but provided a specific exclusion of $1,000 annually for spouses. It was the Congressional purpose to encourage the use of installment or annuity payments for the protection of widows who might otherwise squander the capital. While it is not clear that widowers needed the same protection, the exclusion was made available for all spouses.

Assume a beneficiary, other than a spouse, is entitled under a $50,000 policy, to annual payments for 20 years of $3,000. Further assume the insured died after August 16, 1954. Since the face amount of the policy is tax free, the beneficiary may exclude from income $2,500 each year, paying tax on the excess. Thus $500 plus dividends would be taxable each year.

If payments for life had been elected, with no period certain (a rare option) the face amount would be divided by the beneficiary's life expectancy. Assume this, in the above case, to be 10 years and the annual payments to be $5,400. Here the amount to be excluded each year would be $5,000 (the face amount of the policy divided by the life expectancy of the beneficiary). This $5,000 exclusion continues for the actual life of the beneficiary, so that it is possible that he may receive more than his capital tax-free if he outlives his expectancy.

Usually the option will contain what is called a refund feature. When, as in the above case, payments are guaranteed for 15 years certain, the contingent rights of the second beneficiary to receive payments (if the primary beneficiary died prior to the expiration of the 15-year period) have a measurable value. This value, determined from tables issued by the Commissioner, must be subtracted from the face amount, to ascertain the sum that may be received as return of capital by the primary beneficiary. Assume the value of these contingent rights to be $5,000. The primary beneficiary then determines his annual exclusion by dividing $45,000 ($50,000—

$5,000) by his life expectancy. If this is assumed to be 20 years, his exclusion would amount to $2,250 each year.

All of the above examples have assumed a beneficiary other than a spouse. A spouse, in addition to the exclusion designed to insure the return of the face amount tax-free, has an additional "interest element exclusion" of $1,000 a year. Thus if the capital exclusion is $3,500, and the annual payments $4,700, a spouse is taxed on only $200 a year. This makes the selection of installment or annuity options attractive where a husband or wife of the insured is the beneficiary.

15.12 Transfer for value rule

There are a few situations where the proceeds may be subject to income tax in whole or in part, even though received by reason of death. The statute makes it clear that if the contract has been assigned for a valuable consideration any profit will incur a tax unless the transfer was to the insured, a partner of the insured, a partnership of which he was a member, or a corporation in which he was a stockholder or officer, or was received in a nontaxable exchange or reorganization. Thus if A, an insured, sells a $25,000 policy on his life for $5,000 and the purchaser subsequently pays $5,000 in additional premiums, receipt of the $25,000 proceeds will represent a taxable profit of $15,000. Congress apparently felt that this type of investment was more like the purchase of stock or property with the expectation of gain than would be the purchase of a new policy, because in the latter case the insurable interest requirement makes it most probable that such policies are designed to serve normal insurance objectives. But query if the few policies purchased for speculative or investment purposes is sufficient to justify a rule that in the great majority of cases works real hardships.

Let us look at a few typical examples.

Son-in-Law borrows $5,000 from Father for a business venture, assigning his policies as collateral. The venture fails and Father takes over ownership of the policies in satisfaction of the debt and continues the premium payments thereafter. Has Father made an investment? Should he be taxed on the profit when he would not be if he had taken out a new policy on Son-in-law's life?

Son has a $20,000 policy on which he has paid ten annual premiums. He needs funds to complete the home he is building. Father takes over the policy in exchange for $3,000, its cash value, and thereafter pays the premiums. Should this situation be treated differently from that in which Son, about to surrender the policy because of the premium burden, instead, at Father's suggestion, gratuitously assigns the policy to Father, who thereafter pays the premiums? In each case, Father's motivation is the same, that is, the moral responsibility he feels for Son's dependents.

This exception serves little useful purpose, and is in many cases a trap for the unwary. The purchase of existing policies presents no greater tax avoidance opportunities than the purchase of new policies and, therefore, there is no basis for the different tax treatment. So long as the exception remains law, however, all dealings with existing policies must be scrutinized; the uninformed will continue to be trapped. A sensible solution would be to apply the rule only where the purchaser did not have an insurable interest but efforts to persuade Congress to adopt this change have, to date, failed.

15.13 Proceeds as compensation

The proceeds will be exempt only if received by a donee-beneficiary. Thus if A, a lawyer, agrees to render legal services to B in exchange for B's promise to name him beneficiary of his life insurance policy, the proceeds will be fully taxable to A, when received, as compensation income. This may be only one aspect of the transfer for value rule. But even without such a rule, the result would undoubtedly be the same. The cases have held that a legacy may be treated as compensation and is not within the exclusion for bequests, and the same reasoning applies to the insurance proceeds.

In *Rhodes* v. *Gray* an employment contract provided that the employer would pay premiums on a life insurance contract on the life of the employee and on his death, pay to his designee benefits equal to the proceeds of the policy. The policy named the employer owner and beneficiary. Each year as the employer paid the annual premium he deducted it as additional compensation. In 1954 on the death of the employee the proceeds were collected by the employer and paid over to the employee's son pursuant to the terms of the agreement. The son claimed the payment as tax-exempt as an amount received under a life insurance contract. The Commissioner contended the amount was taxable as a death benefit (except for the statutory exclusion for the first $5,000). On these facts, largely because the employer had charged the premiums as additional compensation to the employee, the Court held that the employee was the equitable owner of the policy; therefore the proceeds did not represent compensation income. While not in issue, obviously each premium payment as made constituted taxable compensation income.

15.14 Proceeds as dividends

Suppose a policy is owned by a corporation on the life of A, its president. Other stockholders include B, C, and D, sisters of A. The corporation names B, C, and D as beneficiaries of the policy. On A's death and receipt of the proceeds by B, C, and D, each will be held to have received dividend income, assuming the corporation had earnings and profits in at least the face amount of the policy. This result seems sound since the moment before A's death the corporation owned a valuable asset, i.e., the unmatured claim against the insurance company. With A's death this asset shifted to the stockholders and the statute makes it clear that any distribution of corporate property to stockholders constitutes a dividend to the extent of earnings and profits. The recent *Ducros* case, a case of very doubtful authority is contra to the rule stated above. In that case a Mr. Small was president of a corporation, Mr. Ducros was treasurer. The corporation purchased and owned a policy on the life of Small. It originally designated itself beneficiary. This was later changed to name Mrs. Small and Mrs. Ducros as beneficiaries. The question involved in the case was whether the share of the proceeds received by Mrs. Ducros, a stockholder, was taxable to her as a dividend. The Tax Court held against Mrs. Ducros but on the novel theory that the contract was not life insurance within the meaning of the tax-exempt provisions of the Code but rather a wagering contract. This was because she had no insurable interest in Mr. Small's life. The Circuit Court properly held this error. The corporation to whom the policy had been issued had an insurable interest and this is all under local law that is required. But the Court further held that there was no dividend income since the corporation did not distribute its own funds. This seems clearly wrong. The corporation owned the valuable rights in the contract; these shifted at Small's death to stockholders. There was thus a distribution of corporate assets, the insurance, to the stockholders and wherever corporate property shifts to stockholders dividend income results to the extent of the corporation's earnings and profit. In the opinion of the author, no reliance should be placed on this case as an estate-planning tool.

15.15 Proceeds as alimony

Installments paid to a divorced wife may constitute alimony payments, taxable in full as such. The result here depends on the nature of the wife's claim to the payments. Suppose Husband agrees to pay Wife $300 a month for her life, whether she survives him or not. He secures the postdeath payments by an insurance policy on his life. All payments received by his wife after his death are taxable in full under the alimony section. On the other hand, if he agrees to pay her $300 a month during their joint lives and in addition transfers to her all ownership in a policy on his life, agreeing to pay all future premiums, each future premium constitutes additional alimony to the wife as paid to the insurance company. In this latter case the wife does not receive the proceeds as alimony. They represent the return on an investment owned by her. However, she would seem to be a purchaser for value, in that the policy was transferred in partial settlement of her marital claims. Hence her profit would constitute ordinary income in the year received.

As the last four sections indicate the proceeds are exempt from tax only if received by a donee-beneficiary. It should also be noted that the foregoing discussion relates only to proceeds received by reason of death. A completely different set of rules govern where the payments are received during the lifetime of the insured.

Income tax—proceeds received other than by reason of death

15.16 In general

Code Section 72 requires the inclusion in income of amounts received during the insured's life under a life insurance or endowment contract, to the extent such amounts exceed the investment in the contract. Payments may be received on maturity or surrender of the contract or as dividends or on a sale. Assume A purchases a $25,000 endowment policy to mature at age 65. If he dies prior to maturity his beneficiary will receive the proceeds by reason of death and they will be exempt from income taxation, subject to the exceptions noted above. But if the policy matures while A is still alive, the profit will be taxable as ordinary income. The gain is the difference between the net premiums paid and the amount of proceeds received. The dividend distributions received prior to maturity represent adjustments of costs rather than a distribution of earnings. This is true whether they are used to reduce the premiums or received in cash. Assume gross annual premiums of $1,500, with dividends of $300, and payments over a 15-year period. Here the investment in the contract would amount to $18,000 ($1,200 multiplied by 15). The profit would be $7,000.

15.17   Lump sum payments

If this full $25,000 is received in a lump sum by the owner of the policy, he must report $7,000 as ordinary income. The profit is taxable as ordinary income since the gain represents interest that has accrued over the years. Prior to the 1964 amendments to the Code taxpayers were allowed to spread their gains of this type as though they had been received over a three-year period. Because of the new general averaging provisions where taxpayers can *in effect* spread over the rough equivalent of a five year period, by virtue of the divide-by-five-multiply-by-five rule, the three-year spread for gain on the maturity of endowment contracts was repealed.

But since in many, if not most, cases the averaging rule will not prove particularly helpful because of the requirements as to what constitutes averageable income it may still be desirable to spread the tax on these gains though the election of one of the installment options.

Prior to the 1954 Code an unfortunate pitfall existed under the 1939 Code. The standard policy provisions provide for the payment of a lump sum unless one of the options has been elected. Suppose A purchased an endowment contract to mature at age 65. If he elected an option after maturity, even though only a day or two thereafter, he was treated as having constructively received the proceeds and as having then deposited them with the company. The result was that the full gain was immediately recognized. On the other hand, if the election had been made a few days before maturity, no immediate gain was recognized since the principal sum was at no time unconditionally available to him. This was an obvious pitfall for the uninformed. Happily Congress has now provided for an additional 60-day grace period, where the option selected is of the installment or life income type. This means that if the election is made at any time before the expiration of 60 days after maturity, the gain may be spread over the years in which the payments are made in accordance with the rules discussed in sections 15.19 or 15.20. It should be noted that this grace period is not available where the interest option is elected. This is undoubtedly due to the fact that in most cases where this latter option is selected it is accompanied by a privilege to withdraw the full amount at any time and the possession of this power, of course, gives rise to immediate recognition of gain.

15.18   Interest option

If the insured elects the interest option, the interest payments constitute income, just like interest on any other deposit. If the principal may be withdrawn at pleasure, the entire profit is immediately taxable. If the terms of the option prohibit any invasion, prior to maturity, the recognition of the gain will be delayed until the date when the principal becomes unconditionally available to the beneficiary. Presumably, if this right does not accrue until the death of the beneficiary of the interest payments (the insured) the receipt of the principal by the secondary beneficiary will, to the extent of the profit, represent income in respect of a decedent under Code Section 691. See section 3.10.

15.19   Fixed years installments

Under the 1939 Code a distinct advantage resulted from the selection of the fixed years installment over the life income option. If A had an $18,000 investment in a $25,000 face amount policy and elected to receive $2,000 a year for 15 years, none of the payments were subject to any tax until he had received back his entire capital. Thus, for the first nine years he would have received $2,000 a year tax-free. Under the 1954 Code a portion of the gain is taxed each year. The taxpayer is required to determine what is called an exclusion ratio. He takes his investment in the contract and his expected recovery and determines from these the percentage of each payment that may be treated as return of capital. Thus, in the case put, his expected return is $30,000, his cost $18,000. Here

$1,200 or 60 percent of each payment of $2,000 is tax-free; the excess is taxable as ordinary income. At the end of the 15 years he will have received back, free of tax, his $18,000 ($1,200 multiplied by 15).

The above example assumes that the payments commenced in or after 1954. If the payments had in fact commenced prior to 1954, for example in 1950, then our taxpayer would have received back under the old rules $8,000 tax-free, prior to 1954. To compensate for this he must reduce his investment in the contract by these tax-free recoveries before computing his exclusion ratio under the 1954 Code. Thus his cost would be $10,000 his remaining expected recovery $22,000 and his exclusion ratio 5/11 or 45.45 percent. The life insurance companies on request will furnish from their records the exclusion ratio in any particular case.

15.20 Life income payments

While the old rule as to fixed installments was highly favorable to the taxpayer the 1939 Code rule on life income options was grossly unfair in that it operated in such a way that annuitants rarely, if ever, lived long enough to get their capital back tax-free. Under the old annuity rule the portion of each payment equal to 3 percent of the cost was taxed as income and the balance treated as return of capital. Assume a cost of $17,000 with payments of $1,080 a year. Three percent of the cost or $510 was taxed as income, the excess was considered return of capital. The annuitant would have to live 30 years to get his capital back.

Under the new Code an annuitant determines the same exclusion ratio as under the fixed years option except that his expected recovery is based upon his life expectancy. Assume A in the above example had a 20-year expectancy. His expected recovery would be $21,600 ($1,080 multiplied by 20). The ratio of his investment ($17,000) to his expected recovery is about 78 percent. Once the ratio is determined for a particular contract it remains fixed despite the fact that the annuitant may outlive his expectancy. Thus in some cases annuitants will recover more back than their original investments, tax free.

Generally the problem of determining the exclusion will be complicated by the presence of a refund feature; i.e., the life income option will be for life, with 10 or 20 years certain. As noted earlier, this right to have the payments survive the death of the annuitant, has an actuarially determinable value and this value must be subtracted from the investment in the contract before computing the exclusion. The Commissioner has issued tables from which this figure may be determined. Again, the exact exclusion ratio for any particular contract may be obtained on request from the insurer.

A further adjustment must be made in any case where payments commenced prior to 1954 by reducing the investment in the contract by the amount of tax-free recoveries enjoyed under the pre-1954 rules before the computation of the exclusion under the 1954 Code is made.

15.21 Proceeds used to discharge obligations

It should be noted here that the above discussion assumes payment to the owner of the contract. If payment is directed to be made to another in discharge of a receivable or as compensation or as alimony, it will be taxable in full to the actual recipient. The owner of the contract, since it is being used to satisfy his obligation, will be treated as constructively receiving the payments and he will be taxed accordingly. The actual recipient will be taxed according to the classification of the payment, i.e., as compensation or alimony income.

15.22 Gain or loss on sale or surrender of policy

Any gain on the sale of a policy formerly received the benefit of the capital gain provisions of the Code, since the contract was a capital asset. The recent *Phillips* case and several others that have followed it now make it clear that on the sale of a policy the profit will be taxed as ordinary income on the theory that the gain is essentially ordinary income in character.

No loss is recognized on a sale or surrender of a policy. The result is justified by the fact that the taxpayer actually has no loss. He has had the protection of the contract over the years, which is the very thing he bargained for.

15.23   Exchanges of policies

Under the 1939 Code if a policy was exchanged for a different policy gain was recognized to the extent of the excess in value of the new policy over the net premiums paid for the old policy. To avoid the recognition of this gain the new Code now provides that no gain is to be recognized on the exchange of:

1. A life insurance contract for another life insurance contract, an endowment contract, or an annuity contract.

2. An endowment contract for another endowment contract, if the contract received provides for payments beginning at a date not later than the date payments would have begun under the old contract, or for an annuity contract.

3. An annuity contract for another annuity contract.

Note that the exchange of an annuity contract or of an endowment contract for a life insurance contract continues to be a taxable exchange. The reason is to prevent avoidance of tax due on maturity of endowments and annuities by conversions to life insurance contracts.

Estate taxation

15.24   Possible tests of inclusion

The estate taxation of life insurance has had a long and changing history. Originally only proceeds payable to the executor were included as part of the gross estate. But it very quickly came to the attention of Congress that, in the words of the House Ways and Means Committee in the Report on the 1918 Act, "wealthy persons have and now anticipate resorting (to named beneficiary designations) as a method of defeating the estate tax" and that "agents of insurance companies have openly urged persons of wealth to take out additional insurance payable to specific beneficiaries for the reason that such insurance would not be included in the gross estate." The law was promptly changed.

From 1918 through 1941, the test of inclusion shifted between ownership of the policy and payment of the premiums with considerable uncertainty on the part of the Treasury as to which represented the sound approach. In late 1941 the Treasury issued a ruling, which the 1942 statute incorporated in the Code, providing for the taxation of the proceeds of all policies (1) owned by the insured or (2) paid for by him. This dual test continued until 1954 when the premium payment test was discarded. Throughout the entire period all proceeds payable to the executor were included in the gross estate, regardless of who owned the contract or who paid the premiums. From time to time it has been suggested that, regardless of ownership, the portion of the proceeds in excess of the cash surrender value ought to be included since this element of value springs directly from the death of the insured. It is not unlikely that this test may be adopted in the future. For the moment, however, there are two tests of inclusion:

1. Proceeds payable to the executor.
2. Ownership of incidents in the policy.

15.25 Payable to executor test

It is immaterial who owned the contract or who paid the premiums, if the estate is designated as beneficiary. The only question is whether the proceeds are payable to the executor or to others. In a number of states insurance, even though payable in terms to the estate, inures to the exclusive benefit of the widow and children free of claims of creditors and is not administrated as part of the estate. The cases have held such insurance is in fact payable to designated beneficiaries. These cases arose under the special $40,000 exemption for insurance to named beneficiaries that existed prior to 1942 but are equally applicable to the payable-to-executor test under the current law.

The Regulations provide that insurance payable to the insured's estate includes "insurance effected to provide funds to meet the estate tax and any other taxes, debts, and charges which are enforceable against the estate. The manner in which the policy is drawn is immaterial so long as there is an obligation, legally binding on the beneficiary, to use the proceeds in payment of taxes, debts and charges."

Insurance will rarely be made payable to the executor. Generally this has the undesirable effect of subjecting the proceeds to the claims of creditors and to costs of administration, such as executor's fees, without any particular advantages. Frequently, however, the proceeds will be payable to a trustee with the thought that he will make the cash available for death costs through the purchase of assets from the estate of the insured. Here care should be taken to authorize but not to direct the trustee to make such purchases. Further in the case of policies used as collateral to secure loans (unless the proceeds would otherwise be included under the ownership test) it should be made clear that the insured is primarily liable for the obligation, and that the policy owner shall be entitled to reimbursement from the estate of the insured, if the collateral is used to satisfy the debt.

On the whole this test has raised a few problems.

15.26   Ownership test

Happily the premium payment test has been discarded. The only present basis for including the proceeds in the estate of the insured when paid to a named beneficiary is ownership at the time of his death of one or more incidents in the policy. Incidents of ownership include the power to change the beneficiary, to assign the policy, to borrow upon it, to surrender it, or to exercise any of the other contract rights or privileges. The insurance contract, like other property, may be freely assigned by the insured in a gift or sale transaction under which he can transfer all his right, title and interest to another. It is also possible, however, to transfer limited interests to others, retaining some of the privileges and rights in the policy. To free the proceeds from estate tax the insured must divest himself of *all* rights and powers in the contract. Assuming his willingness to part with his ownership there are no technical difficulties to the accomplishment of the objective, except that here, as elsewhere, the instrument must eliminate any substantial possibility of reverter.

The Regulations [Regs. 20.2042-I(c) (2)] have long provided that where an insured is sole stockholder of a corporation the entire proceeds of life insurance on his life must be included in his estate as through control of the corporation he has indirectly the power to change the beneficiaries, assign the policy, etc. This has never been burdensome as the amount of the proceeds was not included in valuing his stock. But the Treasury recently stated (Rev. Ruling 71-463) that the rule applied equally to a 75 percent stockholder. This would result in including, for example $100,000 (face value of a policy) in his gross taxable estate rather than $75,000, his proportionate interest in the corporation.

This ruling seems clearly wrong and created such a furor that shortly after it was issued the Treasury announced its withdrawal and indicated that the entire Regulation was being reconsidered insofar as it included within the term "incidents of ownership" a power to change the beneficiary reserved to a corporation of which the decedent was a stockholder (Rev. Ruling 72-167).

15.27 Possibilities of reverter

The Senate Committee Report in connection with the 1954 Code states: "The bill retains the present rule including life insurance proceeds in the decedent's estate if the insurance is owned by him or payable to his executor but the premium payment test has been removed. To place life insurance proceeds in an analogous position to other property, however, it is necessary to make the 5 percent reversionary rule, applicable to other property (see section 14.3) also applicable to life insurance."

This change caused considerable concern among life insurance lawyers. They were fearful that if Husband assigned his entire interest in his contract to Wife, the possibility that it might return to him by inheritance would be regarded by the Service as a possibility of reverter. There does not seem to be any basis for such a fear. Through the whole stormy history of possibility of reverters under the estate tax no one ever contended that if Husband gave Wife General Motors, his possibility of inheriting it from her represented a possibility of reverter and the Regulations now make it clear that the Service agrees. The Regulations specifically state: "The terms 'reversionary interest' and 'incident of ownership' do not include the possibility that the decedent may receive a policy or its proceeds by inheritance through an estate of another or as a surviving spouse under a statutory right of election or a similar right."

15.28   Contemplation of death

Insurance proceeds may be included in the insured's estate under other Sections of the Code. Thus a transfer of a policy without consideration may be held to have been made in contemplation of death if the insured dies within three years after the date of the gift. Life insurance transfers are particularly vulnerable to the contemplation of death section since it is hard to find life reasons for such gifts. Insurance is inherently testamentary in character. Its principal value springs up with death. Its purposes and objectives are associated, in most cases, with death. While it is possible that life motives may predominate, it will be the rare case where the taxpayer is successful in persuading the trier of the facts that the thought of death was not the primary cause of the gift. Many policies have been and will be given away in spite of this objection since there will generally be a substantial chance that the donor will survive the three-year period.

It should be noted that premium payments, like the original transfer, may also be regarded gifts in contemplation of death. Suppose an insured, having paid five premiums, transfers the policy to his son and thereafter pays another five premiums before his death. The IRS until 1971 had taken the position that each premium pays for the same proportionate amount of insurance. In the case put, each premium would be regarded as paying for one tenth of the proceeds and hence as the last three may be found to have been in contemplation of death, three tenths of the proceeds would be included in the estate. But in fact there is no way of telling how much any one premium paid for. In a sense it paid for none since if the last few premiums had not been paid, the face amount would still be due on death under the extended term option in the contract. Nor may it be said that the last premium pays for the excess over the cash value. Because the Courts have found it impossible to determine with any degree of accuracy how much insurance was purchased with the last three premiums, practically all the cases have refused to follow the IRS position and have held that only the dollar amount of the premiums paid in contemplation of death may be included in the gross estate. The IRS now agrees (Rev. Ruling 71-497).

15.29 Community property insurance

The taxation of the proceeds of these policies turn on local law as applicable to the particular fact situation. The policies may have been purchased prior to marriage and premiums paid from separate property or partly from separate property and partly from community property. They may have been acquired after marriage and paid for partly with separate property and partly with community property or wholly from either. The wife may have a vested interest or merely an expectancy in the proceeds.

If the proceeds are payable to the estate, and are community assets under local law, then only one half of the proceeds is considered as receivable by the executor since one-half belongs indefeasibly to the surviving spouse. If, on the other hand, the surviving spouse has only an expectancy or a defeasible interest, should she predecease the insured, the full value will be taxed to the estate of the insured spouse if he is the first to die.

Similarly local law controls where the proceeds are paid to a named beneficiary. Generally only one half of the proceeds of community-owned insurance are includible in the estate of the insured spouse since the survivor indefeasibly owned the other half. The fact that the husband as manager of the community possesses the incidents of ownership over the entire policy in that he can exercise any of the privileges, is immaterial since he holds the incidents over half the policy as agent for his wife. If both divest themselves of all incidents during their joint lives, nothing should be included in the estate of the insured spouse, assuming the transfer of his half interest is not found to have been in contemplation of death.

15.30 *Policies owned on the lives of others*

On the death of the owner of a policy on the life of another, the then value of the unmatured contract represents a valuable asset in the estate of the decedent. Like other property it forms a part of the tax estate, even though ownership passes under the terms of the policy rather than by inheritance. The value to be included is the replacement cost of a similar policy or the terminable reserve on the policy, depending on whether it was fully paid up or is one which calls for the continued payment of future premiums. The gift tax valuation rules, discussed below at section 15.32, are applicable to the estate tax valuation of policies owned by the deceased on the lives of others.

Where the insurance is community property, half of the value of the unmatured contract is included in the estate of the noninsured spouse, if she dies first, since by law she owns one half of the incidents in the policy.

Where the owner of a policy dies before the insured and the insured then dies within six months, it will generally be inadvisable to elect in the first estate the alternate valuation date since this requires the inclusion of the full proceeds in the estate of the owner. See section 3.25 note 3.

Suppose the owner and the insured die under circumstances that the order of their deaths cannot be determined as, for example, in an air crash. Under the Reverse Simultaneous Death Acts there is a presumption that the insured survived. Because of this the Courts have held that only the value of the terminal reserve is to be included in the estate of the owner. However, there are hardly enough cases yet to enable the author to state that this has become a well-settled rule.

15.31 Qualifying insurance proceeds for the marital deduction

See section 9.16.

Gift taxation

15.32 Gifts of policies

The gift tax value of a single premium policy or a fully paid-up policy at the time of the gift, is measured by the replacement cost of a similar contract. Annual premium policies, however, are valued at their terminal reserve plus unearned premium (slightly more than the cash surrender value at the date of gift) except that a newly issued policy will be valued at its replacement cost. The reason for the more favorable rule in the case of policies on which some premiums have already been paid and more premiums remain to be paid is that no replacement cost figure is available, because of the absence of any market for comparable contracts as of the date of gift. The exact value of any contract may be obtained on request from the insurer.[2]

If the donor continues to pay the annual premiums, he will be treated as making gifts each year of the premiums paid.

Gifts of policies and of premium payments qualify for the $30,000 lifetime exemption and also for the $3,000 annual exclusion unless, of course, the terms of the transfer make the gift a future interest. If the assignment is outright to a donee, the exclusion is assured. If it is in trust, the exclusion will be forfeited unless the donee has an absolute and immediate power of withdrawal. See section 10.15. Gifts of policies and of premiums also qualify for the gift-splitting privilege if the donor is married and his wife consents. See section 8.18. On such gifts to spouses, the availability of the gift tax marital deduction will depend on whether the nature of the transfer qualifies the gift by excluding it from the terminable interest rule or by bringing it within one of the exceptions to that rule. See section 10.19.

15.33 Inadvertent gifts of proceeds

A pitfall to watch in policies owned by one other than the insured is the inadvertent gift of the proceeds which occurs

---

[2] The Regulations 25.2512–6 give the following example:

A gift is made four months after the last premium due date of an ordinary life insurance policy issued nine years and four months prior to the gift thereof by the insured, who was 35 year of age at date of issue. The gross annual premium is $2,811. The computation follows:

Terminal reserve at end of tenth year	$14,601.00
Terminal reserve at end of ninth year	12,965.00
Increase	1,636.00
One-third of such increase (the gift having been made four months following the last preceding premium due date), is	$ 545.33
Terminal reserve at end of ninth year	12,965.00
Interpolated terminal reserve at date of gift	13,510.33
Two-thirds of gross premium ($2,811)	1,874.00
Value of the gift	$15,384.33

on the maturity of a policy by reason of death or otherwise when a person other than the owner is named beneficiary. In these cases, it is a good general rule that the owner should always name himself beneficiary. If the insured designates another as beneficiary of an endowment contract, a taxable gift will occur when the policy matures by reason of the insured's attaining the stated age. Thus, if A takes out a $20,000 policy to mature at age 65, naming B as revocable beneficiary, B will receive the face amount of the policy on A's 65th birthday. On these facts, A has made a gift to B of $20,000 on the maturity date. A might have made a gift in a much lesser amount by irrevocably assigning the policy to B before maturity, since its value at the earlier time would be considerably less than the face of the policy.

The same rule applies where the proceeds are received by reason of death. Assume that Father purchases and assigns to Mother a policy on Father's life. The children are named revocable beneficiaries. On Father's death Mother will be held to have made a taxable gift to the children. The reason for this is that up to the very moment of Father's death, Mother owned all the incidents in this policy. With Father's death and at Mother's direction, the valuable rights under the contract shifted from Mother to the children. She lost her contract rights, the children gained them. The courts have held that the gift is of the face amount of the contract, rather than the cash surrender value.

Since, under the Code, gifts of policies may free the proceeds from estate tax upon the death of the insured, many contracts are being and will be assigned in gift transactions. In these cases persons other than the insured will be the owners and if inadvertent gift taxes are to be avoided care must be taken that the owners designate themselves rather than others as beneficiaries.

A variation of the problem discussed in this section occurs when Mother owns the policy on Father's life and irrevocably elects the interest option with principal payable at her death to her children. Here she has made a gift of the remainder interest, and further, because it represents a transfer with income retained for her life, the principal will be part of her gross estate at her death.

Life insurance in estate planning

15.34   Outright gifts of policies

A life insurance contract has much to recommend itself as gift property.

1. Generally the donee feels no richer after such a gift. If Father gives Son 1000 shares of General Motors, Son will immediately develop a sense of independence and security of which Father may disapprove. Father will no longer enjoy the satisfactions that belong to the holder of the purse strings. The stock represents immediately realizable wealth, carrying with it the temptation to convert it, at least in part, into spendable cash. On the other hand, the insurance contract is rarely thought of as disposable except under the most pressing circumstances. Stock is productive of immediate income; the policy, on the other hand, is burdened with future premium payments that call for Father's continued help. These factors will appeal to many donors who are willing to give provided their donees' enjoyment may be indefinitely postponed.

2. Father's financial position, as a practical matter, remains much the same. He feels no poorer. Insurance policies are rarely thought of as available assets in business or investment planning. Generally they are thought of only in terms of their death values.

3. The gift tax cost of the transfer of a policy is generally nominal compared with the estate tax saving achieved. The transfer of a $100,000 face amount policy will incur gift tax on its present value or, if a new policy, on the amount of the initial premium. See section 13.32. This will practically always be less than a tenth or a twentieth of the value of what is removed from the gross estate. To remove $100,000 of other assets requires property of that value to be given. In the great majority of cases no gift tax will be paid on the transfer of insurance. Frequently no encroachment on the lifetime exemp-

tion is necessary since the annual exclusions of both donor and spouse are available where the gift is to the children and for gifts to the spouse the gift tax marital deduction is available. Further, policies may be split into two or more contracts so that the gifts may be spread over two or more years and among several donees.

For the above reasons many donors are willing to give their policies when they would be unwilling to consider any other gifts.

But there are pitfalls to avoid. To remove the proceeds from the gross estate the donor must divest himself of all interest in the policy. He should be careful to eliminate any possibility of reverter[3] and, most important, the gift must be real and not a sham. As with other transfers something more than a change in the paper title is required. Too often an insured will request an assignment of ownership to his wife, comply with the formalities and return the policy to his box. Has he really made an assignment or has he only pretended to assign it? As the Supreme Court noted in the family partnership cases: "Things may not be what they seem." The *Doerken* case referred to below indicates that the taxation of life insurance proceeds does not turn on nominee ownership but on actual ownership. In addition to fulfilling the formal gift requirements there must be an intent to give.

This intent will evidence itself by the assignment and also by the conduct of the parties. Later conduct may belie the words used in the assignment, just as such conduct was found to have done so in many of the family partnership cases. See section 11.6, for a general discussion of sham transfers.

On the assignment of a policy the donor should transfer the actual possession of the contract to his donee. He ought not to continue to use the contract as collateral for his personal loans. He ought not obviously to control the beneficiary designation. Thus if Father transfers the policy to Son, who is married, if Mother continues as beneficiary, it tends to disclose

---

[3] Where the possibility of reverter has a value in excess of 5 percent of the face of the policy the proceeds are includible in the estate of the insured. See section 15.27.

that Father is really sitting in the driver's seat. Premium notices ought to go to Son. He ought to make the actual payments, even though Father furnishes the funds. In short, Son ought to behave like the owner. Father ought not to behave like the owner. To the extent Son does behave like an owner he will develop a sense of ownership and the risks of a holding that the transfer was a sham will be correspondingly eliminated.

In *Doerken,* the decedent owned the policy according to its terms. On paper he had all the rights in the contract. But, in fact, the policy had been purchased with corporate funds, carried as an asset on the corporate books and the corporation was named beneficiary. The Court held that the corporation was the real owner; that Doerken was merely its nominee. The Commissioner may well use this case to attack formal transfers where assignors continued to treat policies as their own. Hence donors who continue to pay the premiums will be wise to take precautions to rebut any inference that the assignments were understood by all concerned to be for tax purposes only.

Where the assignments are outright, care should also be taken to avoid the return of the contract to the insured by inheritance. Hence the donee ought to execute a will specifically bequeathing the property to some family member other than the insured or the insurance endorsement ought to provide for ownership to shift on the death of the donee to a designated family member.

In many cases, in spite of what has been said above, insureds will hesitate to part with their policies, particularly those with substantial cash surrender values. These contracts will frequently represent the principal cash asset to be relied upon in case of need. This will be true where the estate owners' assets are chiefly in nonliquid investments. Here it may be important to study the contracts to determine the wisdom of continuing the premium payments. Assume Father has $100,000 face amount of policies purchased 20 or 30 years ago, with cash surrender values of $55,000 and net annual premiums of $2,000. The insurance at risk is only $45,000. If Father is in a 60 percent income tax bracket, it takes $5,000 gross income to produce the needed $2,000. If his estate tax bracket is 35 percent and his state inheritance tax bracket 10 percent, the net value of the insurance at risk, to his beneficiaries, is slightly less than $25,000. Here the premium cost may be too great for the net insurance protection, particularly if he can exclude the unneeded $5,000 from his gross taxable income.[4] In these circumstances it may be more profitable to elect paid-up insurance in a reduced amount.

As an additional step it will frequently be possible to purchase new insurance to offset the reduced maturity values with premiums that will frequently be less than the $2,000 for the old policies and give these to the children. In this way Father will retain the cash surrender values, in the event of need, and yet eliminate a substantial part of the insurance coverage from his estate.

15.35 Gifts of policies to trusts

No tax benefits arise from the creation of revocable insurance trusts. They do, however, have the advantage of providing for trust management of assets, if this is preferred over the use of the optional settlements in the policy.

The creation of irrevocable insurance trusts with policies on the life of the grantor or his spouse at one time offered attractive tax-saving opportunities if the trust was also funded by the insured, with securities, the income from which was used to pay the premiums. The present statute, however, taxes the income from such trusts back to the grantor on the theory that it is being used for his benefit. See chapter 14. For this reason trusts of this type have fallen into disuse. The income tax advantage subject to the unlimited throwback rule may still be obtained if the policies are on the lives of persons other than the grantor or his spouse.

Where it is not possible to fund the trust with assets belonging to another, there will be times when it may be desirable to

---

[4] By controlling the dividend policy of the family owned business corporation, for example.

create an unfunded irrevocable trust with policies on the life of the grantor. The objection to the outright gift of the policies is that the proceeds will become a part of the taxable estate of the donee. Thus if Father gives his policies to Son, Son's estate will be increased by the proceeds. This can be avoided by putting the policies in trust for Son and granting the various nontaxable powers discussed at section 5.14. However there is a major objection to this plan in that the premium payments thereafter made will not qualify for the annual exclusions since they will constitute gifts of future interests. Hence the choice is between forgoing the annual exclusions and keeping the property out of the estate of the donee or obtaining the exclusions and subjecting the property to later estate tax. While no rule of thumb is possible, donors in general prefer the exclusion. The estates of their donees can generally be kept at reasonable amounts through making all testamentary gifts to them in trust. There will, however, be exceptions, where the unfunded irrevocable trust to hold policies on the life of the grantor outweighs the disadvantage of using up the lifetime exemption and then paying small annual gift taxes on the premiums paid to sustain the policies. The particular facts of each case must be studied to determine the preferable plan.

15.36 Wife insurance

Prior to 1948 it was important to insure the life of the spouse who had the major share of the family wealth in order to provide the necessary funds to meet death costs. Thus if Husband had an estate estimated at $300,000 and Wife's assets were nominal, the federal estate tax on Husband's death would have amounted to $62,700.[5] There would obviously have been no tax on the death of Wife.[6] With the introduction of the marital deduction, however, it became possible, by redrafting Husband's will, to reduce the tax at his death to $17,900, an

---

[5] Before the credit for state death taxes paid.

[6] This assumes the wife either predeceased the husband or, if she survived, his estate would pass to her in such a way as to avoid the "second" tax.

amount that Husband's executors could generally manage to raise without selling assets at sacrifice values. But the reduction in tax was conditioned upon Wife's surviving him. Hence the costly risk to be insured against was the premature death of Wife, rather than that of Husband. This would, in the long run, be the event that might increase his estate taxes by $45,000. However, since the increased tax bill, due to the premature death of Wife, is payable only at Husband's later death, it is immaterial whether the insurance is on the life of Husband or Wife. Generally it will be on Wife's life since she will, in most cases, be the younger of the two and also women have a longer life expectancy. These two factors mean that the premiums on a $50,000 policy will be less if Wife is insured rather than Husband.

1. The policy should be owned by Wife, whether it is on her life or his, since her estate, by assumption, is nominal in amount.

2. Care should be taken to avoid the policy passing to Husband on Wife's death by having Wife execute a will leaving the policy in trust, with authority in the trustee to use the proceeds to purchase assets from Husband's estate.

3. Wife should be named beneficiary, if the policy is on Husband's life, to avoid the gift tax problem suggested in section 15.33.

In many cases it will be advisable to vest the ownership in the children, in order to keep the proceeds out of the estate of Wife, particularly as her estate will become substantial (if she survives Husband) as a result of the marital deduction bequest. If the children are over 21 this will not present any problem. The gift may be outright or to an unfunded trust. It may be advisable to put it in trust, giving each child an absolute power of withdrawal. The existence of the power will assure the annual exclusions for each premium payment. The children may be relied upon not to exercise the power in view of the family objective of having the funds available to render Father's estate liquid. Use of the trust, as a practical matter, is more likely to accomplish the objective of having the funds used to purchase assets from Father's estate.

If the children are under 21, it will be important to use the trust plan since, if the proceeds become payable and are needed before they attain majority, there will be no assurance that their guardian may legally use the funds to purchase non-liquid assets from Father's estate. Doubts have been expressed as to whether a trust for a minor holding only life insurance contracts will qualify for the exclusion under the new 1954 Code Section 2503 (c)[7] (see section 10.17). Further, the case law is uncertain as to whether the absolute power of withdrawal held by an infant is enough to qualify the trust for the exclusion. See section 10.15. However, it is believed, that if the Wife is not to own the policy, a trust is preferable in the case of minor children even at the risk of uncertainty as to obtaining the annual exclusions for the premium payments.

15.37 Grandfather-grandson insurance trusts

A favorite and highly advantageous plan is for Grandfather to purchase insurance on the life of Father (his son) for the benefit of Grandson. Simply put, the premium payments are removed from Grandfather's estate, the insurance proceeds form no part of Father's estate, yet the proceeds will serve normal insurance objectives at his death. For the reasons stated in discussing Wife insurance, section 15.36, the trust technique will be found preferable to the outright gift since Grandson will usually be a minor. The ideal arrangement is for Grandfather to create a funded insurance trust with the trustee owning the policy, paying the premiums and designating itself beneficiary. To illustrate the plan let us assume certain facts. Grandfather has an estate of about $500,000 with annual income of about $40,000. Father's income is about the same.

If Grandfather transfers $100,000 in securities to the trust for the ultimate benefit of Grandson, he will incur gift tax of about $9,000, if a widower, of about $2,500 if Grandmother

---

[7] Since the statute contemplates that income and corpus must be available for distribution to the minor in the discretion of the trustee, using income for premium payments arguably makes the income unavailable for the uses the Section contemplates.

is still alive. The gift will reduce his potential federal estate taxes by between $30,000 and $32,000. The $4,000 of income the trust produces will bear tax at the 20–22 percent bracket instead of a 58 percent bracket or 45 percent, depending on whether Grandmother is living. The trustee will be directed to purchase insurance on the life of Father. This will eliminate any necessity for Father carrying insurance and paying premiums out of income after it has been taxed at a minimum of 45 percent. Thus the trustee can buy at least two and one-half times as much insurance as could either Grandfather or Father with the same gross income. Further, on Father's death the proceeds will escape all estate tax because Father does not own any incidents in the policy. The proceeds may be made available to Father's executor through the purchase of assets from his estate. Note that the trustee should be authorized but not directed to make such purchase. See section 13.25.

It is probably wise not to give Father a special power of appointment over the trust assets since this might conceivably be construed as an indirect ownership of incidents in the policy. But there is no reason why the trustee may not be authorized to distribute corpus to Father, thus making him a discretionary beneficiary, without loss of the tax advantages, if this is desired.

The plan provides:

1. A reduction in Grandfather's estate tax.

2. A substantial annual income tax saving within the family subject to the unlimited throwback rule. See section 6.12.

3. The avoidance of any necessity for Father to carry large insurance protection.

4. The elimination of the insurance proceeds from Father's estate.

5. The creation of an estate for Grandson, to come into enjoyment at Father's death.

15.38   Short-term insurance trusts

Many donors will prefer not to part with their wealth permanently by irrevocably funding a life insurance trust similar to that discussed above. This will be true of young estate owners and of individuals with large incomes but relatively small estates. They will prefer to retain control over their capital assets but will be interested in any plan that will save income taxes. For these clients, the short-term insurance trust may be attractive. Let us assume an estate owner who is 55, with children 15 and 18. Gifts to such children of fully paid-up life insurance policies on their lives will later relieve them of the need for carrying insurance. Through a 10-year trust such gifts may be made at relatively small cost.

Thus our donor may transfer $50,000 of securities to each of two trusts directing or authorizing the trustee to use the income from Trust A to purchase a ten-pay life policy on child A. The terms of trust B may be the same except that the policy will be on the life of Child B. The trusts will terminate at the end of ten years, at which time the securities will be returned to the donor and the fully paid-up policies delivered to A and B.

The gift tax value of what the donor has given (the income interest for ten years) amounts to $44,160, an amount within his and his wife's lifetime exemptions. The annual exclusions will not be available because the gifts are of future interests. The estate tax consequences are negligible, see section 12.27, but by assumption the donor was not interested in estate tax saving. The income will be taxed initially to the trust and later on distribution to the beneficiaries under the unlimited throwback rule.

15.39 Gifts of insurance to charity

Where the proceeds are payable under a revocable designation to a charity, the full amount of the proceeds will form part of the gross taxable estate with an offsetting deduction for the charitable gift. This may, however, result in more than a wash transaction since the inclusion of the proceeds in the gross estate increases the marital deduction. Thus if Jones has $200,000 of other assets and $100,000 of insurance payable to a charity, the marital deduction will be $150,000 and only $50,000 will be subject to estate tax. If the charity had been irrevocably named beneficiary, the marital deduction would be limited to $100,000 because Jones would presumably have parted with all incidents of ownership. On the other hand if Jones had irrevocably assigned the policies during life to the charity he would have obtained annual income tax deductions for the premium payments as charitable gifts. Hence the problem is to weigh the advantages between the value of the annual income tax deduction during life as against a larger marital deduction at death.[8]

While insurance proceeds will occasionally be used to satisfy charitable obligations, it will generally be better to use other assets in order to keep the estate as liquid as possible so that death costs can readily be met without having to sell assets at sacrifice values.

15.40   Insurance-annuity contracts

Prior to the 1941 adoption of the premium payment test many insurance companies offered combination policies under which it was possible for anyone to purchase any amount of insurance without regard to age or health, provided he would purchase an annuity contract in a specified amount at the same time. For example, an insured, age 70, in poor health, could for $105,000 purchase a $100,000 life contract and a $3,000 life annuity. What the companies did was to precisely balance the risks. Assume the life policy cost $73,000 and the annuity $32,000. Also assume the loading charges, commissions, etc., amounted to $3,000 and $2,000 respectively. If the insured lived for 25 years, the company lost money on the annuity but made a profit on the insurance. If the insured died the day after the policy was issued, the company lost heavily on the

---

[8] Query the soundness of the plans that suggest an irrevocable transfer of a policy with a retained right, in conjunction with the charity (an adverse party) to change the beneficiary or the options under the contract as a means of obtaining both a current income tax deduction and the swelling of the estate for the purpose of enlarging the marital deduction.

insurance, but made a big profit on the annuity. Since the risks counterbalanced each other, the loss on either one was exactly offset by the profit on the other.

These contracts were widely purchased because of the specific insurance exemption under the 1939 Code (continued until 1942) of $40,000 for insurance paid to named beneficiaries. In many cases where larger policies were purchased, the purchaser would irrevocably assign the insurance (hoping thereby to remove the face amount from his estate) and retain the annuity contract (thus, in effect, reserving income for life).

The Supreme Court in *Helvering* v. *LeGierse* held, in a case where the decedent owned $40,000 of life insurance under one of these combination contracts, that the life insurance contract was not "insurance" within the meaning of the $40,000 specific exemption since the insurer assumed no risk. In substance, the transaction was like a bank deposit for life with guaranteed interest. Because of this case, estate planners felt that the insurance proceeds would be included in the estate of the insured, even though he had given away the contract, on the theory that he had made a transfer with a reserved life estate. However, in *Fidelity-Philadelphia Trust Co.* v. *Smith,* supra, the Supreme Court recently held, to the surprise of many, that the proceeds of such an insurance contract, which has been irrevocably assigned by the insured, were not part of her taxable estate in spite of the retained annuity contract.

Revenue Rulings following that case have effectively discouraged any revival in the use of these plans. Rev. Ruling 65-69 accepts the *Fidelity Philadelphia Trust Co.* holding that the proceeds of the life insurance portion of a single premium life-annuity contract combination are not includible in the gross estate of an insured as a transfer with income retained where the proceeds are payable to named beneficiaries and all rights under the insurance portion of the contract have been irrevocably assigned. However, the Tax Court has recently held such proceeds includible under section 2039 as a payment under an annuity contract purchased by the insured-annuitant.

The second ruling holds that since the insurance portion of

these contracts is not true "insurance" within the meaning of the Code, citing the *LeGierse* case, the proceeds are not excludible from gross income under Code Section 101(a). For this reason the ruling (65-57) holds that the proceeds are subject to income tax to the extent they exceed the aggregate of the net premiums paid for the contract designated as a life insurance contract. The substantial income tax that would thus be payable at death would seem to sound the death knell to the use of these plans.

16

Valuing the business interest

16.1   Introduction

Generally the most perplexing problem in planning an estate is presented by the business interest of the client. If it is easily valued and if the estate owner has adequate assets to meet his death cost and a family member capable of taking over and managing the business, the problem is readily solved by disposing of the business interest to individual legatees or to the residuary trust. But, in the great majority of cases, it will be impossible to determine with any degree of certainty the value of the business interest in dollars. This interest of uncertain value may represent the principal asset in the estate, and if there is no ready market for its sale, liquidation will almost always result in a substantial loss in value. For these reasons it has become extremely common for estate owners to arrange in advance for the sale of their business interests at death. It is usual to fund these agreements with life insurance in order to assure the payment of the purchase price. Such agreements may be made for any one of the following reasons.

1. The business interest may not be readily salable.

2. The going concern value may be substantially in excess of liquidation value.

3. The owners of the interests may be relatively few in number.

4. Estate liquidity may be a pressing problem.

Advantages of business purchase agreements

16.2   To the owner first to die

Death not only robs a man's dependents of his earning capacity, it may partially destroy the capital value of his business. If a business is liquidated for lack of a purchaser of the enterprise as a unit, all the intangible values disappear. Goodwill or going concern value cannot exist apart from the underlying business assets. In practically all businesses the whole is worth more than the sum of the parts. Clients and customers who over the years have developed a habit of doing business with a firm, do not easily drift away. A reputation for honesty, reliability, excellence of product, etc., attaches to a name and continues in spite of changes in management or ownership. A group of employees learns over the years to function efficiently. These intangibles represent vital factors in the valuation of a business, if the business is to be sold as a unit. If the business is to be liquidated, they disappear like smoke into thin air. Hence the preservation of some of the substantial values in a business depends on its sale as a going concern.

If no arrangement is made for the sale of the interest before the death of the owner, his executor will generally find himself in a poor bargaining position. Thus, a contract for its later sale represents the most effective way in which an estate owner may preserve the full value of his interest for the benefit of his family.

16.3 To the survivor

The survivor, if the purchase price is not burdensome, will be rid of estate interference and the introduction of a new and strange voice in the management of the enterprise. He may continue the same salary and dividend policies or change them to suit his wishes, a most unlikely possibility if his associate's widow is now a co-owner. As the Court put it in the *Emeloid* case:

Harmony is the essential catalyst for achieving good management; and good management is the sine qua non of long term business success. Petitioner, deeming its management sound and harmonious conceived of the (agreement) to insure its continuation. Petitioner apparently anticipated that should one of its key stockholder-officers die, those beneficially interested in his estate might enter into active participation in corporate affairs and possibly introduce an element of friction. Or the estate not being bound to sell to . . . petitioner might sell it to adverse interests. The fragile bark of a small business can be wrecked on just such uncharted shoals.

16.4 The agreement

The type of agreement, the logical purchaser, and the terms of payment will vary from business to business and will be affected by whether the business is conducted as a sole proprietorship, a partnership, or a corporation. The question of determining the overall purchase price, however, will be present in all cases and will frequently present the most difficult problem. This chapter will therefore be devoted to questions of valuation. In the next chapter, there will be discussed the peculiar problems which may arise because of the form in which the business is carried on.

Valuation

16.5   In general

The problem of how to value the business interest is always a difficult and perplexing one. The time of death, the then condition of the business, the effect at that uncertain future time of inflation or of depression, and many other unknown and unknowable factors, make fixing a price seem a hopeless task or at least a task fraught with many dangers. There are, however, several general approaches worth studying. Objections may be raised to each. None is entirely satisfactory. Certain businesses may lend themselves better to one than the others. Certain businessmen may prefer one over the others. Particular objectives may dictate the choice, as where it is desired to freeze the estate tax value of the business interest. In each situation each approach should be examined and the one that seems best suited selected. The various methods may be grouped under five headings:

1. Fixed price;
2. Average earnings formula;
3. Appraisal;
4. Book;
5. Varying combinations of the above.

16.6   Fixed price

Assume A and B as the contracting parties, having in mind that A may be the owner and B a key employee, or A and B may be partners, or A and B may be fellow stockholders. Assume they use the fixed price method and agree that the business is worth $50,000. The only thing they can be certain of is that it will not be worth $50,000 when the first one dies. It may be worth considerably more or considerably less. The business may expand or contract. Inflation may create additional values or depression may destroy existing values. Thus a price fixed to control at an uncertain future date, possibly years away would be, at best, a gamble. This uncertainty may be remedied, however, by a requirement that the parties revalue the business each year, and that the last valuation control. Theoretically such a solution seems ideal. Practically speaking, however, it represents no solution at all, because the parties never get around to the yearly revaluation. They are always too busy with more immediate and pressing matters.

But let B get sick. Now, if the price originally set appears, in the light of changed conditions, to be too low, B sends for A to visit him in the hospital but A insists that B is too sick to trouble himself with business matters. If the price is too high, A wants to discuss it immediately but B will request a postponement until he is released from the hospital. His doctor does not want business problems to delay his recovery! One or the other is going to be slow to sit down to a revaluation and the equal bargaining position contemplated by the contract has disappeared. Rarely does this method by itself represent a satisfactory solution, though in combination with the appraisal method it may serve well in many cases. Thus the price may be agreed upon with a requirement in the contract for yearly revaluations plus the added provision that if no revaluation has been made within 18 months of the date of death, then the price shall be determined by appraisal.

16.7 Formula based on earnings

What an asset earns is a measure, in substantial part at least, of its value. Thus a 4 percent bond should sell at less than a 6 percent bond, other factors being equal. But we find that, as a matter of fact, 6 percent bonds frequently sell for less than 4 percent bonds. The reason of course, is that the security is more doubtful. There is not the same certainty that the 6 percent bond will be paid in full at maturity. A stock paying $3 a year may sell for $30, a 10 percent return. Another stock may pay 60¢ and sell for $30. In this latter case there is only a 2 percent return but investigation will undoubtedly disclose that this latter stock has growth possibilities, more attractive to many investors than current dividends. A stock widely traded, on a recognized market, should be worth more than the identical stock, if no market for its sale exists. Many factors enter into value. Earnings are only one. Security, stability, growth, marketability are some of the other more important considerations.

Nevertheless a capitalization of earnings to determine the value of a business is perhaps the most common method used in the many situations where value becomes important. The other factors may be taken into consideration by the multiple used. Thus one business may be valued at ten times average earnings for the past five years, another at three times average earnings for the past six years. On stock exchanges, public utilities may sell at 12 to 15 times current earnings while food and clothing stocks sell at 10 times current earnings. Automotive stocks may sell at 7 to 8 times earnings while amusement company stocks sell at 4 or 5. A moment's reflection will indicate why this is true. There is comparatively little risk in the public utility investment. Come a depression people still need and use telephones, gas, water, electricity, etc. If earnings drop too low, state regulatory bodies will permit rate increases. True, food and clothing must still be purchased. They are about as essential as electricity and gas but there is no price protection and so the risk is somewhat greater. Cars are sacrificed before food, amusements before cars, etc. The price is governed by the risk. New industries will sell for less than established ones. But the reverse of this will be true when an old industry is being replaced by a new one. The whole problem is extremely complex and perhaps what is said here tends to oversimplify it. But the important fact is that people buy and sell businesses, bankers lend on the security of businesses, employees risk their futures on the stability of businesses, and in all of these cases, their judgments of value are predicated in large part on the earnings history. There has, therefore, come to be recognized a multiple for most common types of businesses which, in the judgment of the particular industry, if applied to average earnings over a stated number of years, depending on the business cycle for the industry, will reflect the value of the business.

A and B will know or can easily discover the multiple for their industry. Adjustments for a particular business due to peculiar abnormalities may have to be made. Thus salaries may be out of line, earnings or losses for particular years may be due to nonrecurring circumstances, etc. The multiple itself may vary from time to time with changes in economic conditions, but it apparently enjoys a degree of stability that warrants its use.

The advantage of determining the purchase price by, say, five times the average earnings over the last five years rather than using the fixed price is that the purchase price is more likely to reflect the value at the time of death. Perhaps greater weight should be given to the earnings of the two years immediately preceding death. Any number of adjustments will occur to the businessman and his advisers based on the peculiarities of his particular business. It is believed that this method has more merit than the fixed price.

16.8 Appraisal

Provision may be made for an appraisal of the business by two appraisers, one being appointed by each side; if they cannot agree, then by a third appraiser, appointed by the other two whose determination of value shall be final. The certified public accountant regularly auditing the books of the company may be designated as the sole arbiter of the value. Whether appraisers or the company's accountant serve, instructions may be given in the contract such as that goodwill shall be ignored or valued in a particular way. There is much to recommend this method as assuring the fairest current value.

16.9 Book

This will almost always be found to be unrealistic since the books reflect cost rather than market value of assets in most instances. Generally goodwill is carried at nominal cost. But this method may fit well in a plan which combines some of the other methods.

16.10   Combination of methods

Here, some assets may be required to be valued at book, such as fixtures, accounts receivable, raw materials, etc.; others by appraisal, such as buildings and machinery, finished merchandise; still others, such as goodwill, at a times earning rate.

In the valuation of business interests for tax purposes the Treasury sometimes uses what is called the Year's Purchase Formula. The method is to allow out of average earnings (5 to 10 years) a return of 10 percent on the appraised value of the tangibles. The excess is then attributed to the intangibles, which are capitalized upon a basis of not more than five years' purchase. This means that 5 times the excess average earnings represent the value of the intangibles.[1]

The Committee which prepared the ruling upon this method stated:

The foregoing is intended to apply to businesses of a more or less hazardous nature. In the case, however, of the valuation of goodwill of a business which consists of the manufacture and sale of standard articles of everyday necessity not subject to violent fluctuations and where the hazard is not great, the Committee is of the opinion that the figure for determination of the return on tangible assets might be reduced from 10 to 8 or 9 percent, and that the percentage for capitalization on the return upon intangibles might be reduced from 20 to 15 percent.

Of course, the above formula is subject to many variations. It represents at best a starting point.

16.11   Typical clauses

A typical valuation clause combining the several methods, is illustrated by the following:

The certified public accountant who regularly audits the books of the business shall calculate and certify to the net value thereof. In making

---

[1] Assume a business with average earnings of $35,000 and plant and equipment with a value of $200,000. Under the formula $20,000 of earnings would be attributed to the physical assets, the remaining $15,000 to goodwill. This gives the goodwill a value of $75,000 (5 times $15,000); the total business a value of $275,000.

the computation he shall value goodwill at three times average net profits of the business, before taxes, during the last three years; he shall value finished merchandise on order at the selling price, other finished merchandise on hand at cost or market, whichever is higher; he shall value fixtures and machinery at book value, less depreciation; raw materials and supplies at cost or market, whichever is higher, outstanding accounts at book value less 2 percent. To this he shall add cash on hand or in banks. Any assets not otherwise provided for shall be appraised by him at their fair market value. From the total of these assets he shall deduct any and all business liabilities, including contingent liabilities making the best estimate thereof that the circumstances, existing at the time of estimate, permit. All of his determinations, so made, shall be final and conclusively binding on the parties hereto, their executors, administrators and assigns.

A typical clause providing for an appraisal of the business interest is illustrated by the following:

The executor or administrator of the deceased partner and the surviving partner shall each appoint one arbitrator who together shall agree upon the valuation of the business interest of the deceased partner. In the event the two cannot agree, they shall appoint a third arbitrator and the decision of the majority shall be binding on both parties. In addition to all other assets of the business considered in arriving at the valuation of the interest, goodwill, if any, and the proceeds of any life insurance paid by reason of the death of the deceased, shall be included therein.

16.12   The regulations

The problem of valuation is always a difficult one. There is no ready answer. The Regulations state:

The fair market value of any interest of a decedent in a business, whether a partnership or a proprietorship, is a net value equal to the amount which a willing purchaser whether an individual or a corporation, would pay for the interest to a willing seller, neither being under any compulsion to buy or to sell. The net value shall be determined on the basis of all relevant factors including—

a) A fair appraisal as of the applicable valuation date of all the assets of the business, tangible and intangible, including goodwill;

b) The demonstrated earning capacity of the business; and

c) The other factors set forth in Reg. Section 20.2031–2(f) and (h) relating to the valuation of corporate stock, to the extent applicable.

Special attention should be given to determining an adequate value of the goodwill of the business in all cases in which the decedent has not agreed, for an adequate and full consideration in money or money's worth, that his interest passes at his death to his surviving partner or partners. Complete financial and other data upon which the valuation is based should be submitted with the return, including copies of reports in any case in which examinations of the business have been made by accountants, engineers, or any technical experts as of or near the applicable valuation date.

Purchase price as determinative of estate tax valuation

16.13   Arm's length purchase agreements

Assume A and B each owned one half of the stock of the X corporation whose principal asset was its goodwill. They entered into an agreement under which the suvivor was to have an option to purchase for a limited time after the death of the other all of the shares which the latter owned at the time of his death. Each was free to sell his shares during life. The price was to be determined by the value of the tangible assets, excluding goodwill. A died. The tangible assets, excluding goodwill, were valued at $50,000, and B paid A's executor $25,000 for A's half interest.

The estate tax return reported the following assets:

Residence...		$ 25,000
Stocks (other than X Corp.).............................		$ 40,000
Bonds..		$ 10,000
Stocks in X Corp.......................................		$ 25,000
Total Assets...		$100,000
Less		
Exemption..................................	$60,000	
Administration Expenses....................	$10,000	
		$70,000
Taxable estate.............................		$30,000
Federal Estate Tax..............................	$3,000	

The Commissioner would and should revalue the X stock by including the full value of the tangible assets, $25,000, plus a figure, which for illustrative purposes we will assume to be $100,000, for goodwill, on the theory that the option did not fix the market value of the shares for estate tax purposes. This action would increase the gross estate to $200,000, the taxable estate to $130,000 and the tax to $29,700. While the tax is thus increased by $26,700, the estate is not entitled to more than the agreed $25,000 for the stock. Thus this asset would cost the estate more in taxes than it was worth in dollars to the estate.

There are situations, such as the above, in which the restrictive price will have no effect on the tax valuation. There are other situations in which, while it does not determine the value, it will somewhat depress the value below market price. There are still others in which it will freeze it at the sales price level.

In *Estate of John C. Strange,* there was an agreement between two brothers, engaged in business in a closed corporation, which provided that upon the death of either, the survivor might acquire the stock of the other upon payment of $10,000 to his estate. Payment was made following the decedent's death. The fair market value of the stock at death was stipulated to be $238,126.54. The Board of Tax Appeals held that the option price of $10,000 was the proper amount to be included in the decedent's gross estate as the value of his stock.

In *Commissioner* v. *Benzel* a father and son had become estranged. The father, a majority stockholder, and the son, an employee of the corporation, entered into a contract by which the son agreed to continue to work for the company in return for an option to purchase his father's stock at the latter's death at a price which turned out to be considerably less than the value of the stock at the later date. The option price was held to fix the value for estate tax purposes.

In *Tompkins* the parties agreed that the partnership should carry and pay for $25,000 of insurance on the life of each of the two partners. On the death of either, the survivor was to receive the proceeds of the insurance on the decedent's life with the right to purchase the interest of the deceased for $25,000. It was also agreed that upon the payment of the

$25,000 to the estate of the deceased, the survivor was to become the sole owner of all the partnership assets, including the insurance policy on his own life. All premiums were paid by the partnership and charged to partnership expense. The right to change the beneficiary was reserved to each insured. Because $15,000 of the insurance on each life contained a double indemnity provision and because partner A died as a result of an accident, partner B received $40,000. He elected to exercise his option and, interpreting the agreement to require the payment of all the insurance proceeds, paid $40,000 to the estate of the decedent. Held: The insurance proceeds were part of A's taxable estate because he owned an incident in the policy, i.e., the right to change the beneficiary, but no amount was to be included on account of the value of his interest in the business.

In view of the above cases a study of the effect of restrictive agreements on value would seem desirable.

1. Where the agreement requires the estate to sell the decedent's interest at a fixed price but there is no similar restriction to prevent his selling his interest while he lives, the full market value of the shares will be included in the gross taxable estate of the decedent.

In *Matthews* the court in so holding said:

> The question was recently considered by this Court in *Claire Giannini Hoffman*. There, a decedent during his lifetime had given his brother an option to acquire, upon his death, whatever interest he might then have in a securities business operated as a partnership and in certain notes of the nominal partners, upon the payment of the balance then due on a promissory note of the decedent and the payment to his estate of a sum equal to 20 percent of the value of the assets of the partnership. We held that the fair market value of the property at the date of decedent's death and not the option price was the measure of the value at which it should be included in the gross estate. The restrictions there imposed upon the property by the option agreement did not become effective until the death of the decedent and did not affect its value until after his death. That was the situation in the present case. The option agreement was to apply only to the stock which might be owned by the decedent at the time of his death and decedent was under no obligation to retain ownership of any of the shares until his death. He was free up to the very moment of his death to sell or otherwise dispose

of the shares for the best price obtainable. The right terminated with and by reason of his death. Likewise the right of the optionee to purchase the shares came into existence at the time of and by reason of decedent's death.

2. Where the restriction requires that the estate first offer the stock interest to the survivor at a fixed price before selling to others, the option will have a depressing effect on the value of the interest, but it is only one of many factors to be considered. Thus in *Worcester County Trust Co.* the Court held that a provision in the articles of incorporation that shareholders desirous of transferring shares should first offer them to the directors, who might buy them for the use of their corporation at their book value, did not fix the market value of the stock, but that such restriction would have a depressing effect upon its value and should have been considered in determining its worth for estate tax purposes:

> The taxpayers contend that the effect of this amendment is to fix the market value of the stock at its book value. The Board, however, took the position that it had no effect whatever on market value. . . . We cannot agree with taxpayers that the amendment set the value of the shares at their book value on the critical date. The amendment did not prohibit sales of the stock except at book value, nor did it fix book value as a call price at which at the behest of the corporation the stock must be sold. It fixed a limitation on the price obtainable by a shareholder for his shares only if he wished to sell and if the corporation at that time wishes to buy. We do not believe that the Board was correct in saying that the "restriction leaves the value unaffected" for the reason that it "only restricts the field of available purchase in the first instance." In our view it must be said that the restriction necessarily has a depressing effect upon the value of the stock in the market.

3. But these holdings are to be distinguished from the cases where (1) the decedent's right to dispose of his interest during life was subject to the agreement and (2) where the decedent's estate was obligated to sell. Thus in the *Benzel, Strange,* and *Tompkins* cases, any sale during life would have been subject to the agreement and the option to purchase was in the survivor; the decedent's executor in each case was obligated to sell. It is true in all these cases that the survivor may fail to

exercise the option, thereby enriching the decedent's beneficiaries. But the enriching event is the failure to exercise the option, not the death, and this has all the earmarks of an inter vivos gift. The courts have properly held that the waiver of such right will not change the frozen estate tax value.

16.14   Purchase agreements within the family

The cases cited above involved business contracts, made at arm's length. Transactions within the family may well be different.

Assume that Father, owning 500 shares, and his son, owning 100 shares, in a corporation, enter into an agreement that neither will offer his shares for sale without giving the other the first opportunity to buy at book value less whatever worth may be attributed to goodwill and that in the event of the death of either the other may purchase the decedent's interest within 90 days at the same price.

That Father may have made a tax-free gift immediately suggests itself. The consideration is clearly disproportionate. What Son has given up with his lesser number of shares, and longer life expectancy, is measurably and substantially less than what he gained. While his rights under the agreement are contingent, they would bring many times what Father's rights would in the open market. The relationship normally precludes the supposition of an arm's length transaction. Because the rights acquired by Father are substantially less than the consideration given, a possible gift in the amount of the difference results. Under the agreement Father retains his stock interest until death. Only at that time will the rights created by the contract in favor of Son come into enjoyment. This, of course, would be equally true were the transaction between strangers at arm's length and the consideration given by each substantially equal; but the estate tax provisions requiring the inclusion of lifetime transfers in the gross estate are inapplicable to transfers for a full and adequate consideration in money or money's worth. Because of the gift element in the father-son contract, the full value of the shares at the date of death may be included in Father's gross taxable estate.

Generally it will be found undesirable to fix in advance the amount to be paid other than by appraisal of assets, including goodwill, where the relationship of the parties to the contract indicates the absence of an arm's length bargaining transaction. Agreements between Father and Son will almost always be suspect and the net effect of a predetermined formula may, therefore, be to fix the minimum rather than the maximum estate tax value. If the business is worth less at the time of death than the amount Son must pay under the agreement, this higher value will control. But if the business is worth considerably more than the agreed price the Commissioner may disregard it and assess the present worth. In many cases involving close family members the parties may be better off without any predetermined formula for arriving at the purchase price other than an agreement to pay the fair market value of the interest at the date of death.

17

Proprietorships, partnerships,
and corporations

Problems common to all three types of business organizations

17.1 In general

Business purchase agreements generally contemplate the purchase of the business interest by key employees in the case of sole proprietorships, partners or the partnership itself in the cases of partnerships, and fellow stockholders or the corporation itself in corporation case. In order to assure the availability of adequate funds to make the purchase the agreements are almost universally funded by life insurance policies on the lives of the sellers. This use of life insurance raises a few problems common to all purchase agreements. Does the prospective buyer have an insurable interest in the life of the seller? Are the premium payments deductible as business expenses? Who should own the policy? Who should be designated beneficiary?

17.2 Insurable interest

It is well recognized that the buyer of a business interest has an insurable interest in the life of the seller whether the buyer be an employee, partner, fellow stockholder of the seller, a partnership, or a corporation in which the seller is an owner or active executive. The buyer in each of these situations has an interest in the continuance of the business as a successful enterprise. Note the quotation at section 16.3 from the *Emeloid* case. Further, the very existence of the agreement puts the buyer under a contingent liability to pay a sum of money at an uncertain future date. This is true whether the agreement is to buy out the interest of his associate at death or either at death or retirement, whichever event first occurs. He has an economic interest in the seller's life in all these cases since his business or employment may be adversely affected by the premature death of the seller. While doubts may have existed 50 years ago, the question of insurable interest is no longer a troublesome problem.

17.3   Deductibility of the premium payments

No deduction is allowed for the premium payments as business expenses or under any other heading of expense. The Code makes this clear. Code Section 264 denies any deduction for premiums paid on any life insurance contract covering the life of an officer or employee or any person financially interested in any trade or business of the taxpayer when the taxpayer is directly or indirectly a beneficiary under the policy. Since the purchase price will be paid from the insurance proceeds, the payor will always be directly or indirectly a beneficiary of the policy. The disallowance of any deduction is justified by the fact that the proceeds will be received free from income tax. Since the proceeds are tax free there is no reason to permit the deduction of the premiums. Such a deduction would, in fact, confer a double benefit.

17.4   Ownership of policies

The policies on the life of the prospective seller should be owned and paid for by the prospective buyer and he should be designated as beneficiary. In some of the earlier cases the insured either owned incidents in the policy on his own life or his estate was named beneficiary. Either of these arrangements required the inclusion of the proceeds in the estate of the insured under the ownership test or the payable-to-the-estate test. This created the risk that both the insurance proceeds and the value of the business might be taxed in the estate of the insured decedent. Happily, it is now clear that this double inclusion will not occur. There is, however, a definite cost basis advantage in having the prospective buyer own the policy on the life of the prospective seller, and receive the proceeds either directly or through a trustee for his benefit.

In the *Legallet* case, O'Neil and Legallet, equal partners, agreed that the survivor would purchase the interest of the first to die. Each applied for insurance on his own life, naming his wife as beneficiary. The premiums were paid for with partnership funds. It was agreed that the proceeds of the insurance would count as full or part payment of the interest of the first dying partner. O'Neil died at a time when his interest was worth $56,000. His widow received $25,000 from his insurer and $30,936 in notes from Legallet. Legallet later sold some of the merchandise and accounts receivable. In litigation over the amount of his profit on these sales, it was held that he could not include the insurance proceeds as part of his cost basis for determining taxable gain. He did not own the insurance, collect the proceeds, or pay them over for the interest he acquired. It seems clear that if Legallet had owned the policy on O'Neil's life, received the proceeds and applied them as part of the purchase price, his cost basis for the assets purchased would have included both the notes and the amount of insurance.

What really happens in the Legallet-type arrangement is that the buyer acquires the assets at a greatly reduced price, since the purchase price is the value of the interest minus the amount of the policy and hence the cost basis for the assets purchased is very much less than it ought to be.

17.5 Advisability of a trustee

In some cases it may be advisable to include a trustee or escrow agent as a party to a business purchase agreement. Walter Freyburger, who has had wide experience in the practical operation of these agreements points out in "Business Purchase Agreements Funded by Life Insurance," a booklet published by New York Life Insurance Company, that use of a trustee may prove valuable in that:

1. A disinterested party will have the custody of the agreement, insurance policies and documents which have been executed to carry out the agreement.

2. Upon the death of a party, the trustee will take the necessary steps to see that the terms of the agreement are complied with. He will file proof of death of the insured and collect the proceeds payable under the policy. He will deliver the policies on the lives of the survivors to such parties and receive the consideration set forth in the agreement. He will also deliver to the survivors the certificates of stock owned by the decedent, if a stock purchase agreement is involved, or, if there is a partnership, the assignment of the interest of the decedent in the partnership or a waiver by the executor of the estate of the decedent to an accounting. He may be required to deliver to the executor an agreement on the part of the survivors to pay all debts of the partnership. There may be various documents which it will be his duty to obtain and deliver.

3. An experienced trustee, such as the trust officer of a corporate trustee, may be in a position to render valuable suggestions to the parties as to contingencies that should be considered in a purchase agreement in the interest of promptness and simplicity of administration.

4. The estate of the decedent, and especially his widow, may be more satisfied that they are getting a fair deal, if the payment of the purchase price for the decedent's interest and the delivery of the necessary documents of title are carried out by a disinterested trustee.

Sole proprietorships

17.6 The logical buyer

In the proprietorship cases the logical buyer will generally be a key employee or several key employees. They are the ones most interested in assuring continuance of the business and most concerned in its control after the death or retirement of the owner. To them the business will have a greater value than it would have to outsiders. Frequently it will be necessary to grant them salary increases in order to enable them to pay the premiums on the insurance policy on the life of the owner that is to provide the source of the purchase money. To the extent that such increases do not make the salaries unreasonable they will be deductible by the owner as compensation paid. It is true, that, in effect, he is himself providing the purchase price by such action. But this is only partially true because of the income tax deductions. Further his estate may be better off through this action since the keymen will pay a higher price than outsiders due to the greater value of the business to them.

17.7   Types of businesses

Business profits are attributable, in any business, partly to invested capital, partly to personal service. The lawyer, the doctor, the accountant, the real estate agent, require little capital to operate successfully. On the other hand, the merchant or manufacturer may have substantial amounts of capital tied up in inventory or work in progress. In some businesses capital may be a major factor, in others a very minor factor. This will be true whether the business is a sole proprietorship, partnership, or a corporation. However the tax consequences of any sale will vary depending on the form of the organization and the nature of the assets.

17.8   Classification of assets

The assets used by a sole proprietor in his business may consist of all or part of the following: improved real estate, stock-in-trade or inventory, fixtures, receivables, goodwill. Any sale during his life may contemplate a covenant not to compete, as a method of protecting the goodwill purchased. Wherever the sole proprietor, or his executor after his death, sells the business, he is treated not as selling a single unit or asset but rather as selling so many separate items of property and, for purposes of computing the taxes on such a sale, a portion of the purchased price must be allocated to each class of assets. This will frequently be done in the contract of sale. If not, it must be done at the time the income tax returns are filed by the buyer and seller (subject to revision by the Commissioner) based upon the fair market values of the different items. The importance of the allocation in tax dollars will become apparent when the tax classification of the different classes of assets is considered.

1. *Improved real estate*   This represents a Section 1231 asset. Subject to the depreciation recapture provisions of the Code its sale during the life of the sole proprietor will result in capital gain, if sold at a profit, but ordinary loss, if sold at less than its tax cost. If the sale occurs after the death of the sole proprietor, it will be a capital asset in the hands of the executor since, it is not property used in the executor's business, it being assumed that the business interest is to be sold rather than continued by the executor or the beneficiaries. Because it becomes a capital asset in the hands of the executor or legatees the sale will result in capital gain or loss, depending on whether the purchase price is more or less than the fair market value at date of the proprietor's death or six months thereafter if the optional valuation date[1] is used and the sale occurs more than six months after the date of death. If the sale occurs within the six-month period and the valuation date is six months after the date of death then the market value at date of disposition determines the cost basis. As a practical matter there will rarely be either gain or loss, since the sale will occur so shortly after the date of death that the sale price will be used to establish value at date of death.

2. *Inventory*   The inventory, in the sense here used, refers to the items held for resale to customers in the ordinary course of business. Any gain will be taxed as ordinary income, any loss will be deductible in full if the property is sold during

---

[1] Under prior law the optional valuation date was one year after the date of death.

the life of the proprietor. If the sale occurs after his death the inventory will be transformed into capital assets, again because it comprises property which now meets the capital asset definition in that the inventory is not held by the executor for sale to customers in the ordinary course of business. Again it is unlikely that there will be any gain or loss attributable to the sale of the inventory by the executor.

3. *Fixtures* These are items used in the trade or business and like the improved real estate are Section 1231 assets in the hands of the proprietor, capital assets in the hands of the executor.[2]

4. *Receivables* These are capital assets or ordinary income assets depending on the method of accounting used by the proprietor. If he is on an accrual basis, they will have been taken into income as earned and thus become capital items. If he is a cash basis taxpayer, the portion of the purchase price allocable to the receivables will result in ordinary income to him. If the sale occurs after his death, the receivables of the cash basis taxpayer become "income in respect to a decedent" items and hence on their sale by the executor produce ordinary income.

5. *Goodwill* The goodwill represents a capital asset, both to the proprietor and, after his death, to his executor. But if a sale occurs during life and a portion of what is really being paid for goodwill is specifically allocated to a covenant not to compete, that portion becomes ordinary income to the proprietor, deductible as an expense by the buyer. See section 13.9.

17.9   Illustrative cases

In considering what assets are to be transferred and how the purchase price is to be determined and paid, it will be important to consider the types of assets held. This may best be illustrated by three examples, a drug store, a doctor's practice, and a gift shop which manufactures its own products.

---

[2] There may be some depreciation recapture under Section 1245.

	Drug store		Doctor's practice		Gift shop	
	Cost	Market value	Cost	Market value	Cost	Market value
Building..........	$15,000	$30,000	$15,000	$30,000	$15,000	$ 30,000
Inventory..........	18,000	22,000	–0–	–0–	–0–	28,000
Fixtures..........	4,000	4,000	8,000	12,000	4,000	3,000
Receivables........	6,000	6,000	–0–	18,000	8,000	8,000
Goodwill..........	5,000	10,000	–0–	15,000	–0–	50,000
	$48,000	$72,000	$23,000	$75,000	$27,000	$119,000

The drug store purchases its inventory and the price is relatively stable, hence there is little difference between cost and market value. It reports its income on an accrual basis and hence receivables have a cost basis equal to the face amount. Presumably the value is the same. It is assumed that it purchased its goodwill for $5,000.

The doctor sells only services; hence no inventory. His fixtures have a value in excess of cost. This is due to the accelerated depreciation permitted under the 1954 Code. His receivables have no cost basis as he uses the cash method of accounting. Goodwill has no cost since he built it himself.

The gift shop has no cost for its inventory. It is a novelty shop whose employees carve the products from wood in the area, paint pictures and scenes on canvas, etc. Cost of labor and materials may have been expensed. Hence, the inventory has no cost. Its goodwill, developed over 40 years, has no cost but a value 3 times the average earnings. The basis for the value is the long period of existence, a large mail-order business, and its reputation throughout the country among vacationers.

The table showing the gift shop inventory as zero is obviously exaggerated since some items of labor and materials should be charged to cost of goods rather than to expense. The Revenue Service would clearly frown on the procedure of expensing all costs of labor and material. The allocation, however, of salaries in this area is often vague, and not infrequently inventory costs may be found to be negligible. The extreme illustration is designed to point up the problem.

If the drug business is sold during the life of the proprietor, for $72,000, there will be long-term capital gain on the real estate of $15,000;[3] $4,000 ordinary income on the inventory and $5,000 long term gain on goodwill. If instead of a full payment for the goodwill the purchase price is fixed at $67,000 plus $5,000, payable at $1,000 a year, for a covenant not to compete, the Buyer may deduct these $1,000 yearly payments, the Seller must treat them as ordinary income in the years received. There will then be neither gain nor loss on the sale of the goodwill.

If the sale occurs after the death of the proprietor there will be neither gain nor loss since all the items will become capital items with stepped-up cost basis in the hands of the executor.

If the doctor sells his practice and the assets used in his practice for $75,000, he will realize capital gain on the building and fixtures[4] and goodwill, but $18,000 of ordinary income on the receivables. If the sale is by his executor there will be no capital gain because of the stepped-up cost basis but the amount paid for the receivables will be taxed as ordinary income. Whether the sale takes place at retirement or at death it may be advisable to withhold the receivables and designate the Buyer as agent to collect. In this way the gain may be spread over the period actually required to collect these accounts.

If the gift shop is sold during life there will be capital gain on the real property[5] and goodwill, ordinary loss on the fixtures, neither gain nor loss on the receivables but ordinary income on the full value of the inventory. If the sale is made by the executor, there should be neither gain nor loss since the sales price will almost invariably be used to determine the estate tax value, and as noted above the inventory items' become capital assets in the hands of the executor.

With these basic considerations in mind the estate planner will have to decide whether, a fixed dollar amount, a times-earnings formula, an appraisal method, or a combination of

---

[3] Subject to depreciation recapture.

[4] Same as 3.

[5] Same as 3.

these methods should be adopted. Sometimes book value will be used for certain items such as receivables, fixtures, inventory, an appraisal for real estate, and a times-earnings formula for goodwill. See section 16.11. The answer can only be determined by the facts of each individual case. Sometimes to keep the price down certain assets may be withdrawn such as the real estate or receivables.

It is important to note here that the rules discussed above relate to sole proprietorships. The rules as to partnership interests and stock in corporations differ considerably. These will be dealt with later in this chapter.

17.10   Transfer-for-value rule

Assume the price has been determined, the insurance acquired by the keyman and the obligation to buy and to sell assumed by the execution of a contract. Suppose that later the keyman dies or resigns. He (or his estate) now owns a policy on the life of a person in whom he (or his estate) no longer has an interest. It may, of course, be sold to the proprietor or surrendered. Frequently the contract will give the proprietor an option to purchase it. If he does it, he ought to be in a position to select a new keyman and transfer the policy to him for its current value. Unfortunately the tax laws make this impractical because of the rule that if any person, with stated exceptions, purchases an existing policy of life insurance on the life of another, any profit will be subject to income tax. This means that if the substituted keyman purchases the policy for its cash surrender value, say $5,000, pays $3,000 in additional premiums and then collects the face amount of $50,000, he will have $42,000 of additional income to be taxed at ordinary rates.[6] The effect of this would be to have half or more of the proceeds eaten up by taxes and the purpose of the insurance defeated. The 1954 Code corrected this inequity with respect to partnerships, and (to a lesser ex-

---

[6] Subject to the averaging provisions of the Code.

tent) corporations but nothing was done to eliminate the adverse tax consequences in sole proprietorship cases. If this situation arises the owner may make the new keyman a junior partner and thus bring him within the partnership exception. See section 17.16. In many cases this may be found preferable to purchasing a new policy, even assuming that the owner is still insurable.

17.11 Principal contract clauses

The following provisions will be found in most agreements.

1. *Restriction on sale of business during life, without the consent of the keyman*   This is important if the purchase price is to fix the estate tax value. See section 16.14.

2. *Purchase of insurance and payment of premiums by the employee*   It is important that the keyman promise to keep the insurance in force in order to insure the payment of the purchase price.

3. *Right in the proprietor to purchase the policy in the event the contract is cancelled for any reason*   He represents the logical buyer and at the time of cancellation he may no longer be insurable. Customarily the price is the then cash surrender value and this seems fair to both parties unless the sale occurs shortly after the issuance of the policy.

4. *Method of determining the purchase price*   See sections 16.6 to 16.11.

5. *Provisions for notes and other security in the event the insurance proceeds are insufficient to pay the purchase price in full*   The security available in each individual case will vary. Sometimes the keyman may be required to incorporate the business and assign all the stock as collateral for the unpaid balance.

6. *Termination of the agreement*   The agreement should cease to be effective:

   a) if the proprietor becomes bankrupt or insolvent,

   b) if the keyman dies, discontines his employment or is discharged, *c*) if the keyman permits the policy to lapse,

d) if the keyman dies within 60 days or other stated period after the death of the proprietor. It seems unfair to require the purchase if the keyman does not live long enough to actively operate the business.

Partnerships

17.12 The logical buyers

The partnership interest may be purchased by another partner or by the partnership. The latter arrangement constitutes a liquidation of the partner's interest. If the contract provides for the sale of the interest to the surviving partner or partners it is called a buy-and-sell agreement. If it provides for the liquidation of the partner's interest by the partnership itself it is called an entity plan agreement. Probably a majority of partnerships use the entity rather than the buy-and-sell method. The choice will depend on a number of factors all of which should be carefully considered in relation to the facts of each particular case. The entity method had become standard practice before the 1954 Code because of the transfer-for-value rule and because courts had come to recognize that a partnership interest was a separate asset, distinct from the underlying partnership assets, in the hands of the partner or his executor. Changes in the 1954 Code, which will be discussed later, have, to a large extent, eliminated the differences that these rules caused and hence the decision is no longer heavily weighted in favor of the entity method, as it may still be in the corporation cases.

17.13 Tax rates

Since the partnership is a tax reporting rather than a taxpaying entity, it makes no difference in the income taxes paid by the individual partners, which method is adopted. See section 17.21, discussing this factor in the corporation cases.

17.14   Amount of insurance needed

The entity method, under which the partnership purchases, pays for, owns, and is beneficiary of the insurance, is said to require, if the purchase price is to fairly reflect the value of the partnership interest to be liquidated, a larger amount of insurance on the life of each partner. Assume two partners A and B. The value of the partnership is $200,000. Under the buy-and-sell method each partner would buy $100,000 on the life of the other. He would own the policy, pay the premiums, and receive the proceeds. The $100,000 would be sufficient to buy the interest of his deceased partner, paying its full value, $100,000. However, if the partnership owned the policies, on the death of the first partner, its assets would increase from $200,000, plus the cash surrender of the policies, to $300,000. Thus the interest of the deceased partner on liquidation ought to bring $150,000. Of course, it would be possible to provide for a valuation, which excluded the insurance proceeds, but query if such a clause is fair to the estate of the deceased partner. The Regulations state that if the insurance is owned by or payable to a partnership or corporation the proceeds of the insurance are considered as an asset of the partnership or corporation for the purposes of first, determining whether the agreement was supported by a full and adequate consideration and second, determining the value of the decedent's interest, if the agreement is not considered to have been entered into at arm's length.

Generally the parties when dealing at arm's length, will want this asset to be included in fixing the value of the interest of the deceased owner. Nor is the fact that a larger amount of insurance may be required necessarily an objection to this method since the larger policy assures a larger capital payment to the estate of the deceased owner.

17.15   Payment of premiums

Except for the possibly larger policies under the entity plan, the cost is the same to the partners under either method. No deduction is allowed for the premiums paid, whether paid by the partners or the partnership. But the entity method provides for ease and assurance of payment. The burden of the premiums, while the same, is easier borne as a business expense than as a personal one. Further the partners feel a greater assurance that none of the policies will be permitted to lapse if the common purse is responsible for the annual premium payments.

A special problem exists where there is any substantial disparity in the ages of the partners. Thus suppose A is 50, B 40, C 30. Generally the youngest man will have the smallest draw but will be saddled with the largest premium burden if the cross purchase method is adopted. This inequality in the premium burden disappears when the entity method is used, since the total premium payments are made before the division of profits is computed.

17.16   Transfer-for-value rule

A major objection to the buy-and-sell method existed under prior law. Suppose we had three partners, A, B, C. Under a buy and sell agreement, A purchased insurance on the lives of B and C. B purchased on the lives of A and C, and C on the lives of A and B. Now if A died, B and C would collect the proceeds on the policies on A's life and use them to pay for their interest. The estate of A would then own policies on B and C, in whose lives A's family no longer would have any interest. In order to continue the agreement, B would like to buy the policy on C's life and C the policy on B's life. Under the old transfer-for-value rule, this was not practical. However, if the partnership owned the insurance on all the lives, no transfer was necessary when a partner died. For this reason the entity method became the standard plan to use. Happily, the 1954 Code eliminated this stumbling block to the buy-and-sell method as to partnerships (but not as to corporations, see section 17.26) by providing an exception to the transfer-for-value rule where the sale of the policy is to a partner or partnership of which the insured is a member. Thus this factor is no longer a consideration in the choice of the method to use.

17.17   Classification of assets

Although the 1954 Code recognizes the partnership interest as a capital asset, limitations are imposed on the extent to which the proceeds on a sale or liquidation of a partnership interest can qualify for the favorable capital gain treatment. Under prior law the sale of a partnership interest became a favorite device for turning ordinary income into capital gain. Assume a law partnership under the terms of which A had an interest in as yet unrealizable receivables, both work completed and work in progress, having a fair market value of $75,000. His interest in the capital assets, books, furniture, fixtures, etc., were worth about $10,000. If A continued as a partner, the $75,000, when collected, would be taxable to him as ordinary income. Suppose he sold his partnership interest for $85,000, the cost basis of his interest being $10,000. The courts allowed him long-term capital gain on the $75,000 profit. The same advantage accrued to the seller of a partnership interest where the value of the inventory was very greatly in excess of its cost basis to the partnership.

In order to eliminate this conversion of ordinary income into capital gain through a sale the 1954 Code now taxes to a selling partner the share of the purchase price allocable to unrealized receivables and substantially appreciated inventory. The term "unrealized receivables" is used to apply to any rights to income which have not been included in gross income under the method of accounting employed by the partnership. Thus its principal application is to cash basis partnerships which have acquired contractual rights to income from services or sales. It also covers work in progress and so has the application to a limited extent in the case of accrual basis partnerships. Substantially appreciated inventory refers to the cases where the fair market value of the inventory is more than

377

120 percent of the partnerships basis for the inventory and amounts to more than 10 percent of the fair market value of all partnership property.

Where the partnership interest is liquidated by payments from the partnership, rather than a sale, the rules are the same, i.e., the retiring partner or his estate gets capital gain treatment on the share paid for his interest except for that portion of the price attributable to unrealized receivables or substantially appreciated inventory but with the following additional exception: Any payment attributable to goodwill, except to the extent that the partnership agreement specifically provides for a payment for goodwill, constitutes ordinary income. Thus the parties may, in effect, control whether the portion of the price paid for goodwill shall receive capital gain or ordinary income treatment. It will generally be to the advantage of the remaining partners to make it taxable as ordinary income to the retiring partner or his estate since they will then be entitled to deductions for the amounts so paid.

17.18   Illustrative cases

The application of the above rules may be illustrated by the same examples used in connection with a sale of a sole proprietorship, by assuming in each of these cases that two partners A and B, each own a 50 percent interest in the partnership. For convenience the tables of assets are repeated here. For those who are troubled by the absence of any liabilities assume cash (also not included) equals the payables.

	Drug store		Doctors A and B		Gift shop	
	Cost	*Market value*	*Cost*	*Market value*	*Cost*	*Market value*
Building..........	$15,000	$30,000	$15,000	$30,000	$15,000	$ 30,000
Inventory.........	18,000	22,000	–0–	–0–	–0–	28,000
Fixtures..........	4,000	4,000	8,000	12,000	4,000	3,000
Receivables.......	6,000	6,000	–0–	18,000	8,000	8,000
Goodwill..........	5,000	10,000	–0–	15,000	–0–	50,000
	$48,000	$72,000	$23,000	$75,000	$27,000	$119,000

On the sale of A's interest in the drug store during life for $36,000 his profit of $12,000 would be taxed as long-term capital gain, assuming he had owned the interest for at least 6 months. The inventory item receives capital gain treatment because its market value is not sufficiently in excess of cost to cause it to be classified as substantially appreciated inventory. The partnership interest would continue as a capital asset in the hands of A's executor and while a sale by him would be a taxable transaction, the new cost basis, i.e., fair market value at date of death, would prevent the recognition of any gain, since as a practical matter the sale price would be used to determine the value at the date of death.

On a liquidation of A's interest, during life or at death, the result would be the same if the contract provided that the purchase price included the goodwill. If no reference were made to goodwill, presumably the $5,000 profit allocable to the excess over its cost would be ordinary income.

These results would follow whether the payment was in a lump sum or spread over several years or even if in the form of a fixed percentage of the earnings over a period of years. On the question of allocation of payments over several years, see the illustration below from the Senate Finance Committee Report.

On the sale of Dr. A's interest during life he would have capital gain treatment[7] on the share of the purchase price allocable to his capital interest (all assets except the unrealized receivables). Thus $9,000 of his profits would be taxed as ordinary income. If the sale occurs after death, the cost basis of his partnership interest would be increased to market value at date of death, thereby eliminating any capital gain, but the portion of the price allocable to his share in the receivables would still be taxed as ordinary income. If instead of a sale the partnership liquidated A's interest the agreement will determine whether the payment attributable to goodwill shall be taxed as ordinary income or not. Thus if the agreement of liquidation provided for the payment of the appraised values of his half interest in the real estate, fixtures (equipment) plus $6,000 a year for three years, the latter $18,000 would be tax-

---

[7] Subject to the depreciation recapture provisions of the Code.

able to him or his executor as ordinary income and each of the $6,000 payments would be deductible by Dr. B as paid.

The Senate Finance Committee Report gives the following illustration:

Partnership ABC is a personal service partnership and its balance sheet is as follows:

	Assets			*Liabilities and capital*	
	Adjusted basis	*Market value*		*Adjusted basis*	*Market value*
Cash................	$13,000	$13,000	Liabilities......	$ 3,000	$ 3,000
Accounts			Capital:		
receivable......	–0–	30,000	A...........	10,000	21,000
Fixed assets.........	20,000	23,000	B...........	10,000	21,000
			C...........	10,000	21,000
Total..............	$33,000	$66,000		$33,000	$66,000

Partner A retires from the partnership in accordance with an agreement whereby he is to receive $10,000 a year for 3 years, a total of $30,000, for his partnership interest. The value of A's capital interest in the partnership, for purposes of Section 736(b), is $12,000 one third of $36,000, the sum of $13,000 and $23,000, the fair market value of fixed assets). The accounts receivable (unrealized receivables) are not included in A's capital interest in the partnership under Section 736(b). Since the basis of A's interest is $11,000 ($10,000, the basis of his capital investment, plus $1,000, his share of partnership liabilities), he will realize a capital gain of $1,000 on the sale of his interest in partnership property. The balance to be received by him, $18,000, constitutes payments under Section 736(a) and is taxable to A as ordinary income.

The $10,000 A receives in each of the three years would ordinarily be allocated as follows: $4,000, payments for the capital interest (one third of the total payment of $12,000 for the capital interest), and the balance $6,000, payments under Section 736(a). Of the $4,000 attributable to A's capital interest, $333 is capital gain (one third of the total capital gain of $1,000), and $3,667 is return of capital. The partnership will be entitled to a deduction under Section 736(a)(2) of $6,000 during each of the 3 years.

If the agreement between the partners provided for payments to A for 3 years of a percentage of annual income instead of a fixed amount, a portion of each payment, determined under regulations, would be treated as paid for A's capital interest, based upon its $12,000 value at the time of his retirement. The balance would be treated as a distributive share of partnership income to A under Section 736(a)(1).

The consequences of a sale or liquidation in the case of a partnership interest in the gift shop would be the same as the doctor partnership, since substantially appreciated inventory is treated in the same way that unrealized receivables are treated. Note the importance here of whether or not a liquidation payment is specifically provided for the good will.

17.19   Entity versus buy-and-sell method

No hard and fast rule can be laid down as to the preferable method to use. Where unrealized receivables or substantially appreciated inventory is likely, it will generally be advisable to spread the payments over several years under either method. Where goodwill represents a substantial asset, liquidation may be preferable to purchase since the deductibility of the price of this item will generally be of greater value to the continuing partners, than will the disadvantage of its inclusion in the gross income be to the retiring partners or his estate, particularly if the purchase price is spread over several years.

The trend in the past in the partnership cases had been toward the entity plan and seems likely to continue.

Corporations—sales or liquidation of entire interest

17.20   Corporations electing to avoid corporation tax

The 1958 Congress added new Subchapter S to the 1954 Code. This permits certain corporations, through unanimous action by their stockholders, to elect not to be subject to the corporation income tax. Where this election is made the stockholders must include in their own individual income for tax purposes the current taxable income of the corporation, whether distributed or not, without the benefit of any dividend exclusion or credit. Thus it has become possible to eliminate the "double" tax on corporate income with respect to corporations that qualify.

Any corporation may qualify if it has ten or fewer individual stockholders and only one class of stock. The stockholders may include an estate but not a trust and none may be nonresident aliens. All stockholders must consent. Once the election is made it continues until revoked. Revocation may be accomplished by the consent of all shareholders and it will automatically occur if (1) a new shareholder does not consent upon becoming such or (2) if more than 20 percent of the gross receipts of the corporation consist of personal holding company income. Once an election is revoked or terminated a new election may not be made for five years thereafter.

The character of the income does not follow through to the stockholders. Generally all income will be taxed as ordinary income. The only exception is that any long-term capital gains of the corporation are taxed as such to the stockholders. Assume a corporation's taxable income, after salaries paid to its owners, A and B, amounts to $20,000 (no capital gains). The corporation will pay no tax, and A and B will each add $10,000 to their personal reportable incomes whether the profits are distributed to them or retained by the corporation. Each shareholder increases the basis of his stock by the amount of the retained earnings with which he has been charged. On a later distribution (or where corporate losses are passed on to him) he reduces his basis.

There appear to be many estate and tax-planning opportunities through the use of these new sections. But a word of caution would not be amiss. Until more experience is gained, elections should be made only after all factors have been carefully weighed and expert advice obtained. It is clear, for example, that insurance premiums on stock redemption agreements do not become deductible because of this election, though some at first jumped to this hasty conclusion. The stockholder is not taxed on his undistributed share of the current earnings and profits but on his share of the current taxable income, frequently a quite different figure.

1. A businessman or group of partners may now obtain the advantages of limited liability, perpetual existence, and ease of transfer without having to pay the corporate tax.

2. Sole proprietors and partners could for a time through incorporation and the election to avoid the corporate tax become participants in qualified pension and profit-sharing plans, an advantage long denied them because they were technically not "employees." The Tax Reform Act of 1969 has limited the deductions for contributions for stockholder employees of Subchapter S corporations to the lesser of 10 percent or $2,500 of compensation for years beginning in 1971 and thereafter.

3. Many other fringe benefits denied employers but available to employees may now be available to sole proprietors and partners through incorporation (without corporate tax). These include (*a*) group life, (*b*) accident and health insurance, (*c*) exempt compensation in case of illness, etc.

If a corporation elects to take advantage of Subchapter S the considerations favoring a stock redemption (other than the question of tax rates) will have relevance. See sections 17.23 to 17.28. Generally electing corporations, like other corporations, will tend to favor the redemption method.

17.21   Sale or redemption

As in the partnership cases the business purchase agreement may take the form of a buy and sell contract, i.e., the individual stockholders may agree to purchase the share of any deceased stockholder or it may take the form of a stock redemption agreement, i.e., the corporation may agree to redeem the shares of the stockholder first to die. Since stock is a capital asset, its sale will produce either capital gain or loss. This is true whether the stockholder or his executor makes the sale. In the latter case there will rarely be any recognized gain or loss since the executor acquires a stepped-up basis on the death of his decedent. A complete redemption of all the shares of a single stockholder also receives capital gain treatment. The nature of the corporate assets is immaterial. Hence, except for a collapsible corporation, the partnership problems discussed in section 17.17 do not exist.

Generally the contract will take the form of a stock redemption agreement, even though this may entail the purchase of somewhat larger policies by the corporation on the lives of each stockholder for the reasons set forth at section 17.14, than would be necessary if the surviving stockholders agreed to purchase the stock of any deceased stockholder.

Some doubt was cast upon the rule that a redemption of all the shares of a single (unrelated) stockholder results in capital gain by the recent *Zipp* and *Holsey* cases.

In *Zipp,* the owner of 48 of the company's total of 50 shares had given 46 shares to his sons. The corporation then redeemed his remaining two shares for $93,000. But the facts indicated that there was no bona fide gift to the sons; that what really happened was a sale of the shares to the sons with the payment of the purchase price to be made by the corporation. Hence, the payment was treated as a constructive dividend to the sons. It was as though they had withdrawn the money and paid it over to their father. In *Holsey,* where there were two stockholders, the tax court had held that a redemption of all the stock of one stockholder was a constructive dividend to the other. Holsey had an option to purchase the shares of his fellow stockholder. He transferred it to the corporation which then used it to effect the redemption. This case was later reversed on appeal. But query, even on the Tax Court's theory if both Holsey and Zipp did not have some of the sham elements or lack of "business purpose" in the mechanics of what was done that characterized the Court Holding Company type of transfers (see, section 13.15). In any event, they are a far cry from the typical stock redemption agreement. It is not believed that there is any substantial risk that a complete redemption of the stock of one stockholder will be treated as a constructive dividend to the remaining stockholders under the normal stock purchase agreement. The Tax Reform Act of 1969 provided that under regulations to be issued by the IRS a distribution that results in the receipt of cash or property by some stockholders and an increase in the proportionate ownership interest of other stockholders may cause the latter to be treated as receiving taxable dividends, but the House and Senate Committee Reports make clear that this regulatory power is not to be extended to isolated redemptions.

17.22   Tax rates

If we assume two stockholders, each in a 50 percent income tax bracket and annual premiums on the insurance used to fund the agreement of $2,500, the buy-and-sell method requires an additional $5,000 to be withdrawn by the stockholders to purchase the same amount of insurance, since only the net, after taxes, is available to the stockholders for premium payments. If the corporation's profits are less than $25,000, the additional payment, if allowable as a deduction for compensation paid, will benefit the corporation only to the extent of 22 percent. If the corporation is in the 48 percent bracket (the rate on the excess over $25,000) the deduction will be worth slightly more than its cost to the stockholders. But there will always be the risk that these payments may be taxed as dividends, should the Commissioner determine that maximum salaries are already being paid and therefore disallow the deduction of the additional amounts as excessive compensation.

The stock redemption method eliminates these problems since the corporation pays the premiums and owns the policy, hence only $2,500 of corporate funds is needed. Consideration of the tax rates generally suggests the redemption technique, particularly when the ease of payment and assurance of continuation of the policies arguments are added. See section 17.15.

17.23   Unreasonable accumulations tax

It is sometimes suggested that, as the policies acquire substantial cash surrender values, the corporation may run the risk of becoming subject to the special tax on unreasonable accumulations. This tax is designed to force the distribution as dividends to stockholders of accumulated earnings in excess of $100,000 that are not needed in the business. Specifically it imposes a tax for 27½ percent on the first $100,000 (over the $100,000 exemption) and 38½ percent on the excess if the corporation is availed of for the purpose of avoiding surtax on its stockholders by permitting earnings to accumulate unreasonably. However, the now famous *Emeloid* case makes it clear that providing cash through insurance to redeem stock upon the death of one of the owner-managers represents a valid business purpose. Since that decision it has become generally recognized that funding redemption agreements with life insurance policies does not create any real risk of running afoul of the unreasonable accumulations tax.

The recent *Pelton Steel Casting Company* case has caused many to worry that the tax on unreasonable corporate accumulations may hamper the use of stock redemption agreements. This case held that the use of accumulated earnings to redeem the stock of two stockholders did not relieve the company from the unreasonable accumulation tax. Suppose a corporation used as an excuse for a large accumulation that possibly its buildings might be destroyed by fire and that it preferred to act as a self-insurer. Such an argument would be given short shrift. With fire insurance available and the universal method of protecting against the risk, the accumulation might well be deemed unreasonable. May not this be the real explanation of *Pelton?* Accumulating profits in the form of cash or in investments unrelated to the business or the use of profits to purchase life insurance may be alternative methods of providing cash to retire stock. But one represents the generally recognized method of providing the full cash for an event, uncertain as to time, and the other a rarely, if ever, adopted one. Where cash is accumulated year by year its inadequacy in the earlier years and its full availability for other purposes, tends to suggest that the real motivation may be other than to provide a fund to insure performance of the typical type stock redemption agreement.

*

17.24   Certainty of performance

Under the laws of practically all states a corporation may redeem its shares from surplus but not out of capital. This may, in particular cases, present some problems. Generally, however, the receipt of the proceeds will produce the needed surplus. Further, a surplus can usually be artificially created either by corporate action reducing the capitalization of the corporation or in some cases by a revaluation of assets to reflect current values. Local law must be carefully considered to determine what, if any, difficulties, the possibility of a lack of available surplus may pose if the redemption method is used.

17.25 Survivor's cost basis

If the buy-and-sell method is used the survivor increases the cost basis of his investment in the business. Thus if A and B had each invested $10,000 in a company originally and if A purchased B's stock for $25,000, A's cost basis for the business, of which he is now the sole owner, would be $35,000. If, however, the stock redemption method is used, A's cost basis remains at $10,000 since that is all he ever invested. This is true even though he is now sole owner, just as he would be if the buy-and-sell method were used. But the importance of this failure to get a stepped-up basis can be overemphasized since it will become significant only if A sells his shares during his life.[8] Even then, he gets capital gain treatment.

17.26 Transfer-for-value rule

There is one real stumbling block to the buy-and-sell method where there are more than two stockholders. As previously noted the proceeds of life insurance are received free of income tax except where the policy has been purchased for a valuable consideration. A purchaser of an existing policy will be taxed on any gain, i.e., the excess of the proceeds over what he gave for the policy plus subsequent premiums paid by him. There are, however, exceptions to the exception. If the purchaser of the policy is the insured himself, a partner of the insured, a

---

[8] With death the stock gets a new cost basis, fair market value at date of death.

partnership of which he is a member, or a corporation in which the insured is a shareholder or officer, then its purchase does not have the effect of making the proceeds partly taxable.

Suppose we have three stockholders, A, B, and C. They use the buy-and-sell method, A purchasing insurance on the lives of B and C; B on the lives of A and C; C on the lives of A and B. Now if A dies, B and C will collect the proceeds of the insurance they own on the life of A and use them to buy his interest. The estate of A will still own the policies on the lives of B and C. In order to continue the agreement between B and C, B would like to buy and the estate of A would like to sell, the policy it owns on C's life. But if B purchases it then any gain over what he pays plus the later premiums, will be taxable to B as ordinary income when the proceeds are collected. This potential income tax liability may defeat the very purpose of the insurance since it may very substantially reduce the cash available to B to pay for C's interest. But if the redemption method is used the corporation continues to own the policies and no transfer is necessary. Further, it is possible for the corporation to purchase existing policies from its shareholders when the agreement is entered into if the stockholders prefer this to having the corporation purchase new insurance.

17.27 Family member parties

Where the owners are closely related persons or entities the constructive stock ownership rule may make a redemption of an entire interest dangerous. For purposes of determining whether the entire interest is redeemed a stockholder is treated as owning the stock owned directly or indirectly by or for his spouse (if not legally separated), his children, his grandchildren and his parents. In addition stock owned by a partnership or an estate or a trust is treated as being owned proportionately by the partners or beneficiaries. An estate or partnership is treated as owning stock owned by the beneficiaries or partners and stock owned by the beneficiary of a trust is considered as owned by the trust, unless the interest of the beneficiary is a remote contingent interest. If 50 percent or more of the stock of a corporation is owned by any person he is considered as owning the stock owned by the corporation in the same proportion that his stock ownership bears to the value of all the stock in the corporation. Thus, close family cases must be specially considered.

Assume Father and Son each own 50 percent of the stock of the X Corporation. Father's will leaves his estate equally to Son and Daughter. The Corporation, after his death, redeems all the stock owned by the estate. This would not constitute a redemption of an entire interest since the estate, under the constructive ownership rule, is treated as owning the stock of the Son because the statute provides: "Stock owned directly or indirectly by . . . a beneficiary of an estate shall be considered as being owned by the . . . estate." The suggested redemption would therefore fall under the rules of a partial redemption discussed in the sections that follow immediately. See particularly section 17.32.

17.28 *General preference for redemption method*

The stock redemption method will be found preferable in the great majority of cases. Corporate dollars will frequently be cheaper than stockholder dollars. Premium payments seem less painful. The continuance of the policies in force seems more likely. The transfer-for-value rule where there are more than two stockholders is a strong argument for its use. The cost basis problem is generally not too important nor is the fear of the unreasonable accumulation tax as great as before the *Emeloid* case. Only where a partial interest is to be redeemed or where the contract is between closely related individuals or entities is the buy-and-sell method likely to have advantages that outweigh its disadvantages and this will be true only in a limited number of cases.

Corporations—sales and redemptions of partial interests

17.29   Reasons for partial sales or redemptions

Frequently it will be desired to provide for the sale or redemption of a part only of the interest at death or retirement. The value of the interest may be so great as to make the purchase of the entire amount too costly. The Seller may prefer to leave part of his interest in the company, particularly in the form of preferred stock, as an investment. The constructive ownership rule (see section 17.27) may cause the redemption of an entire interest to be classified for tax purposes as a partial redemption.

17.30   Sales

The sale of a part interest, like the sale of an entire interest, will entitle the seller to capital gain treatment except for the rare sale of Section 306 stock. This special classification given certain stock received as a stock dividend was introduced in the 1954 Code to overcome the decision in the *Chamberlin* case. In that case a corporation had a large surplus. The stockholders were anxious to get these earnings or an equivalent amount of cash into their individual hands but at capital gains rates, and without loss of control. This was accomplished by first having the corporation issue a nontaxable preferred stock dividend to the common stockholders who immediately thereafter sold the entire preferred issue to a life insurance company. The basic position of the stockholders remained the same after the sale, as the corporation was now in a position to redeem the preferred any time it was desired to eliminate the investment of the owner of the preferred. This device was commonly known as the "preferred stock bail out."

First, the 1954 Code made all stock dividends paid in stock

of the declaring company nontaxable. But all such stock dividends, other than common on common, bear the stigma of "Section 306." The label also attaches to stock (other than common) received in a corporate reorganization, split off, split up, or spin off, to the extent that it is substantially the same as a stock dividend or if it was received in exchange for Section 306 stock, or any stock which has a substituted or transferred basis determined by reference to the basis of Section 306 stock. The taxable event was made the disposition of Section 306 stock rather than its issuance. If the stock is redeemed the proceeds are taxed as a dividend to the extent of the earnings and profits at the time of the redemption. If the stock is sold the amount realized is treated as gain from sale of property which is not a capital asset, i.e., as ordinary income to the extent of the shareholder's allocable share of the earnings and profits at the date of distribution. To the extent that the amount realized is in excess of the amount that would have been a dividend if the corporation had distributed cash instead of stock, the excess over the adjusted basis is capital gain.

There are certain exceptions to the application of these rules making the proceeds of such a sale or redemption ordinary income. They do not apply:

1. On a sale, other than to a related person under the constructive ownership rules, which terminates the entire interest of the stockholder including stock constructively owned.

2. On complete redemption of all the stock of the shareholder or on a partial or complete liquidation or redemption, as those terms are defined in the Code.

3. If the Commissioner is satisfied that the distribution of the stock and its later sale or redemption was not in pursuance of a plan having as one of its principal purposes the avoidance of income tax.

Section 306 stock is not likely to cause problems in buy-and-sell and stock redemption agreement. The usual pattern will be an issue of preferred on common in order to reduce the amount to be sold on retirement or death or to continue the preferred investment. Since the 306 stock will be the preferred this is the stock that will be retained. Thus the sale of the common will not have adverse tax effects on retirement nor will a later disposition of the preferred stock as, in the words of the Committee, "the subsequent disposition of the (preferred) would not ordinarily be considered a tax avoidance disposition since he had previously parted with the stock which allows him to participate in the ownership of the business."

A sale by the executor or beneficiary of such stock will not suffer the disastrous effects of Section 306 stock since the stock loses its 306 stigma on the death of the owner.

17.31 Partial redemptions

Partial redemptions receive capital gain treatment unless the redemption is "essentially equivalent to a taxable dividend." This exception is necessary to prevent too easy avoidance. Assume Corporation X has 300 shares of common stock outstanding, A, B, and C each owning 100 shares. At the end of the first year of business they have earnings and profits of $30,000. If a dividend is declared each will receive $10,000 of ordinary income. Suppose, however, the corporation redeems 10 shares of each stockholder. Ought the $10,000 received by A, B, and C, after deduction of the cost basis attributable to these shares, receive the favorable capital gain treatment? It is true each now owns only 90 shares but what difference does this make? Each still owns one-third of the corporation, has the identical voting power, the identical interests in profits and on dissolution, etc. Clearly such a redemption is essentially equivalent to a dividend. But suppose only ten shares of A's stock is redeemed. Here the answer is less clear but the case law has long been settled that a distribution need not be pro rata in order to constitute a dividend. There may be too great a risk that the shareholders have in mind redeeming ten of B's shares next year and ten of C's the following year. Hence it is likely A will be treated, in the case supposed, as having $10,000 of dividend income. Before 1954 the tests were vague and uncertain and there was always the risk that any partial redemption might be treated as a dividend if less than the entire interest was redeemed.

The 1954 Code specifically provides that certain partial redemptions shall not be treated as dividends. There are two specific exceptions: disproportionate redemptions and redemptions to pay death taxes. If the taxpayer cannot bring himself within the terms of these exceptions the question is left, as it was before 1954, for a determination on the facts of each particular case as to whether it was substantially equivalent to a dividend.

17.32   Disproportionate redemptions

A redemption will be considered substantially disproportionate and therefore receive capital gain treatment if:

1. The percentage of all voting stock owned by the stockholder immediatly after the redemption is less than 80 percent of the percentage of the voting stock which he owned immediately before the redemption. This 80 percent rule also applies to all common stock, whether voting or nonvoting and;

2. The shareholder immediately after the redemption owns less than 50 percent of the total voting power of all voting stock.

In determining these percentages the constructive ownership rules discussed in section 17.27 are applied.

Some examples will illustrate the application of these rules:

1. Before redemption A owned 40 shares of common out of 100 outstanding or 40 percent. If only his stock is redeemed his ownership must be reduced from 40 percent to less than 32 percent. 13 of his shares must be redeemed so that he will own 27 after the redemption, 27 being less than 32 percent of the then outstanding 87. Note that the less than 50 percent requirement is not present since he never owned more than 50 percent.

2. A before redemption owned 70 percent of the 100 outstanding shares. The corporation redeems 35. The redemption

will not qualify since after the redemption he will still own more than 50 percent of the then total voting power of all voting stock.

The rules of constructive ownership will not apply if there is a redemption of all the shares actually owned by the shareholder and the following conditions are met:

a) Immediately after the distribution, the shareholder has no interest in the corporation (including an interest as officer, director, or employee), other than an interest as creditor, and does not acquire any such interest (other than by bequest or inheritance) within ten years from the date of distribution, and files an agreement to notify the Commissioner of any such prohibited acquisition.

b) No portion of the stock redeemed was acquired within a ten-year period from a person, the ownership of whose stock would be attributable to the shareholder under the constructive ownership rule.

c) No such member of the distributee's family owns (at the time of distribution) stock, the ownership of which is attributable to the distributee and which was acquired from the distributee within the ten-year period ending on the date of the distribution, unless such stock so acquired is redeemed in the same transaction.

However, the restrictions of (*b*) and (*c*) do not apply if the acquisition or disposition did not have as one of its principal purposes the avoidance of federal income tax.

Thus a redemption of all the shares of a retiring stockholder may be dangerous if other members of the family also own shares in the corporation which are not redeemed, unless the above conditions can be complied with. Also if the beneficiary of the estate of a deceased shareholder also owns stock the redemption of the shares owned by the estate may, in some cases, fail to qualify as disproportionate. For these reasons where the business purchase agreement involves several members of the family, it may be necessary, unless the above conditions can be met, to use the buy and sell method or to limit the redemption to an amount necessary to pay death taxes. See section 17.33.

17.33 Redemption to pay death taxes

Code Section 303 provides that the redemption of stock in an amount not in excess of the death taxes (federal and state), funeral and administration expenses shall not be treated as a dividend provided:

1. The stock redeemed constitutes a part of the decedent's gross estate.

2. The amount does not exceed state and federal death taxes, administration and funeral expenses allowable as deductions under the federal estate tax.

3. The value of all the stock to be included in determining the value of the decedent's estate is either (a) more than 35 percent of the value of the gross estate or (b) more than 50 percent of the taxable estate. For purposes of the 35 percent and 50 percent requirements, stock of two or more corporations shall be treated as a single corporation if the value of each included in the decedent's estate is more than 75 percent of the value of the outstanding stock of each such corporation.

4. The distribution must be made within the period of limitations for the assessment of the federal estate tax, i.e., 3 years after the estate tax return is filed or within 90 days after the expiration of such period. Further time is provided if a petition is filed with the Tax Court putting the estate tax in litigation.

The objective of the provision was explained in the Senate Committee Report as follows:

It has been brought to the attention of your committee that the problem of financing the estate tax is acute in the case of estates consisting largely of shares in a family corporation. The market for such shares is usually very limited, and it is frequently difficult, if not impossible, to dispose of a minority interest. If, therefore, the estate tax cannot be financed through the sale of the other assets in the estate, the executors will be forced to dispose of the family business. In many cases the result will be the absorption of a family enterprise by a large competitor, thus tending to accentuate the degree of concentration of industry in this country.

A few examples will illustrate the coverage of the Section.

1. X leaves an estate of $500,000 consisting of $200,000

worth of X Co. stock. Taxes, funeral, and administration expenses total $150,000. X company redeems $150,000 worth of his stock, or any lesser amount. This distribution may not be treated as a dividend since his stock ownership represents more than 35 percent of his gross taxable estate.

2. X leaves an estate of $1,000,000 in part consisting of $200,000 of X stock. Debts and administration expenses amount to $100,000. Marital deduction $450,000, charitable bequest $100,000. His taxable estate, after considering the $60,000 exemption, amounts to $290,000. If we assume taxes, funeral, and administration expenses are $160,000, a redemption of X stock in any amount not in excess of $160,000 may not be treated as a dividend.

3. X leaves an estate of $300,000 consisting of stocks and bonds in a large number of companies. There is also included $200,000 of the stock of X Co. which he had given his son two years before his death, on the theory that it was a gift in contemplation of death. The Corporation redeems $100,000 of X stock from his son. The redemption may not be treated as a dividend, if X's taxes, funeral and administration expenses exceeded the sum of $100,000, without regard to whether or not the proceeds of the redemption were needed or used to pay the taxes, etc.

4. X leaves an estate of $500,000 consisting in part of the stock of X Corporation ($50,000 in value); Y Corporation ($75,000 in value) Z Corporation ($100,000 in value). He owns all of the outstanding stock of each of these corporations. The three corporations, since each meets the 75 percent requirement, may be regarded as a single corporation in determining whether the 35 percent of the gross or 50 percent of the taxable estate requirement is met. Obviously the 35 percent of the gross taxable estate test is satisfied.

This provision will prove useful in cases where it is not possible to have a disproportionate redemption and the redemption method is preferred to the buy and sell agreement.

The Tax Reform Act of 1969 permits accumulations in the year of death or later years to redeem stock to pay death taxes and provides that no inference is to be drawn from this change that earlier accumulations for this purpose represent unreasonable accumulations.

Corporations—entire stock owned by one stockholder

17.34   One man corporations

Wherever 80, 90 or 100 percent of the stock of a corporation is owned by a single stockholder peculiar problems are presented. If the entire control is to pass to key employees the buy-and-sell method is obviously the answer. If the value of the interest is too large for them to purchase and pay for, a nontaxable stock dividend may be the answer, with the common now substantially reduced in value, to be purchased under the usual buy and sell contract.

The stock redemption, other than a redemption limited to the amount necessary to pay death taxes, will pose dividend problems if it is less than a complete liquidation, since no matter how much is redeemed the estate will still have more than 50 percent of the voting stock.

While the buy-and-sell method is frequently the only practical one it is not a completely satisfactory solution because of the transfer-for-value rule. If the keyman, after entering into the contract and procuring the insurance, dies or resigns, it is impractical for the succeeding keyman to purchase the existing policy because any gain will be subjected to income taxes on the death of the insured stockholder. The 1954 Code exception to the transfer-for-value rule is limited to sales to corporations of which the insured is a stockholder or officer.

Corporations—summary

17.35   Summary

1. In general the stock redemption method will be found preferable to the buy-and-sell method.

2. This will be true in most partial, as well as complete, redemptions of the deceased owner's interest because of the disproportionate redemption rules and the redemption to pay death taxes provision of the Code.

3. Where the fact situation creates a danger that a complete or partial redemption may not satisfy the disproportionate redemption requirements because of the constructive owner-ship rules, the redemption may be limited to an amount not in excess of death taxes and funeral and administration expenses or the buy-and-sell method may be adopted but with the recognition that at a later date the transfer for value rule may cause difficulty if the surviving owners desire to continue the business purchase agreement among themselves.

4. The one man corporation, like the sole proprietorship, will generally find the buy-and-sell method the better one and again the transfer-for-value rule may, at some future date, make it less than ideal.

Index

(References are to Sections)